Local democracy, civic engagement and community

MANCHESTER
1824

Manchester University Press

Local democracy, civic engagement
and community

Manchester University Press

Local democracy, civic engagement and community

___

From New Labour to the Big Society

Hugh Atkinson

Manchester University Press
Manchester and New York

distributed exclusively in the USA by Palgrave Macmillan

Published by Manchester University Press
Oxford Road, Manchester M13 9NR, UK
and Room 400, 175 Fifth Avenue, New York, NY 10010, USA
www.manchesteruniversitypress.co.uk

Distributed in the United States exclusively by
Palgrave Macmillan, 175 Fifth Avenue, New York,
NY 10010, USA

Distributed in Canada exclusively by
UBC Press, University of British Columbia, 2029 West Mall,
Vancouver, BC, Canada V6T 1Z2

British Library Cataloguing-in-Publication Data
A catalogue record for this book is available from the British Library
Library of Congress Cataloging-in-Publication Data applied for

ISBN   978 0 7190 7911 5 hardback

First published 2012

Typeset
by Action Publishing Technology Ltd, Gloucester
Printed in Great Britain
by TJ International Ltd, Padstow

Contents

Contents

Figures

Abbreviations

ACEVO	Association of Chief Executives of Voluntary Organisations
AMS	Additional member system
APBB	All-Party Parliamentary Beer Group
BBPA	British Beer and Pub Association
BIS	Department for Business, Innovation and Skills
BNP	British National Party
CABE	Commission for Architecture and the Built Environment
CBN	Community Broadband Network
CHC	Community Health Council
CLD	Commission for Local Democracy
CLG	Department of Communities and Local Government
CoSLA	Convention of Scottish Local Authorities
CPRE	Campaign to Protect Rural England
CPS	Centre for Policy Studies
CSR	Comprehensive Spending Review
CSV	Community Service Volunteers
DCMS	Department of Culture, Media and Sport
DCSF	Department for Children, Schools and Families
Defra	Department of the Environment, Food and Rural Affairs
DETR	Department of the Environment, Transport and the Regions
DLTR	Department of Local Government, Transport and the Regions
EHRC	Equalities and Human Rights Commission
ERS	Electoral Reform Society
ESRC	Economic and Social Research Council
FPTP	First past the post
GLA	Greater London Authority
GLC	Greater London Council
IDeA	Improvement and Development Agency
INLOGOV	Institute for Local Government Studies
IPPR	Institute for Public Policy Research
JRT	Joseph Rowntree Trust
LAA	Local Area Agreement
LGA	Local Government Association

LGiU	Local Government Information Unit
LGR	Local Government Review
LINks	Local Involvement Networks
LSP	Local Strategic Partnership
MP	Member of Parliament
NALC	National Association of Local Councils
NCVO	National Council of Voluntary Organisations
NDC	New Deal for Communities
NEF	New Economics Foundation
NFSP	National Federation of Sub-Postmasters
NGO	non-government organisation
NHS	National Health Service
NLGN	New Local Government Network
NSPCC	National Society for the Prevention of Cruelty to Children
OCS	Office for Civil Society
ODPM	Office of the Deputy Prime Minister
PCT	Primary Care Trust
PFI	Private Finance Initiative
PR	Proportional Representation
SAZ	Sport Action Zone
SCP	Sustainable Communities Plan
SNP	Scottish National Party
SNT	Safer neighbourhood team
SOLACE	Society of Local Authority Chief Executives
SRB	Single Regeneration Budget
STV	Single transferable vote
UN	United Nations
VCO	Voluntary Community Organisation
VIRSA	Village Retail Services Association

Preface

I first got the idea for this book about three years ago. For some time I had wanted to explore the links between local democracy, civic engagement and community. I had a broad idea in my head but what I lacked was a conceptual framework. I explored various ideas, but it was on a bird-watching holiday in Norfolk that my thoughts took on more of an analytical feel. It must have been the combination of fresh air and the occasional pint of bitter that stimulated the old grey matter! I have a long-standing experience of local government and local democracy, first as a local government officer, then as an elected local councillor and finally as an academic and researcher. This book is hopefully the culmination of that experience.

For all its limitations, local government is an important locus for political participation, accountability and democracy. It can act as forum for local groups to state their case and thus help shape the democratic process. Just as importantly, local government and local democracy can act as an important counterweight to central government that, despite its perennial rhetoric of decentralisation, is reluctant to cede power. Beware of central government bearing gifts of localism, one might say!

The book may only have my name on the cover but it would not have been possible without the support and guidance of a number of people. First of all I would like to thank Tony Mason of Manchester University Press for his help and support in getting this book published. I am also very grateful to my colleague Stuart Wilks-Heeg for his invaluable insights and comments on my original proposal for this book. I would also like to put on record my thanks to an old colleague of mine, Dr Mike Hickox. His encouragement and support (notwithstanding the odd barbed comment) has been central to my academic development and critical thinking.

Deep thanks also to Chris Wood. Without his support, sheer professionalism and friendship through a very difficult time I would not have finished this book. I would also like to thank my daughter Donna for her love and support for Mr Hugh. Finally, I owe so much to my wife and colleague Ros Wade. She has been a constant source of support and reassurance during the writing of this book, commenting on drafts and proofreading the manuscript. Her blend of considered advice, combined with the odd drop of brutality, kept me on the straight and narrow when I needed it most.

Hugh Atkinson

Introduction

This is a book about local democracy, about community and civic engagement in Britain. It was conceived as a counterweight to the many negative accounts that seek to dominate our political discourse with their talk of political apathy and selfish individualism.

Barack Obama made the point effectively in the American context long before his successful bid for the Presidency. In an interview given to the *Chicago Reader* newspaper on 8 December 1995 he set out his now well-rehearsed argument about the need for change in the way the USA does its politics. For Obama, too much of the emphasis in political debate rested on 'that old bootstrap myth: get a job, get rich and get out'. 'Our goal must be' said Obama 'to help people get a sense of building something larger. The political debate is now so skewed, so limited, so distorted. People are hungry for community. They miss it.'

I was reminded of Obama's point about the hunger for community early on the morning of Monday 2 February 2009. The snow that had started on the previous Sunday evening had continued to fall throughout the night. I awoke from my slumbers in my house in South London to find a thick carpet of snow, more than a foot deep in places. Cars were snowed in and local roads impassable. The stillness and silence were something to behold. What struck me most, however, was the attitude of local people. It was not just the children happily playing in the snow that struck me, but the behaviour of their parents and other adults. Deprived of their cars, they were out on foot, off to the local store in search of supplies or just simply to enjoy the magic of the moment as the pristine white snow lay all about.

Something truly fascinating started to happen. Perfect strangers smiled at each other and engaged in conversation. A community was emerging out of the snow. Across the city in Primrose Hill something similar was happening. In an item in the *Guardian* newspaper a local resident and mother was watching her daughter happily sledging down the snowy slopes. 'Mummy' said the little girl 'everyone is much nicer when there is snow. Everyone talks to you' (*Guardian*, 4 February 2009). Out of the mouths of children as they say! Press reports and anecdotal evidence from across the country painted a similar picture. It was a neat counterpoint to the gainsayers of community.

It was if a window had opened up allowing individuals to crawl through and become part of a community. With the opportunity there, countless people were happy to grasp it. Sadly, and perhaps unavoidably, this particular window soon closed as the snows melted, the roads cleared and people clambered back into their cars and carried on with their busy daily lives.

One snow event does not make a summer, if one is allowed to mix one's metaphors, but it did demonstrate the real if yet latent sense of community and civic spirit that exists. It is a theme that I will return to.

The state of local democracy

There is a widespread view that local democracy in Britain is in deep trouble and that we face a crisis of civic engagement and political participation. Indeed there is available evidence that would appear to lend credence to this viewpoint. This includes low electoral turnout and the significant difficulties that political parties face in recruiting local people both to carry out political activity on the ground and to stand as candidates for election to the council (Power Inquiry, 2006).

However, a central argument of this book is that a deeper analysis of the evidence points to a much more nuanced and complex political terrain with a wide variety of informal and formal activity at the local level. To borrow a phrase from Robert Putnam in his highly acclaimed analysis of civic engagement and community in the USA, the local space has a potential and a vibrancy thanks to its cultivation by 'assiduous civic gardeners' (2006: 16). The difficulties of civic engagement and political participation at the local level are real enough but there are rich seams to be mined and clear opportunities to be grasped. Reports of the death of local democracy are much exaggerated, to paraphrase Mark Twain. It may be a bit poorly at times but it is not time for the undertakers to move in yet.

This book focuses on local democratic politics in Britain over the last decade and a half. It includes an analysis of civic engagement and participation across a range of policy areas and in the context of debates around accountability, legitimacy, and sustainability. It argues that new and alternative forms of civic engagement are opening up at the local level driven by a range of government and non-government actors. These are reshaping the local space.

The period under analysis starts with the election of the New Labour government in 1997 and covers the first year of the Conservative/Liberal Democrat coalition government that came to power in May 2010. The thirteen years of Labour government saw a seemingly never-ending stream of initiatives, the purported aim of which was to revitalise local democracy. The pace of reform was at times frantic, with policy paper succeeding policy paper. However, if students of local democracy hoped for a period of calm and consolidation under the coalition government then they were in for a disappointment. The twin agendas of localism and the 'big society' combined with the large-scale cuts to local authority budgets (some 30 per cent in the period 2011–15) have the potential to radically transform the nature of local democracy and elected local government itself.

Local democracy is in a constant state of flux. One has to check repeatedly to see whether this or that body still exists or if it has been abolished in the name of localism or the 'big society'. Policy announcement follows policy announcement. Ministerial statements abound. Local democracy, for so long the quiet backwater of British politics, has become a lot more interesting!

The book is divided into seven chapters. Chapter 1 looks at theoretical debates as to the meaning of local democracy, civic engagement and community together with a number of related concepts. The issues raised will provide the basis for a more developed analysis in the subsequent chapters. Chapter 2 analyses the widespread view that we face a crisis of local democracy with such evidence as low electoral turnout and declining membership of political parties. However, this chapter will argue that a more nuanced analysis of the available evidence points to a much complex picture with a wide variety of both informal and formal political activity taking place. Chapter 3 looks at the policy agenda around local democracy in the context of the developing nature of central/local relations since 1979. It provides a broad survey of some of the key policy initiatives, ideas and proposals to enhance local democracy that have come from central and local government, together with various policy think tanks and other interested parties. Chapter 4 focuses on the 'crisis' of formal democracy at the local level. This includes the 'decline' in the role of political parties and falling voter turnout at local elections. Possible solutions for a reinvigorated formal local politics are analysed.

Chapter 5 looks at recent developments beyond the realm of elections, political parties and formal political institutions. These include citizen panels, neighbourhood governance arrangements and the use of referenda. The effectiveness, or otherwise, of such measures in boosting civic engagement will be analysed. Chapter 6 focuses on local services and policy attempts to widen public participation in the shaping and delivery of such services. Finally, Chapter 7 looks at the concept of sustainability and regeneration strategies to build sustainable communities, both physical and social. Within this, there is an also an analysis of local strategies to combat climate change.

The last fifteen years have seen a variety of policy initiatives that have sought to reshape local democracy and elected local government. Yet, they have often been contradictory in nature. Under New Labour, the narrative was one of reinvigorating local government and empowering local communities with an emphasis on decentralisation of political power. Yet, in practice, government policy often veered towards more central control with the imposition of more and more targets and continuing restrictions on local government's room for financial manoeuvre. Under the coalition government, the narrative has been one of localism and the 'big society'. But the reality has at times fallen short of the rhetoric. From continuing restrictions on the ability of local councils to determine their own level of council tax through ministerial pronouncements on bin collections central government seems to have difficulty in letting go. And yet, despite all this, local democracy still remains a vibrant terrain of innovation, civic engagement and participation, and dynamic community activity.

1

The theoretical context

Introduction

I will look first at theoretical debates as to the meaning of local democracy and related concepts. We need to establish an understanding of such concepts before we are able to appreciate and comment on the welter of empirical evidence, debate and opinion that is available to us. Such an understanding will help set the scene for the analysis in subsequent chapters of the status and health of local democracy.

In the nineteenth century, the well-known Prussian politician Otto Von Bismarck stated that *politics is the art of the possible*. More broadly, we can understand politics as being about conflicts between groups and the resolution of these conflicts. As Hague and Harrop note, it is 'the process by which groups make collective decisions' (Hague and Harrop, 1987: 3). Groups can range from formal political institutions such as cabinet, parliament and political parties through to local tenants' groups and voluntary organisations. Political decisions can be determined in a variety of ways. These can include diplomacy, negotiation, voting and, in extreme cases, violence. What makes such decisions essentially political is 'their collective character, affecting and committing those who belong to the group' (Hague and Harrop, 1987: 3).

Healy *et al.* argue that 'A redefinition of politics and the role of elected representatives' is necessary if we are to enhance political and civic engagement (Healey *et al.*, 2005: 42). Indeed this is most certainly true. Whilst we need to acknowledge the importance of formal political institutions and political parties, we need to construct a way of doing politics that is about more than petty squabbles, sound bites and wheeler-dealing. In other words, we need a politics that addresses and confronts the social and economic challenges that face communities and individuals in their everyday lives.

At the local level, there are many examples that this is happening already, and we will focus on some of these in subsequent chapters. Research evidence does point to public apathy and distrust about many aspects of formal politics (voting, membership of political parties and a willingness to stand as a local councillor, for example). Yet even here the picture is mixed.

In addition, there is a significant amount of activity and civic engagement beyond the formal realm of politics taking place at the local level. The challenge at the local level is to harness this energy to help drive forward and strengthen formal politics and broader forms of civic engagement in a relationship of mutual benefit and reciprocity.

In the debate about the state of local democracy, words and phrases such as civic engagement, political participation and community enter the debate, often without a clear understanding of what they actually mean. Add to the brew civil society, social capital and public value and the head can really start to hurt! Yet if we are carry out a robust audit of the health of local democracy in Britain, a good dose of theory is essential. Theory provides a framework to help us to understand what is going on, to make sense of the evidence and the arguments, to make an analysis and possibly even to offer prescriptions for the future. In other words it offers us a *context*, it gives meaning to the why and the what, it provides us with an organisational tool without which we may well end up with a random and disparate collection of facts, what has been described as mere empiricism.

To this end, I will now focus on the meaning and definition of six interconnected but distinctive concepts. These are democracy, political participation and civic engagement, social capital, community, civil society and public value. Subsequent chapters will give empirical weight to this theoretical discussion.

How can we conceptualise democracy?

Democracy itself, Beetham argues, 'belongs to the sphere of the political' (Beetham, 1996: 29). It is a sphere 'of collectively binding agreements and policies' and the attempted resolution of conflicts as to how such agreements and policies should be shaped and implemented (Beetham, 1996: 29). It starts from the premise that that we are 'social creatures' whose lives are interdependent on each other and as such require common rules and policies (Beetham, 1996: 29). This does not deny individual choice and individual rights but they have to be seen in the context of this interconnectedness. Notions of democracy are not confined to formal institutions of national and local government but extend to any organisation where there are disagreements to be mediated and objectives and rules to be agreed. This can include national groups such as the Women's Institute and local tenants' associations.

The concept of democracy, its interpretation and implementation is multi-faceted and highly contested. Should democracy, for example, be about responding to the wishes of the majority of the electorate? In that case, how do we deal with the needs and aspirations of minority opinion? Healy *et al.* argue that the real measure of an effective democratic system 'may not be how effectively it converts the will of the majority into political action but how able it proves in standing up for the rights and needs of minorities' (Healey *et al.*, 2005: 38). Larry Flynt once observed that 'majority rule only works if you are also considering individual rights … you can't have five wolves and a sheep voting on what to eat for supper' (see Healey *et al.*, 2005: 38).

The issue of minority rights is important. We only have to look at the example of Northern Ireland to see how the marginalisation of the minority catholic/nationalist community over sixty years led to frustration, social upheaval, political protest and, in some sections of society, the pursuit of the 'armed struggle'. This is an extreme example, certainly, but it does highlight a basic principle. How can the various shades of political opinion in communities receive their proper share of political representation?

The method of election is pertinent here. The system of simple plurality (or 'first past the post' (FPTP), as it is known colloquially) used in UK general elections is a case in point. Look at the example of the 2005 general election. The Labour Party won 356 seats, giving it a majority over all other parties of 66 seats yet only gained just over 35 per cent of the vote. If the number of seats gained had been directly proportional to the votes cast, the Labour Party would have won only 227 seats. In the 2010 general election the Conservatives received just over 36 per cent of the vote (1 per cent more than Labour in 2005) and yet won only 306 seats.

Whilst accepting that some voters may have acted in a different way if the last two general elections had been fought under a system of proportional representation, these examples highlight the ongoing debate about the nature and purpose of elections. Supporters of the FPTP system argue that it produces stable majority one-party government. Proponents of proportional representation, in its varied forms, argue that it results in fairer representation. Both points of view have validity. In essence it is about striking a balance between the exigencies of stable and effective government, on the one hand, and fair representation, on the other. Where that balance lies is the point of contention. FPTP is also the system used for local elections in England and similar arguments pertain here. In Scotland, the situation is different. With the devolution settlement, local government in Scotland comes under the aegis of the Scottish Parliament, thus allowing policy differentiation from England and Wales. In 2007 proportional representation, in the form of single transferable vote (STV), was introduced for Scottish local elections. The implications of this initiative in terms of both political representation and political participation will be analysed in Chapter 4 when I look at formal democracy.

Direct democracy

We can draw a distinction between indirect (or representative democracy) where we elect our representatives, such as members of parliament and local councillors, and more direct forms of democracy, such as referenda where specific questions are put to the electorate. Representative democracy has been the traditional model adopted in the UK but over recent years referenda and other forms of direct democracy, such as citizens' panels and citizens' juries, have become a more familiar sight on the political landscape at national, regional and local levels.

The use of referenda, it is argued, allows the public to express their views more directly. Since 1997 there have been successful referenda that have led to the creation of a Scottish Parliament and Assemblies for Wales and the Northern Ireland. By contrast, in 2007 the people of the North East of England voted against an elected regional assembly. At the local level there have been a number of local referenda in recent years on issues such as the level of council tax and proposals for directly elected executive mayors.

At first sight the idea of local referenda directly seeking out the views of local people seems attractive. But many issues arise here. These include the type of information provided to voters so they can make an informed choice, the fact that the way the question is put can have an impact on the outcome and the relative influence of different groups (Hague and Harrop, 2010: 190–191). Would direct democracy help reinvigorate political participation or would it, as Healy *et al.* claim, lead to 'domination by the most able and most articulate self selectors' (Healey *et al.*, 2005: 42) and thus further marginalise minorities and the socially excluded? I shall look at these issues in more detail when I examine informal democracy in Chapter 5.

Representative government and democracy

In a system of representative government elected politicians, whether they be members of parliament or local councillors, mediate the views of the electorate. This is an indirect form of democracy.

The political philosopher, John Stuart Mill, writing in 1871, argued 'That the ideally best form of government is representative' (Mill, 1975: 179), For Mill, wide public participation in the political process was the key to fully satisfying 'the exigencies of the social state' (Mill, 1975: 198). He went on to argue:

> that any participation even in the smallest public function, is useful; that the participation should everywhere be as great as the general degree of improvement of society will allow; and that nothing less can be ultimately desirable, than the admission of all to a share in *the sovereign power of the state*. But since all cannot, in a community exceeding a small town, participate personally in any but some very minor portions of the public business, it follows that the ideal type of a perfect government must be representative. (Mill, 1975: 198)

So, for Mill, there are two crucial factors for a vibrant and functioning democracy, namely the widest possible public participation and a system of representative government. This is classic liberal democratic theory.

Beetham goes on to draw out a distinction between representative government and representative democracy. It has been argued elsewhere that representative government 'assumes that citizens are passive, that they are incompetent to participate in decisions about complex issues (Stewart *et al.*, 1994: iii). For Beetham, the validity of such a view is open to debate. What is beyond doubt for him is that 'Representative democracy ... cannot be either realised or sustained without an active citizen body' (Beetham, 1996: 30). He then goes on to set out what he refers to as a list of four 'mediating concepts' that set the context for an effective system of representative democracy. These are: authorisation, accountability, responsiveness and representativeness (Beetham, 1996: 31).

First, for Beetham, an essential element of representative democracy is the 'popular authorisation' of those politicians who make governmental decisions by means of elections on the basis of universal suffrage (Beetham, 1996: 31). This is indeed a valid point of view but it does raise certain issues. These include the type of electoral system to be used, such as simple plurality or one of the various forms of proportional representation. Different electoral systems produce different outcomes in terms of the representation of both majority and minority public opinion.

Second, decision makers, Beetham argues, need to be accountable to the electorate on whose behalf they make decisions. Mechanisms to facilitate this include regular elections, effective parliamentary scrutiny of the governmental executive and an independent press. Here public access to the goings on of government is central. Secrecy and obfuscation can be major barriers to the public accountability of politicians and other public officials (Beetham, 1996: 31).

Third, responsiveness goes beyond accountability, making it a requirement that government (elected politicians) 'take note systematically of the full range of public opinion' when shaping public policy and delivering services (Beetham, 1996: 32). Again, of course, this raises a number of questions. For example, what kind of transmission mechanisms should be employed to deliver this? In addition, what weight should be given to minority opinions, a key issue in divided polities such as Northern Ireland?

Fourth, there is the concept of representativeness, which is for Beetham central to notions of political equality or equality of citizenship (Beetham, 1996: 32). Here the requirements include: votes of equal value, a socially representative political class, and an independent press to allow the broadest expression of public opinion. Again of course such requirements raise as many questions as they provide answers, not least amongst them being the balance to be struck between the relative influence of majority and minority public opinion.

Local democracy

What of democracy at the local level? Some readers may recall a 1980s television series called *The Beiderbecke Affair*. In one episode, a local town hall official was quoted as saying that 'Local government is the last refuge of the timid and the poor in spirit'. This is a somewhat jaundiced view to say the very least! However, there is no doubt local democracy is a contested and complex concept which has been at the centre of no little political conflict in Britain, no more so than in the 1980s when the Conservative government of Margaret Thatcher came into direct conflict with a number of Labour-controlled local authorities who, from the perspective of central government, were seeking to challenge their authority.

Writing in 1986, Gyford argued that 'There is now no universally accepted notion as to the proper nature of local democracy', while 'many of those who use the term are simply talking past one and another' (quoted in Beetham, 1996: 28). For Beetham, writing ten years later, 'the terminological confusion Gyford observed had in fact intensified in the last ten years' (Beetham, 1996: 28).

John Stuart Mill's views on local democracy are complex and at times appear somewhat contradictory. Writing in *Representative Government*, he argued that 'It is but a small portion of the public business of a country, which can be well done or safely attempted by the central authorities: and even in our own government [he is referring to Britain] ... the legislative portion at least of the governing body busies itself far too much with local affairs' (Mill, 1975: 363). Thus Mill appears to be making a case for a diffusion of power to the local level.

But later on in the text Mill appears to offer a different view. He states that 'The authority which is most conversant with principles should be supreme over principles, whilst that which is most competent in details should have details left to it' (Mill, 1975: 377). What implications does such a view have for central/local relations and the status of elected local government? For Mill, 'The principal business of the central authority should be to give instruction, of the local authority to apply it' (Mill, 1975: 377). Thus Mill appears to view central/local relations very much in terms of master and servant, where the role of local government is to do the bidding of its central master.

Yet if we delve further, a more complex picture emerges. In a different part of the same text Mill speaks of 'the liberty of the individual, in things wherein the individual alone is concerned, implies a corresponding liberty in any number of individuals to regulate by mutual agreement such things as regard them jointly and regard no other persons but themselves' (Mill, 1975: 125). Mill's reference to the liberty of individuals to regulate by mutual agreement such things as regards them jointly, whilst applicable to local clubs, societies and other voluntary associations, could equally and logically apply to elected local government. Indeed Mill argues that 'knowledge to be most useful must be centralised', but that 'Power may be localised' (Mill, 1975: 377).

Elsewhere in the same book, Mill stresses the importance of elected local government within a proportional electoral system based on universal suffrage. Yet there is conditionality here as Mill recommends 'a greater proportional influence to those who have a larger money interest at stake' (Mill, 1975: 366). Thus Mill appears to be advocating a guided system of representative local democracy.

In addition, his views on intellectual capacity at the local level are far from flattering, arguing as he does that 'local representative bodies and their officers are of a much lower grade of intelligence and knowledge than parliament and the national executive' (Mill, 1975: 375). Fast forward to the last twenty-five years and it could be argued that a not too dissimilar view has held sway in the corridors of power in Westminster and Whitehall!

In more recent times local democracy has had many champions. Above all, local democracy can rest its claim on being the most accessible avenue for political participation. For Jones and Stewart, the argument goes much deeper. Elected local government, they argue, 'should be a guardian of fundamental values. It represents, first and foremost, a spread of political power' (Jones and Stewart, 1985: 5). Chandler has argued that elected local government is an important institution, not merely because of what it does but also of what it ought to contribute to a more democratic and humane society' (Chandler, 1996: viii).

Beetham points to the greater democratic potential of elected local government, as opposed to non-elected local administration politically accountable to central government, in terms of accountability, responsiveness and representation (Beetham, 1996: 40).

The democratic case for local government

Various arguments have been put forward to advance the democratic case for elected local government (Chandler, 2009; Jones and Stewart, 1985). I will consider a number of these. Local government is said to be closer and more accessible to local people than government at the centre, and thus more accountable (Beetham, 1996: 38). There is also an argument that elected local government strengthens and enhances democracy, in that it provides local people with a variety of opportunities for political participation. Such participation can take a variety of forms. These include becoming a member of a political party, being a member of a local pressure group or community organisation, voting in local elections, or standing for election to the local council. Sharpe talks of the 'democratic primacy' of local government 'because it does enable more people to participate in their own government' (Sharpe, 1970: 160). Furthermore, it creates multiple centres of power that act as break on an all-powerful central state (Jones and Stewart, 1985). In other words, elected local government encourages and facilitates political pluralism. In 1986 the Widdicombe Report, an investigation into the political and policy workings of local government, stated that 'the case for pluralism is that power should not be concentrated in one organisation of state, but should be dispersed, thereby providing political checks and balances and a restraint on arbitrary government and absolutism' (Widdicombe, 1986: 48).

In addition there are a range of differing and diverse communities with a variety of challenges that require focused and differentiated responses beyond the scope of a single central authority. Responding to such diverse interests is a key element of the democratic process. Finally, Beetham has argued that the electoral process at the local level gives an 'incentive for policy makers and service providers to develop more responsive modes of consultation (and a legitimate ground for citizens to demand them) that are lacking in a non-elected administration' (Beetham, 1996: 39). The argument here is that local elections provide downward accountability to local people and an upward transmission mechanism for collective and individual expression. In other words, they keep local policy makers on their toes. Goldsmith has spoken of the role of local government 'as the advocate of the locality' (Goldsmith, 1986: 2).

The democratic case for local government is, however, not beyond challenge. Voter turnout at local elections is relatively low, with an average of around 35 per cent over recent years. Such apparent voter apathy suggests some weakness in local democracy. Some commentators point to the unrepresentative nature of the FPTP system used for local elections in England and Wales (save for elections to the Greater London Assembly, where a system of proportional representation is used), suggesting some form of proportional system such as that introduced for Scottish local elections. It is also argued that voters are increasingly seeing local elections as an opportunity not to pass judgement on local political regimes and the quality of local services, but to express their views on central government policies. Such developments weaken the notion of local accountability. In addition, the argument that local government can act as an advocate for a locality is weakened, it is argued, due to the fact that Britain 'has larger, less community based local authorities than almost any other liberal democracy' (Chandler, 1996: 2). Furthermore, successive central government policies over two decades that have sought to restrict the role of local government and reduce its autonomy have weakened local democratic accountability. This 'in turn encourages the seepage of power to the centre, which further reduces electoral choice and local accountability' (Beetham, 1996: 41).

I shall assess and weigh the balance of these conflicting arguments in subsequent chapters.

Political agency and the role of political parties

Earlier on in this chapter we noted in our discussion of the nature of politics that there is a broad recognition that a great many of the social problems and policy challenges that face us cannot, on their own, be addressed by individual action alone but require a collective response if political change is to be achieved. Such a view still holds true despite the fact that this collectivist view has come under concerted pressure in the last twenty years with neo-liberalism's stress on markets and individualism.

Yet even neo-liberalism has found expression in that venerable collectivist institution, the good old political party, with conservative and even social democratic parties embracing and expounding its philosophy. Political parties have fallen out of fashion in recent years in Britain. Falling membership and the dwindling band of party activists at the local level give weight to this point of view (see Chapter 4). Yet political parties still have an intrinsic role to play. Social and political change do not simply happen, but need an agency to drive them. For Beetham, the agency that best fits the bill is the political party (Beetham, 1996: 47). Belonging as it does 'to both civil society and the state ... it is uniquely placed to link democratic initiatives in the two' (Beetham, 1996: 47). If it can measure up to the task it has a key role to play in the democratisation of politics in Britain at the national and local level. I shall return to the role of political parties in Chapter 4.

Political participation and civic engagement

It is very important not to underplay the importance of the formal political process. For, as Skidmore *et al.* argue, 'Universal representative rights remain ... a necessary condition for democracy and an often too fragile an asset in many parts of the world' (Skidmore *et al.*, 2006: 48). They go on to contend that 'The decline of more active forms of participation [such as] political parties or pressure groups, trade unions or community groups, parks committees or faith based organisations has weakened representative democracy' (Skidmore *et al.*, 2006: 48). Now whilst they make a valid point about the need to view politics and democracy from a broader perspective than simply voting, they conflate a number of factors here. Whilst there is evidence to show that the trend in membership of political parties has been downwards over the last decade, there is a great deal of evidence to suggest that broader forms of what one might term civic engagement in the shape of activities such as membership of pressure groups, local community groups and volunteering are very vibrant. I shall return to this in Chapter 2.

In the ongoing debate about the vibrancy or otherwise of local democracy a variety of phrases and concepts have been utilised. They are often used interchangeably with a meaning that is not often clear. Community participation, political participation, political engagement, civic engagement and just plain engagement all form part and parcel of the local lexicon. Of course, there is debate about the meaning of these concepts. Terminological exactitude is unlikely, possibly even undesirable (we may obsess with it at the expense of good analysis), but broad working definitions are important if we are to make sense of and calibrate the social and political reality. For the purposes of this study, I shall draw out a distinction between two of these concepts: political participation and civic engagement.

We can observe political participation in what one might term the 'formal realm' of politics. This would include voting, joining a political party and standing for elected office. But political participation goes considerably further than this. Political science emphasises just as strongly the key importance of what one might term the 'informal realm'; that is, the myriad of activities that take place outside traditional politics. These include taking part in demonstrations, signing petitions and lobbying your local council.

Civic engagement includes the above activities but it is more, much more. It captures a much broader range of national and local activity. It can involve setting up a local tenants' group, joining your local RSPB group, running a voluntary local drop-in centre, serving in a local community shop, being a member of a non-government organisation (NGO) or charity, campaigning for equal opportunities, or working as a volunteer in your local citizens' advice bureau. To ignore all this activity gives only a partial and limited picture of what is going on in the social world. It is the difference between viewing the world of nature through a 14-inch black and white portable television or a 32–inch widescreen colour model. (See Figure 1.)

Wilks-Heeg and Clayton talk of the 'growing recognition of the symbiotic relationship between political participation and more everyday day forms of civic engagement' (Wilks-Heeg and Clayton, 2006: 102). Such interaction

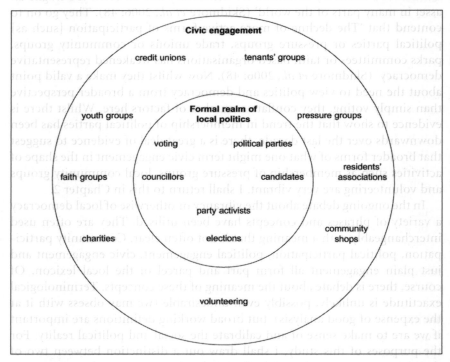

1 Formal democracy and civic engagement

between groups and individuals results in the formation of networks of trust and cooperation (Wilks-Heeg and Clayton, 2006: 102). This is the 'social capital' that the American political scientist Putnam refers to (Putnam, 2000). It is a necessary ingredient for a vibrant and connected local democracy and it is to this that I now turn.

Social capital

The concept of social capital has developed to a significant degree from the work of social scientists in the USA. It has gained much of its current prominence with Robert Putnam's reformulation of the concept in his classic study of US community and civic engagement (Putnam, 2000). He argues that just as physical capital (for example, a screwdriver) and human capital (for example, a university education) can increase productivity both individually and collectively, so too can social contacts and interactions between individuals and groups. It is these social contacts and interactions that are at the heart of social capital (Putnam, 2000: 18).

However, the concept of social capital is not new. Indeed its roots can be traced as far back as 1916 to the writings of L. J. Hanifan in the USA. Hanifan was the state supervisor of rural schools in West Virginia. He believed strongly that community involvement was essential if schools were to be successful. It was in this context that he expounded his views on the meaning of social capital. His views are worth quoting at some length because they set out clearly the core of the concept. For Hanifan, it referred to 'those tangible substances that count for most in the daily lives of people: namely good will, fellowship, sympathy and social intercourse amongst the individuals and families who make up a social unit' (see Putnam, 2000: 19). Left to his own devices 'the individual is helpless socially'. Yet:

> If he comes into contact with his neighbor, and they with their neighbors, there will be an accumulation of social capital which may immediately satisfy his social needs and which may bear a social potentiality sufficient to the substantial improvement of living conditions in the whole community. The community as a whole will benefit by the cooperation of all its parts, while the individual will find in his associations the advantages of the help, the sympathy and the fellowship of his neighborhoods. (Hanifan, quoted in Putnam, 2000: 19)

As Putnam notes, social capital can 'be simultaneously a private good and a public good' (Putnam, 2000: 20). He gives the example of organisations, such as the Rotary Club and the Round Table, which raise funds to provide finance and other support for groups, such as the elderly and deprived children. At the same time, membership of such organisations offers individuals opportunities to make new personal acquaintances and friendships and a route into potentially rewarding business networks. Such processes, Putnam notes, foster 'sturdy norms of reciprocity' (Putnam, 2000: 20). Putnam's observation here is important for, as he notes, 'A society characterized by generalized reciprocity is more efficient than a distrustful society' (Putnam, 2000: 20). In other words, social capital has the potential to shape and enhance formal political participation and broader forms of civic engagement.

Yet as always the social world is a complex one full of both opportunities and threats. Things can be rosy if you are inside a network but, as Putnam notes, 'the external effects of social capital are no means always positive' (Putnam, 2000: 21) and 'can be directed towards malevolent purposes' (Putnam, 2000: 22). In a British context this might include the capture of tenants' groups by local racist networks. Less malevolent but still socially exclusive is the exploitation of social capital by local power elites to block the building of affordable housing in leafy suburbs.

In an attempt to conceptualise the problem, Putnam draws a distinction between what he calls 'bridging social capital' (which is broadly inclusive) and 'bonding social capital' (which tends to exclusivity) (Putnam, 2000: 23). Of course, like all concepts they have their imperfections and do not always fit neatly with social reality. But they do provide a helpful framework for analysis.

Bonding social capital

Some networks and the social capital that spring from them can be rather homogeneous, inward-looking and exclusive. This can either be by necessity or choice or a mixture of the two. This is what Putnam defines as 'bonding social capital' (Putnam, 2000: 23). In the UK context, at one end of the scale this might include some women's groups and groups made up of specific ethnic identities. As Putnam argues, the social capital that arises out of such groups can be good for 'undergirding specific reciprocity and mobilising solidarity' (Putnam, 2000: 22). In addition, it can 'provide crucial social and psychological support for less fortunate members of the community' (Putnam, 2000: 22). At the other end of the scale we might include the Freemasons and golf clubs with high membership fees. Networks here create their own social capital but they tend to be built on social and financial exclusivity.

Bridging social capital

Here networks are much more outward-facing and have a membership which is much more diverse and inclusive. In the US context, Putnam refers to examples, such as the Civil Rights Movement and ecumenical religious organisations (Putnam, 2000: 22). In the UK context, examples might include local fair trade groups, environmental campaigners, credit unions and community shops. For Putnam, 'bridging social capital can generate broader identities and reciprocity, whereas bonding social capital bolsters our narrow selves' (Putnam, 2000: 23).

Linking social capital

A third type of social capital that we can identify is that of 'linking social capital'. This needs to be viewed in the context of attempts by central and local government to boost political and civic engagement. It is argued, for example, that by encouraging voters to play a role in the decisions that shape local services such participants build relationships with public officials and institutions which, in turn, give 'their community access to valuable external resources like money, support or political leverage' (Skidmore *et al.*, 2006: 9). Such relationships between communities and those in formal positions of power have been described as 'linking social capital' (Skidmore *et al.*, 2006: 9). It is 'linking social capital', Skidmore *et al.* argue, 'that policies to promote community participation in governance have the best chance of influencing' (Skidmore *et al.*, 2006: 9).

The meaning of community

'Community' is a concept often used but not always well understood or explained. In both sociology and politics the meaning of community has been a matter of debate over a number of decades and it remains a contested concept. It can be a community of place, linked to a location such as a residents' group or a local community choir. It can also be a community of interest such as the Make Poverty History campaign or the education community. It can also be about sexuality/lifestyle, such as the gay community, but this is in itself is a very heterogeneous group. Community of interest and place can often overlap – for example, local campaigns to stop the felling of woods to build a local bypass that encompass both local concerns and broader sustainability issues. On a wider scale, we often hear reference to the community of nations or to the global community. Community can be local, regional, national and global.

Communities can also be linked to ethnic roots. We often hear talk of the black community, the Asian community and the Muslim community but what does this mean? It is surely not possible to speak of such groups as if there were homogeneous entities. Rather, through their heterogeneity they embody a myriad of different views, aspirations and ways of looking at the world. But these terms can act as a useful shorthand.

We also need to the address the issue of how the interests of such communities are expressed and mediated. We hear often of community leaders. Indeed government is often seen to call on such leaders for policy advice and information. Yet there are real issues relating to legitimacy here. How representative, for example, are such 'leaders' of those on whose behalf they purport to speak? How are they elected or selected? To whom are they accountable? Although these are difficult and thorny issues it is true to say but they do not in themselves negate the notion of community. Community may not always be easy to identify and describe. It is perhaps somewhat like an elephant, often difficult to describe but you know one when you see one!

For the purposes of this book we can view community as the interaction between individuals or groups by virtue of some common/shared interests or physical location that helps to shape and develop a sense of common purpose through the production of what we have described earlier as social capital. Such social capital can be measured as the collective value of all social networks (who people know) and the inclinations that arise from these networks to do things for each other.

Civil society

Linked to the concepts of social capital and community is the idea of civil society. It has been argued that 'Civil Society is contested territory' (Edwards, 2008: vii). Yet the search for the meaning of civil society is an important element in any discussion about civic engagement, community and local democracy. It is a complex and problematic concept that has over time produced a variety of different and sometimes conflicting interpretations. These have included its relationship with the state, the relative emphasis on individual or collective action, the relative weighting of political democracy and the democracy of the markets (in today's parlance, the citizens/consumers debate). If we take a brief journey through history we can see evidence of this. In ancient Greece writers and thinkers such as Aristotle viewed civil society as being fused with the state.

Bottery notes that the origins of civil society in Ancient Greece were based on the view of a 'civil society coterminous with the State ... the end point of individual development was ... through a realisation of political life – the polis was the pinnacle of human development' (Bottery, 2000: 196). Edwards makes a similar point. He argues that 'Aristotle's polis was an *association of associations* that enabled citizens (or those few individuals that qualified) to share in the virtuous tasks of ruling and being ruled. In this sense the state represented the *civil* form of society civility described the requirements of good citizens' (Edwards, 2008: 6). As Sullivan notes, for Aristotle, the 'first and final concern of politics is mutual moral cultivation' (Sullivan 1986: 168). In the words of Aristotle citizens 'are drawn together by a common interest in proportion as each attains a share in the good life through the union of all in a form of political association' (Barker, 1962: 111).

Contract theorists such as Hobbes (*Leviathan*, 1681) and Locke (*Second Treatise on Government*, 1689) parted company with this idea of a fusion of individual, civil society and the state as a normative good thing. Both introduced into western political thinking the idea of a contract between individuals in civil society and their rulers albeit from different perspectives. The alternative, as Hobbes pointed out in *Leviathan*, was the survival of the fittest. Rulers could be granted sovereignty by the people, but that sovereignty could also be revoked (Bottery, 2000: 197). Thus, as Bottery notes, 'Civil society here was that element of society which contracted into agreement with rulers … whether this contract was a pessimistic Hobbesian punitive arrangement or a more conditional Lockesian one' (Bottery, 2000: 197).

However, as Edwards notes, notions of civil society took on a different hue in the period from 1750 to 1850 as a reaction 'to a perceived crisis in the ruling social order' (Edwards, 2008: 7). In addition, the rise of the market economy led to an increasing differentiation of interests with 'communities of neighbourhoods' being replaced by communities of strangers' (Edwards, 2008: 7).

Thinkers such as Adam Smith (*The Wealth of Nations*, 1776) viewed matters more through an economic lens. For Smith, the market was the core of civil society where the invisible hand of self-interest would provide the wealth of nations, leading to economic progress and social prosperity, what Adam Ferguson called 'optimistic results from unanticipated circumstances' (quoted in Bottery, 2004: 197). From such a perspective the individual (and their needs and wishes) was at the forefront of civil society. As Bottery notes, 'it created a powerful moral argument that the pursuit of self interest was actually good for society as a whole' (Bottery, 2004: 197). Smith was aware of the dangers of putting the free market at the centre of civil society. Yet it was an idea that came back to centre stage with Thatcherism in the 1980s with adaptations by New Labour after 1997. I shall return to this theme in subsequent chapters.

Modern notions of civil society can usually be traced back to the period of the Enlightenment in the eighteenth century, a period in which the American Declaration of Independence (1776) and the French Revolution (1789) witnessed a breakdown in the traditional models of authority. In this period, thinkers such as De Tocqueville saw civil society as a defence against an over-powerful state that might threaten 'newly realised individual rights and freedoms organised through the medium of voluntary associations' (Edwards, 2008: 7). De Tocqueville was a French sociologist who developed much of his thinking about civil society through his contemporary analysis of the newly emerging United States of America. For him, Americans based their actions on both individualism and equality. Whilst he was concerned that an overemphasis on the individual could lead to an erosion of *civic virtue*, he felt that 'Americans had a strong saving grace in their promotion of equality'. Notions of equality engendered a feeling of mutual respect within the citizenry that helped to facilitate participation in political and associational life (O'Brian, 1996: 6).

One of the key strengths of the emerging America for De Tocqueville was its large number of voluntary associations and its strong focus on localities. For De Tocqueville, the value of such voluntary associations lay in restricting the power of centralising institutions and promoting pluralism.

'Americans of all ages, conditions and dispositions', he declared in his study *Democracy in America*, 'have a constant tendency to form associations' (De Tocqueville, 1945, vol. 1: 114). Fast forward to modern times and the USA where notions of self-government, localism and voluntarism and the fear of an overweening federal government still remain strong. Such an approach has strong links with schools of thought such as communitarianism that I shall consider presently. Yet De Tocqueville was also concerned, as O'Brien notes, that the 'American predilection for material gain would cause them to lose interest in public affairs' (O'Brien, 1999: 6). Such themes have been taken up in more recent times by writers such as Putnam with his study of associational life in the USA and the implications for what has become known as 'social capital' (Putnam, 2000).

Hegel built on past insights such as those of Adam Smith and noted how markets drive individuals to self-interest and this inevitably produces inequality. Hegel saw social life as being comprised of three social spheres – family, civil society and the state (*Philosophy of Right*, 1820). In Hegel's view civil society was deficient. It was, therefore, the role of the state to intervene and provide for the greater good. 'Civil Society is now the problem, the state the solution' (Bottery, 2000: 199). This required 'constant surveillance by the state in order for the *civil* to remain' (Edwards, 2008: 8).

Marx in the nineteenth century and Gramsci in the twentieth century, though with a difference of emphasis, saw civil society as essentially a tool of the dominant class through which it shaped its hegemony in such a way so that people are unable to see the chains that bind them (Bottery, 2000: 199). As Marx stated:

> What is society, whatever its form may be? The product of men's reciprocal action. Are men free to choose this or that form of society for themselves? By no means no. Assume a particular state of development in the productive forces of man and you will get a particular form of commerce and consumption. Assume particular stages of development in production, commerce and consumption and you will have a corresponding social constitution, a corresponding organisation of the family, of orders or of classes, in a word, a corresponding civil society. (*The Poverty of Philosophy*, 1857, quoted in McLellan, 1980a: 142)

Gramsci's view of civil society, McClellan says, denoted 'all the organisations and technical means which diffuse the ideological justifications of the ruling class in all domains of culture' (McLellan, 1980b: 188). Civil society, through the hegemony of the ruling class, was the 'ethical content of the state' (*Selections from the Prison Notebooks*, quoted in McLellan, 1980b: 88). As Edwards notes, however, in Gramsci's view 'civil society was the site of the rebellion against the orthodox as well as the construction of cultural and ideological hegemony' (Edwards, 2008: 8). Thus it had a potentiality to challenge the hegemony.

How can we conceptualise civil society today? We can consider three possible models of civil society: the libertarian, the communitarian and the strong democracy models.

The libertarian model

This model draws a distinction between the *public* and the *private*. It can be traced back to the market insights of thinkers such as Adam Smith. 'Public' refers to big government and 'private' to those of us in the rest of society, 'a domain of free individuals who associate voluntarily in various economic and social groupings that are contractual in nature' (Barber, 1998: 16). From such a perspective, as Bottery notes, 'Individual liberty is then the core value, while government is seen as the enemy, the coercer' (Bottery, 2000: 201). Yet such a model oversimplifies the context within which individuals function and operate. Whilst Bottery may be slightly overstating the case when he critiques the libertarian model with its failure 'to recognise the *yearning* for solidarity and community which many people feel' (Bottery, 2000: 201), community does matter, as subsequent chapters in this book will testify. Up and down the country there are countless examples of individuals in localities coming together collectively to meet difficult challenges and to offer solutions.

If the last thirty years of neo-liberal hegemony, culminating in the 2008 global credit crunch have taught us anything, it is that prosperity and societal well being cannot come from the pursuit of individual self-interest and market solutions alone. The libertarian model may have some merits in its talk of voluntarism and its opposition to conformity but this can be at the cost of parochialism and narrow self-interest. It underplays the role of community, sustainability and citizenship.

The communitarian model

This model is associated with thinkers such as Etzioni (1993) who take issue with the libertarian model. We are not free individuals exercising choice but instead 'are defined by a given set of relationships over which we have no choice; we are born Protestant, Jew, Muslim, into communities we had no hand in fashioning' (Bottery, 2000: 203). Such communities give us identity and provide mutual support in our daily lives. We need them to function. In fact for (some) communitarians we could not exist as human beings without them. But the relationship is reciprocal. Communities themselves need our support and succour if they are to prosper and develop.

This sounds all well and good. Motherhood and apple pie (with custard) comes to mind. But the danger may lie in the detail. While the communitarian viewpoint may offer a 'glue for communities in a fragmented world, it does by defining others as outside of its self' (Bottery, 2000: 204). Furthermore, the glue of communitarianism can bond a society so tightly that its members are suffocated' (Bottery, 2000: 205).

It is one of the main arguments of this book that communities are alive across the length of Britain and that they are an important resource in dealing with the societal and economic challenges of the twenty-first century. Yet we need to sound a word of caution here. For, as Bottery observes, any notion of community 'must be founded as much upon argumentation, difference and tolerance, as it is upon seeking for that which we all have in common' (Bottery, 2000: 204). It is a difficult balancing act but it is one that is crucial to a healthy polity.

The strong democracy model

So there might there be, dare one say it, a Third Way between the overt individualism of the libertarian approach and the potential exclusivity and closed-door nature of communitarianism.

The libertarian model puts an emphasis on voluntarism but tends towards parochialism and self-interest. Conversely the communitarian approach stresses the importance of a public space but which in some cases can exclude certain groups. Addressing such deficiencies, Bottery has put forward a model of civil society with a strong democratic emphasis. It draws a distinction between the public realm (comprising government and its institutions), the private realm (involving the activities of individuals both social and economic) and civil society that is tied 'explicitly to the functions of citizenship', and which celebrates 'the exercise of both rights and responsibilities through open, critical and plural debate' (Bottery, 2000: 206).

As a report by Democratic Audit notes 'democracy lies as much in the vitality of . . . citizens' self organisation in all aspects of their collective life – what has come to be called civil society – as well as their formal relation to government' (quoted in Wilks-Heeg and Clayton, 2006: 103). Pattie *et al.* make a similar point arguing that of civil society 'refers to the formal and informal relationships between people which can be broadly defined as political which operate outside the institutions of the state' (Pattie *et al.*, 2003: 2). This can include individuals joining an interest group, concerned members of the public attending a demonstration, or volunteers doing voluntary work in a local hospital. The scope and extent of this civil society at the local level in Britain will be a matter for subsequent analysis.

Public value

'Public value' is an emerging and, at times, contested concept with differing views, for example about the role of the private sector in the delivery of public services. In essence, it seeks to look beyond neo-liberalism's obsession with money value and economic relations and instead seeks to build an understanding of the central importance of public services as a key element in community cohesiveness and development and the strengthening of civic engagement and social capital.

Increasingly, 'value' over the last thirty years has come to be measured in money terms in relation to profit and efficiency. This is a product of the ideological dominance of neo-liberalism shaping the discourse around public services and the drive to privatisation and marketisation, what has been described as the 'new public management' (Orr and Vance, 2009). In the drive to ape the private sector, some of the intrinsic values of public services have been at best downgraded and at worst cast aside.

Let us take the issue of local post office closures over recent years, a highly contentious policy area which will be discussed in more detail in Chapter 6. Local post offices may not always make a profit and in some cases do not break even. But they have a value beyond that of profit and loss. They provide a point of contact for the community, acting as a resource for groups such as the old and the vulnerable. In addition, they help to develop and underwrite local civil society and shape and build social capital.

In this regard the emerging concept of public value, as opposed to money value, provides us with an important explanatory and analytical tool. Thinking on *public value* has its origins in debates in the Kennedy School of Business in the USA in the 1980s, when educational programmes were being conceived and designed for managers in the public sector, and one of its chief proponents was Professor Mark Moore.

It is a concept that has taken on an increasing currency in Britain in recent years. The concept of public value sought to analyse the role, purpose and *raison d'être* of public sector organisations. For Moore, 'Language ... had previously centred on efficient effective accomplishment of the mission of the organisation and the protection of the public interest' (Moore, 2007). But herein lies the difficulty. For the private sector, one of the key motivations is producing profits and creating shareholder value, what one might label 'private value'. Yet, as Moore has noted, there appeared to be 'no equivalent for the public sector in models of corporate strategy' (Moore 2007). In other words there seemed to be no public value equivalent.

So how has public value been conceptualised and developed in the UK context? It is a contested term, and one not always easily understood, which has taken on a number of forms. Yet, as Horner *et al.* argue, 'The distinction between consumers and citizens remains at the heart of theoretical developments and application of public value in the UK' (Horner *et al.*, 2006: 16). This notion links directly to some of the arguments in the book. Consumers can be seen as atomised individuals making individual choices in the market place. But public services operate in a broader domain.

As Horner *et al.* note, 'In a democracy this [public] value is ultimately defined by the public themselves. Value is determined by citizens' preferences' (Horner *et al.*, 2006: 18). But, as they go on to argue, 'It is only of value if citizens – either individually or collectively – are willing to give up something in return for it' (Horner *et al.*, 2006: 18). This not only takes the form of paying ones one's council tax but giving up one's time, for example as a community volunteer, magistrate, or parish councillor.

In other words, the discussion of public value relates directly to notions of civic engagement and community. Public value is about 'placing individuals as citizens centre stage of the decision making process so that public resources best serve the public's needs and not the self interest of public managers, professionals or the interests of one particular group of citizens' (Horner *et al.*, 2006: 19). It also feeds directly into notions of local democracy and accountability and attempts to tackle the so-called 'democratic deficit' at the local level. The democratic deficit can be defined as the 'the gap between public demands to monitor and control the activities of public institutions and the actual level of control achieved' (Horner *et al.*, 2006: 18).

The gap between the ideal of a democratically controlled National Health Service (NHS), on the one hand, and the existence of largely autonomous health service professionals who appear able to pursue their own agenda 'regardless of democratic wishes' is one possible example (Horner *et al.*, 2006: 18). The outsourcing of local services to private contractors and the increasing use of the Private Finance Initiative (PFI) to build schools and hospitals are other examples. They can create confusion in the eyes of the public as to who is responsible for the service and the method of redress, should they wish to complain. Lines of accountability can also be blurred.

So how does the concept of public value link to the themes of this book? It gets to the heart of the debate about the relative value of markets and the private sector, on the one hand, and public services and the public realm, on the other. The public realm should use markets as a tool instead of being a slave to them, a tendency that has been all too prevalent over the last twenty years. Of course it goes without saying that effective public services which provide real value for money is one goal which we must all strive for. But there is a greater goal of community cohesion and inclusion, social obligation and, dare one say it, a sense of social solidarity and togetherness which good and well-run public services can give us. This is the true value of public services.

Conclusion

This chapter has looked at various theoretical discussions about the meaning of democracy, political participation and civic engagement, social capital, community, civil society and public value. An understanding of such concepts is an important element in helping us to gauge the health of the body politic at the local level. In Chapter 2 I look at survey evidence as to the nature and extent of political participation and civic engagement in Britain. The opportunities for participation and civic engagement go well beyond what one might term the 'formal realm' of politics such as voting and joining a political party. Membership of pressure groups, broader political campaigning on issues such as climate change, activity in the local community and volunteering are equally important elements in shaping a vibrant civil society.

2

Civic engagement and political participation: debates and evidence

---

Introduction

There is a widespread view that democracy at the local level in Britain is in crisis with levels of political participation at an all-time low. Indeed, there is an increasing 'anti-politics' narrative that posits a public alienated from the political class. The public uproar in 2009 over the 'excessive' allowances claimed by some members of parliament (MPs) has fed into this. However, the central argument of this chapter, and indeed of the book itself, is that a deeper and more thoughtful analysis of the available evidence points to a much more nuanced and complex political terrain, with a wide variety of both informal and formal political activity. Democracy at the local level does face real challenges but there are rich seams to be mined and real opportunities to be grasped.

Robert Putnam's study of the USA provides an interesting comparative perspective. Putnam concludes that over the last forty years the country has witnessed a marked decline in civic engagement and notions of community. He talks of 'the complex factors that lie behind the erosion of America's social connectedness and community involvement over the last several decades' (Putnam, 2000: 277). These include the decline of family, pressures of time and money, the growth of big government, the increasing commercialisation of everyday life, the increasing dominance of television and information technology and generational shifts in attitudes to notions of community. (Putnam, 2000: 277–284). The Power Inquiry refers to Putnam's work, stating that 'some years ago there was a fear that Britain was suffering from the same crisis of social capital as that identified in the USA' (Power, 2006: 41).

Some studies seem to reflect a similar downbeat picture in the British context. For example, a report published by the Commission on Urban Life and Faith made the point that 'In the last twenty years Britain had witnessed a widening decline in associational life and traditional forms of political participation ' (Commission on Urban Life and Faith, 2006: 45). Other evidence also seems to paint a similarly pessimistic picture. Commentators point, for example, to the increasingly low turnout in elections (Power, 2006, Electoral Commission). There is also evidence of a decline in the membership of political parties and local political party activism that will be developed in Chapter 4 (Beetham *et al.*, 2008: 42; Bogdanor, 2006).

However, as with all things in the world of politics, matters are not that simple. This brings us back to our earlier theoretical discussions and the need to look beyond the formal realm when considering the level of political participation and civic engagement in Britain today. A closer analysis of the available evidence reveals a complex and sometimes contradictory picture.

Research published by the Power Inquiry, the Economic and Social Research Council (ESRC)-funded Citizen Audit of Britain and the Department of Communities and Local Government (CLG) Citizenship Survey, highlights the myriad of political activity (much of it considered outside the formal realm) at both local and national level in Britain. Work by the Joseph Rowntree Trust (JRT) in a case study of two northern towns presents a somewhat mixed picture, but it too highlights the range of activity taking place at the local level. It argues that 'Democracy lies as much in the vitality of citizens' self organisation in all aspects of their collective life – what has become to be called civil society – as their formal relations to government` (Wilks-Heeg and Clayton, 2006: 193). Furthermore, writers such as Putnam have noted the increasing importance of the symbiotic relationship between political participation, in the more formal sense, and the broader forms of civic engagement that I discussed in Chapter 1 (Putnam, 2000).

I will now consider the evidence by looking at the following eight themes: the state of formal politics, public attitudes to politics, broader forms of civic engagement, involvement in political campaigning and pressure groups, volunteering and the role of charities, community identity and a sense of place, civic engagement and young people and finally the emerging world of the internet/world wide web. What emerges is far less a crisis of political participation and civic engagement and more a colourful kaleidoscope of individual and collective community activity.

The state of formal politics

If we are looking to sustain the thesis that there is a crisis of engagement in Britain we need look no further than turnout at elections. For example, the turnout for the 2001 General Election was a mere 59 per cent, the lowest comparable turnout in British electoral history. In 2005, turnout was up but to a barely respectable 61 per cent. It is true that turnout increased to 65 per cent in the 2010 General Election but this is still a low figure compared to the average from 1945 to 1997. Turnout in local elections remains low, averaging less than 35 per cent. Such figures do not stand comparison with our European counterparts, where turnout is considerably higher.

What factors, then, lie behind such apparent disengagement with the formal electoral process? Findings from the Power Inquiry are illuminating. Power took evidence from a wide range of organisations, groups and individuals. It concluded that the argument that the 'British people's failure to engage with formal democracy resulted from apathy, lack of interest or weak sense of civic duty did not, however, sit well with the evidence' which for Power 'showed a vibrant and innovative realm of participation beyond formal democracy' (Power, 2006: 58). The real explanations lay elsewhere. One of the key findings was that 'people's disengagement with formal democracy was motivated by frustration and alienation' (Power, 2006: 58). People did not feel that the processes of formal democracy gave them sufficient opportunity to affect political decisions. The main political parties were viewed as too similar in their policy offerings and the electoral system was considered to be unfair (Power, 2006: 17).

Such explanations can be equally applied to the challenges facing local democracy, but here the situation is compounded by the fact that thirty years of central government policy initiatives have resulted in a significant erosion of the policy and fiscal autonomy of elected local government. It has been argued elsewhere that local government sought to overcome this process by carving out a creative autonomy in a number of policy areas (Atkinson and Wilks-Heeg, 2000). This not withstanding, commentators have argued that this centralisation of power has contributed to a sense that local government has so little clout that there is little incentive to vote in local elections (Chandler 2009). Such an argument is persuasive but as ever the reality is more complex. For, as Professor John Stewart has wryly observed, 'there is and has long been a problem of low turnout in local elections in United Kingdom. There has not been a golden age of turnouts, disappointing although that is for those who argue that low turnouts are due to increasing centralisation' (Stewart, 2003: 35). I shall return to this issue of local electoral turnout in more detail when I look at local democracy in the formal realm in Chapter 4.

Public attitudes to politics

The Power Inquiry, which published its findings in 2006, was commissioned by the JRT. Its task was to look at the state of British democracy and the extent of political participation and civic engagement. It was a broad-ranging inquiry that took evidence from many organisations and individuals across Britain.

It talks of the myth of apathy (Power, 2006: 58). This might seem somewhat paradoxical given the evidence above concerning public attitudes to the formal democratic process in Britain, but Power argues 'An alternative approach is to explain the British sense of civic duty not as weak but as *essentially non political*' (Power, 2006: 58). It found a strong frustration with, and alienation from formal democracy (Power, 2006: 58). As evidence of this the 2005 Citizenship survey found that only 37 per cent of respondents had trust in parliament (Power, 2006: 35). The seventh Audit of Political Engagement carried out in 2009 (at the height of the MPs' expenses 'scandal') found that public dissatisfaction with MPs stood at 48 per cent. This compares with a 36 per cent dissatisfaction rating in the first audit of political engagement that was published in 2004 (Hansard Society, 2010: 29).

However, local government, that oft-maligned political creature, fared much better in the 2005 Citizenship Survey, with 56 per cent of respondents saying that they had trust in their local council (CLG, 2006a). Linked to this, the seventh Audit of Political Engagement found that 78 per cent of respondents said they were interested in local issues (Hansard Society, 2010: 119). In addition, data from the eighth Audit of Political Engagement showed that 40 per cent of the British public agreed that local councils had a significant impact on their everyday lives. Only the media scored higher, with 42 per cent. Parliament scored only 30 per cent (Hansard Society, 2011: 89). One might tentatively conclude from this that the nearer an institution is to the local community the more trusted and visible it becomes. This is of course a broad generalisation, but such a view does have echoes in the increasing calls in Britain for a greater degree of political decentralisation away from Westminster and Whitehall and the growing discourse around localism and the 'big society'.

Indeed, the Power Inquiry argued strongly that 'The current way of doing politics is killing politics' (Power, 2006: 22). The current system does not respond to changing values and does not adapt to change. Strikingly, 56 per cent of potential voters in 2003 felt they had no say or influence on what government does (Power, 2006: 76).

The available evidence appears to point to a generational shift in attitudes to politics. As Power noted the 'norms supporting political activity have weakened over time' (Power, 2006: 57). It quotes a study by Whiteley that found in 1959 that in a survey 70 per cent of respondents believed that citizens should participate in local affairs to some degree. When asked a similar question in 2000, the figure had fallen to 40 per cent (Whiteley, 2003).

A study by Clarke *et al.* seems to point to similar conclusions. In an analysis of civic duty over time, it found a gradual but significant decline in people's propensity to vote. Respondents were asked if they felt it would be a serious neglect of duty not to use their right to vote. The findings do seem to point to a shift in attitudes through the generations. Of those who first had the opportunity to vote during the premiership of Harold Macmillan,

79 per cent said 'yes'. This declined to 70 per cent in the Wilson/Callaghan era of 1974–79. By the time of the Thatcher era the figure had declined to 50 per cent. Under New Labour, the figure stood at 41 per cent (Clarke *et al.* 2004).

Yet it should be noted that Power's own research casts doubt on this view of a declining sense of civic duty. As he argues, 'It is quite conceivable that respondents [to such surveys] were expressing not apathy, indifference or a weak sense of civic duty but a broader lack of allegiance to formal democracy resulting from a strong sense that existing institutions and processes offer little meaning' (Power, 2006: 58). This is an important point. The widespread furore that broke out in May 2009 over the 'excesses' of the allowance system for MPs left the position of formal political institutions in a state of flux. But the public anger that erupted, as evidenced by opinion polls and the like reflected, perhaps somewhat paradoxically, not a rejection of politics but a lively interest in it, or what one might term an 'engaged apathy'. As the *Guardian* put it 'The cynicism of many voters towards Westminster had been replaced by something much more engaged, but also far more enraged' (*Guardian*, 16 May 2009).

What we are perhaps witnessing, as Power argued, is a 'changing sense of civic duty' (Power, 2006: 58). Power took evidence from the political scientist Pippa Norris who conducted a cross-national survey of political participation in 2002. In her evidence, Norris argued that what we are witnessing is not a weakening of civic duty but rather a population engaged in a repertoire of political activities beyond voting in an attempt to influence decision makers (Power, 2006: 59).

Power goes on to argue that if we accept the weakening sense of duty thesis we might also expect to see a concomitant loss of interest in politics. Let us consider the evidence. The annual Audit of Political Engagement found in the period from 2003 to 2008 that the annual average of those people who had discussed politics or political news with someone else was around 40 per cent (Hansard Society, 2010). However, methodological problems do emerge. The findings of the Audit in 2006 'suggested that politics suffers from a definitional problem ... as only 6 per cent of the British population had, in fact, not discussed any of the seventeen political issues with which they were prompted' (Hansard Society, 2006). The Audit of Political Engagement found that in 2010 58 per cent of the public said they had an interest in politics (Hansard Society, 2011: 65). This supports one of the conclusions of the Power Inquiry that 'interest in political issues is high' (Power, 2006: 16).

The Power Inquiry conducted a survey of 1,025 people who were on the electoral register but did not vote at the 2005 General Election. A number of themes emerge. First, only 19 per cent of respondents gave apathy as the reason for not voting; 36 per cent cited factors such as little difference between the parties in terms of policy or the fact that politicians could not be trusted. Second, the findings highlighted some apparent contradictions in the answers of the respondents. Power noted that '66 per cent declared themselves uninterested in politics' yet at the same time more than 90 per cent of respondents 'identified three or more political issues that really mattered' (Power, 2006: 60). Third, non-voters were asked to choose from a list of factors that might make them more likely to vote. The majority of non-voters (54 per cent) chose politicians both listening to people's views between elections and keeping their policy promises. For eighteen- to twenty-four-year-olds, what one might term the 'lost generation' in terms of electoral politics, the figure rose to 72 per cent (Power, 2006: 60).

The 2005 Annual Audit of Political Engagement found that 53 per cent of those interviewed expressed themselves as fairly or very interested in politics. By 2006, this figure had risen to 56 per cent before falling back to 51 per cent in 2007. In 2009, the figure stood at 52 per cent. In 2010, 53 per cent of respondents said they were interested in politics. Despite these statistical variations interest in politics has remained broadly consistent at 50 per cent or more in the period from 2004 to 2010 (Hansard Society, 2010). (See Figure 2.)

Looking further into the figures, a number of gender and generational differences can be highlighted. Data from the 2010 Audit shows that 58 per cent of men expressed themselves as very or fairly interested in politics as compared to 48 per cent of women. In terms of the generations, the data for 2010 shows that the highest level of recorded interest was amongst the fifty-five to sixty-four age group. 66 per cent of this group were either fairly or very interested in politics. By contrast, only 38 per cent of those aged eighteen to twenty-four expressed an interest in politics, the lowest of any age group (Hansard, 2010: 70). Such findings about young people help to

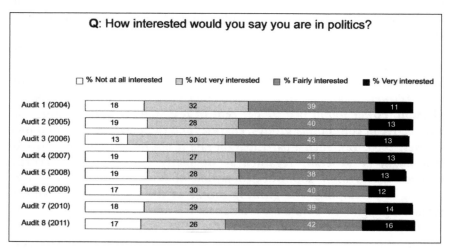

2 Interest in politics

underpin the general impression, as expressed in the media and elsewhere, of a disengaged generation ploughing individualistic furrows. Yet, not surprisingly, the reality is more complex. Some research indicates that many younger people are more attracted to pressure politics than formal party and electoral politics (Power, 2009: 59). They are interested in politics but not the politics of elections and political party manifestos. There is also evidence that younger people aged eighteen to twenty-four are the most likely to engage in volunteering. I shall return to this presently.

What, then, of the public's knowledge of politics? The 2010 Audit of Political Engagement found that 51 per cent of respondents said that they knew either a fair amount or a great deal about politics. This is the highest recorded figure since the audit was first published in 2004. Such figures point to a far from insignificant knowledge of politics amongst the general population but they still leave just under 50 per cent of the population with little or knowledge of politics. The figures are more worrying for those aged between eighteen to twenty-four, with only 35 per cent of respondents who said that they knew a fair amount or a great deal about politics (Hansard, 2010: 62). What, then, are the implications of such findings for the health of the British polity? A number of studies have found that low levels of political knowledge dampen political participation. Pattie *et al.* make the important point 'that raising people's interest in politics generally makes them more active citizens (Pattie *et al.*, 2003: 466).

Broader forms of civic engagement

What comes out of much of the survey evidence, and it is an argument that will be developed in this and subsequent chapters, is that 'it is important not to confuse changing senses of what constitute civic duty and political involvement with a decline in civic duty and political participation' (Power, 2006: 60).

Whilst it is true that the Power Inquiry found significant disengagement with formal politics, it also argued that there is clear evidence of a growing involvement of people in what it terms 'pressure politics' over a number of years (Power, 2006: 17). In a survey of non-voters after the 2005 General Election, Power found that 37 per cent of respondents were members or were active in community groups, charities and campaigning organisations (Power, 2006: 42). Such a participation rate is not insignificant in a group that might be generally regarded as singularly apathetic. This perhaps suggests that a more sophisticated notion of how to influence decision making is developing. The growing profile of the UK Uncut movement (which highlights corporate tax avoidance) is a case in point.

Other available evidence, such as the ESRC-funded Citizen Audit of Britain, also points to a relatively high level of political campaigning outside the formal realm of electoral politics. The brief was to conduct an audit of citizenship in Britain; it set out to examine political participation, voluntary activity, and the values of individuals that underpin civil society. In the words of in its principal authors, it was a 'large multi-wave survey of citizenship in the United Kingdom at the start of the twenty first century' Pattie *et al.*, 2003: 446). Some 3,400 individuals were interviewed face-to-face in one hundred local authorities across Britain. In addition, a large sample of 10,000 people responded to a mail survey.

The Citizen Audit found that over a twelve-month period (2001–2) 62 per cent of respondents had donated money to a political campaign and 42 per cent had signed a petition. In addition, 25 per cent had contacted a public official and 13 per cent had contacted a politician to effect a change in the law or public policy. As the Power Commission noted, such levels of participation are significant (Power, 2006: 42).

The Citizenship Survey paints a similar picture. It is a survey of a representative sample of 10,000 people across England. Since 2005, it has been under the auspices of the CLG. Its research in 2010 found that 34 per cent of respondents had either signed a petition, contacted a public official or lobbied a politician in the previous twelve months (CLG, 2010a: 2).

Involvement in political campaigns and pressure groups

The World Values Survey is a world-wide network of social scientists studying changing values and their impact on social and political life. It has conducted five waves of surveys since 1981. It found that the proportion of British people taking part in demonstrations had gone up from 6 per cent in 1974 to 13 per cent in 2000 (see Power, 2006: 43). In addition, the percentage of Britons taking part in consumer boycotts rose from 6 per cent in 1974 to 17 per cent in 2000 (Power, 2006: 44). The Citizen Audit found evidence of an even more significant rise in this area, with 31 per cent of respondents stating that they had 'boycotted certain products' in 2000 (Power, 2006: 44). The annual Audit of Political Engagement found that in the period from 2003 to 2008 an average of 19 per cent of respondents had taken part in a consumer boycott for political, ethical, or environmental reasons (Hansard Society, 2009: 3).

The Power Inquiry's own research on political activity found that those involved in such community and campaigning activities 'enjoy high morale and commitment' (Power, 2006: 42). Power quotes one local activist who said that such campaigning and activity 'makes a real difference and produces real results that impact on peoples' lives' (Power, 2006: 43). Friends of the Earth (UK) has over 100,000 financial supporters in addition to a myriad of local groups. Greenpeace (UK) has in the region of 154,000 supporters. Developing this theme of political activity outside the formal realm, Power argues that the early 2000s witnessed three of the most widely supported campaign events ever to take place in Britain (Power, 2006: 43).

First, the Countryside Alliance (which calls on policy makers to give more attention to rural affairs) drew an estimated crowd of 400,000 to its London demonstration in 2001. Second, the 2003 Stop the Iraq war demonstration saw an estimated crowd of 1 million marching through the streets of London. And, finally, the Live 8 concert in 2005 (part of the campaign to Make Poverty History) was attended by 150,000 people. Power makes an important point, as these are large numbers.

Evidence from the Citizen Audit also appears to suggest relatively high group membership. The audit found that 40 per cent of people were part of what one might term 'active citizenship', that is members of organised groups. The audit found that 25 per cent of people participated in the activities of an organisation. In total 18 million people were members of an organisation and 11 million were active participants (Whiteley *et al.*, 2003). Such numbers are significant and suggest the high levels of group activity evidenced by the Power Inquiry. Yet much of this activity was not what one might term 'political'. The Citizen Audit found 29 that per cent of people belonged to a motoring organisation. Groups with a potential social or political agenda, such as trade unions, accounted for 9 per cent and resident and neighbourhood associations accounted for 6 per cent; 3 per cent were members of churches. A range of campaign groups, including environmental, animal rights and human rights organisations made up 6 per cent of the total (Whiteley, 2003).

Volunteering and the role of charities

Another way to measure the state of play in relation to civic engagement, community and a sense of civic duty is to look at the extent of volunteering and support for charities in Britain. The Charity Commission's web site lists some 167,000 registered charities. In addition Stephen Bubb, Chief Executive of the Association of Chief Executives of Voluntary Organisations (ACEVO), has argued that 'Rather than turning away from charity, young people in particular are increasingly turning to it and away from more traditional ways of making change happen' (*Observer*, 1 June 2008). I shall return to the issue of young people and civic engagement presently.

Let us look at the evidence in respect of the level of volunteering. Research by MORI on behalf of the Charity Commission shows that public trust in charities is growing (Ipsos MORI, 2008: 4). Furthermore, 75 per cent of those interviewed agreed that 'most charities are trustworthy and act in the public interest' (Ipsos MORI, 2008: 14). Public trust of charities ranks higher than that for central and local government (Ipsos MORI, 2008: 4). The Citizenship Survey also provides an insight into the level of volunteering today. Its survey of some 10,000 people looks at the extent of what it terms 'informal' and 'formal' volunteering. The survey defines informal volunteering 'as giving unpaid help as an individual to someone who is not a relative' (CLG, 2006a: 4). Formal volunteering is defined as 'unpaid leave given as part of groups, clubs or organisations to benefit others of the environment' (CLG, 2006a: 6).

The 2009/10 Citizenship Survey found that 54 per cent of people in England had carried out informal or formal voluntary activity at least once in the last twelve months; 29 per cent of respondents had volunteered at least once a month. In respect of formal volunteering, 40 per cent of respondents had volunteered at least once a year, with 25 per cent saying that they had volunteered at least once every month (CLG, 2010a).

Such survey evidence is important, since such volunteering can give individuals the opportunity to tap into social networks and reach out beyond their immediate social group. This helps to build the kind of bridging social capital we looked at in our theoretical discussions in Chapter 1. Contacts can be made and self-esteem developed. Such volunteering can also help build linking social capital. Through volunteering, individuals may come into contact with local officials and councillors and tap into the local decision making network. This can open up opportunities for the individual by providing access to information and advice.

A study by Wilks-Heeg and Clayton focused on the extent of volunteering in two towns in the north of England, namely Burnley in Lancashire and Harrogate in Yorkshire. In the case of Burnley they found that there were 354 Voluntary Community Organisations (VCOs) in the town that between them attracted 8,500 volunteers, representing 95 per 1,000 of the town's population. That added up to 15 hours per head of population. Turning to Harrogate, there were 605 VCOs in the town, attracting 10,080 volunteers or 67 volunteers per 1,000 of the population. This represents 20,600 volunteer hours per year or 1–3 hours per head of population, considerably down on the figures for Burnley (Wilks-Heeg and Clayton, 2006: 113). But a word of caution is needed here. For as Wilks-Heeg and Clayton acknowledge, we encounter a number of methodological problems here, not least due to the variety of methods used to collect the data in the two towns. Thus making comparisons between the two towns and drawing definitive conclusions 'is highly problematic' (Wilks-Heeg and Clayton, 2006: 113). Indeed, findings from the Citizen Panel surveys in the two towns found that around 20 per cent of Burnley respondents had volunteered formally in the past 12 months, compared to 27 per cent in Harrogate (Wilks-Heeg and Clayton, 2006: 114).

The results of the Citizen Panel surveys showed significant common features in the two towns. Faith groups, trade unions, local voluntary groups, residents' and tenants' groups, sports and social clubs made up the core membership groups in both towns (Wilks-Heeg and Clayton, 2006: 114). In particular, the evidence in respect of faith groups and trade unions was 'particularly striking' (Wilks-Heeg and Clayton, 2006: 115) especially given the apparent decline in church attendance and trade union membership.

Membership of faith groups was around 20 per cent in both surveys; it was the second highest form of group membership in Burnley and the third highest in Harrogate. In addition, there was evidence of the role of faith groups in broader forms of civic engagement (Wilks-Heeg and Clayton, 2006: 116).

The Commission on Urban Life and Faith makes a similar point. Whilst acknowledging that membership of most churches has declined it argues that 'many local church communities, alongside congregations of other faiths, stand out in urban locations as amongst the most vibrant institutions in civil society' (Commission on Urban Life and Faith, 2006: 45). One might use the term 'community group spill over' to describe this process. The Harrogate research highlighted one particular church member who exemplifies this process. In addition to her church membership, she was active in two local campaigns, Make Poverty History and promotion of fair trade. She was a member of the Fair Trade steering group that involves a number of other community groups in the town. She estimated that around 180 members of her local church were involved in some kind of local activity, a significant number given the potential 'ripple effect' of this on other organisations in the area (Wilks-Heeg and Clayton, 2006: 115).

In all, there were forty churches in Harrogate, all of which supported fair trade. Many of these churches also supported other local campaigns such as action on climate change and the environment; all of which adds up to a potentially significant contribution to local community activity amongst faith groups.

In summary, such widespread evidence of volunteering gives weight to the argument of the Power Inquiry 'that very large numbers of citizens are engaged in community and charity work outside of politics' (Power, 2006: 16). It does seem to gainsay the current negative orthodoxy about the decline of community and the weakening of social cohesion. There are commentators, however, who disagree. Professor Alison Woolf argues that people in Britain are actually turning their backs on charity (*Guardian*, 25 May 2008). Woolf acknowledges that the aforementioned citizenship surveys suggest high levels of volunteering but she attempts to cast a critical eye on the available evidence. She suggests, somewhat disparagingly, that charities include bodies such as sports clubs, amateur choirs and a variety of small arts groups in addition to what she describes as 'traditional charities'. Then, in citizenship surveys, she says somewhat sarcastically, you are classified as volunteering if you feed your neighbour's cat or give someone advice.

Let us deal with these two points. First, Woolf seems somewhat dismissive of community choirs and local arts groups. Yet such groups play an important role in creating a sense of community and are an important element of civic engagement. Indeed writers such as Robert Putnam have praised the positive civic and political effect of choirs (Putnam, 2000). Such groups reinforce the point made in the theoretical discussion about the interrelationship between formal political participation and these everyday examples of civic engagement.

Second, feeding the neighbour's cat or giving out advice may seem relatively minor acts. Yet such acts help create the social cement and building blocks that help support and create the kind of social capital I talked about earlier. It is very much the case that the whole is certainly much greater than the sum of the parts. It is often the little things that matter. Big-ticket projects, such as a major regeneration project, often catch the attention, and that is understandable. Yet the kindly support of a neighbour, the friendly chatter of a local hairdresser with her elderly, sometimes lonely, clients matters as much if not more so: a case of from little acorns mighty oaks do grow.

Woolf's broad thesis is that meaningful civic engagement is on the decline. She identifies a number of factors in this, one being the decline in organised religion. Woolf argues that many of the most well-known charities in Britain have varying links to organised religion. She cites the NSPCC, Barnado's, Crisis and the Samaritans as examples of this. She also makes the point that volunteering amongst those who are actively religious is twice that of the general population. With the 'recent precipitous decline in church membership' from Woolf's perspective there are clear implications for the functioning of the charitable sector.

Yet such a view is open to debate. Indeed Woolf herself concedes that churches, through their existing networks, are in a position to respond to social need. We have noted the survey evidence from Burnley and Harrogate that highlighted the role that the churches and other religious institutions played in local community activity. The Commission on Urban Life and Faith makes a similar point (Commission on Urban Life and Faith, 2006: 45).

Community identity and a sense of place

Some commentators paint a pessimistic picture in respect of community and civic engagement. Atkinson, for example, notes the widespread feeling that communities have become weakened over time; a consequence of 'not only market forces and technological change but also the policies of successive governments' (Atkinson, 1994: 1). Dorling *et al.* argue that neighbourhoods in many parts of Britain 'were more socially distinct in 2008 compared to the more mixed neighbourhoods of around 1968' (Dorling *et al.* 2008: 2). This was the product of increased population movement coupled with social, economic and political change (Dorling *et al.*, 2008: 2). The consequences of this are an increasing 'demographic segregation and polarisation' coupled with growing 'social fragmentation and political disengagement' (Dorling *et al.*, 2008: 35). Dorling *et al.* warn of the danger of 'such polarisation and segregation processes' leading to increased feelings of isolation and 'weaker feelings of belonging' (Dorling *et al.*, 2008:

25). Such findings have clear implications for community cohesion and the development of social capital and would appear to be an indictment of public policy in Britain over the last forty years.

However, the findings of the Citizenship Survey appear to cast a somewhat different light. Headline findings for the 2007 Survey show that 75 per cent of respondents said that they had a strong feeling of belonging to their neighbourhood. This shows an increase of 4 per cent as compared to 2003 (CLG, 2008: 7). Moreover, the Survey suggests a relatively high level of community cohesion. For example, it found that 80 per cent of people mixed socially with those of different religious and ethnic groups (CLG, 2008e: 7). Furthermore, 82 per cent of respondents agreed that their local area was a place where those from different backgrounds 'got on well together' (CLG, 2008e: 8), an increase from 80 per cent in 2003 and 2005. The findings of the 2009 Survey were broadly in line with those for 2007. Thus the picture that we see of communities and neighbourhoods across Britain is one of shades of grey rather than simple black and white. The problems facing communities and neighbourhoods are real enough. Such problems are the product of many factors, including wrong-headed government policy, social neglect and decay, poor local services and lack of employment prospects. But amidst the problems there is potential for positive action and outcomes. The Commission on Urban Life and Faith makes this point well. Whilst by no means underestimating the many challenges faced by local communities today, it talks of the 'unprecedented opportunities' for government, church and broader society (Commission on Urban Life and Faith, 2006: 17).

Civic engagement and young people

If there is one section of society that seems to encapsulate the so-called 'crisis of civic engagement' it is the youth of Britain. Research commissioned by the Prince's Trust found that only 9 per cent of adults believe that young people make a positive contribution to their local communities (Prince's Trust, 2008). In addition, 72 per cent admitted to feeling nervous and threatened when they saw young people in the street (Prince's Trust, 2008). Reinforcing this negative image, Women in Journalism looked at a representative sample of stories on a range of topics concerning teenage boys. It found that only 16 per cent of stories about teenage boys and entertainment were positive in nature. Stories about teenage boys and sport was only slightly higher at 24 per cent (Women in Journalism, 2009: 11). In addition, of the 8,269 newspaper stories surveyed, more than half were about crime and young people (Women in Journalism, 2009: 11).

As a spokesperson for the Prince's Trust has noted, 'Reading the great British press it would be easy to think that all our teenagers are involved in gangs and wielding knives' (*Independent on Sunday*, 12 April 2009). But the

Prince's Trust challenges such a stereotype, arguing that 'figures show that that teenagers are more likely to volunteer than any other generation' (The Princes Trust, 2008). This is backed up by the children's charity, Barnado's, which says that in its research it has found that young people do show concern about life in their communities (Barnado's, 2005: 14).

Such statements may seem somewhat counterintuitive but there is evidence of a significant level of voluntary and community activity amongst young people. For example, 275,000 young people took part in Duke of Edinburgh award scheme programmes in 2008. Evidence from the 2005 Citizenship Survey found that younger people (those aged from sixteen to nineteen) were the most likely group to participate in informal voluntary activity at least once a month (CLG, 2006a). In 2009, the figures showed that 55 per cent of young people volunteered formally or informally at least once a month. This was 1 per cent higher than the overall average for the population (CLG 2006a).

The emerging role of the internet/world wide web

The arrival of the so-called 'web2 technology' has brought a step change in the way we interact with our personal computers. No longer are we mere passive recipients of information handed down by official bodies and experts. Web2 technology offers the potential for greater interactivity and the sharing of a multiplicity of ideas and viewpoints that can impact on politics and decision making. We are witnessing the growing phenomena of the political blog, web-based opinion pieces with the opportunity for comment by visitors to the site. In addition, discussion forums such as twitter afford the opportunity for the sharing of information and ideas.

But to what extent does such technology open up a space for greater participation and the democratisation of the political process? The Power Inquiry noted that its brief survey of discussion forums showed that politics and current affairs were amongst the principal topics for discussion (Power, 2006: 44). Live Journal estimates that there are some 78,000 active bloggers in Britain. The UK Poli Blogs website has links to 257 blogs with a specifically political theme (Power, 2006: 44).

Conclusion

There is a widely held view that we face a crisis of democracy, political participation and civic engagement in Britain today. Indeed, low electoral turnout and declining political party membership lend some credence to this thesis. Yet, as I have argued in this chapter, a closer examination of the evidence points to a significant degree of civic engagement beyond the formal realm of politics. This ranges from global campaigns to Make Poverty History, through to national campaigns to protect forests, right down to volunteering in the local community. People are still engaged in the body politic but that engagement now takes a variety of forms.

There might also be another way to look at the extent of local civic engagement. Perhaps we are looking at the issue through the wrong end of the lens. There is some evidence that seems to show that the same number of people is involved as local activists as they ever were. It is just that these activities are spread more thinly than in the past. We seem to have an ever-expanding civic space. Significant changes in the local space over the last decade have seen a shift away from formal local government structures and institutions as the principal locus for policy shaping and service delivery to what has become known as local governance. Whether it is as a participant in a citizens' panel, a member of a local ward assembly, or a parent representative on the governing body of a local school, the sheer range and availability of local activities is there for all to see.

Having carried out this broad survey of the state of play with regard to political participation and civic engagement, Chapters 5–7 will focus on a number of policy initiatives. With this in mind, I now turn to an analysis of some of the major policies, debates and initiatives that have helped to shape the local political space over the last fifteen years.

3

The challenge of local democracy, civic engagement and community: an agenda for change?

Introduction

In the early period of the newly elected Labour government after 1997 the apparent conciliatory tone towards local government was in sharp contrast to the conflicted nature of central/local relations during the Thatcher and Major years. Tighter financial restrictions, rate capping, cuts in central government financial support, increased privatisation of local authority services and loss of policy autonomy all gave the clear impression of a beleaguered local democracy under threat and fighting it seemed for its very existence. Now whilst it has been argued elsewhere that local government fought a smart rearguard action against this full-frontal assault and indeed in a number of areas did succeed in carving out a creative autonomy in a number of respects (Atkinson and Wilks-Heeg, 2000), the threat to British local democracy, whose roots can be traced back some 700 years, was real enough. It should not be forgotten that in the 1980s Nicholas Ridley, the then Secretary of State for the Environment with responsibility for local government, actively considered the abolition of democratically elected local government in Britain. It did not happen, that is certainly true, but even the consideration of such a policy option put into sharp relief the sheer contempt that Thatcherism appeared to have for large sections of local government. It is true that such stridency was toned down somewhat in the Major years but the broad thrust of Conservative policy remained in place; an increasing centralisation of decision making and a closing down of local autonomy.

The landslide victory of the Labour Party in 1997 held out the possibility of a major and positive change in central/local relations. Leach and Pratchett have argued that 'It is too easy to forget the euphoria with which the world of local government welcomed the arrival of New Labour into office in 1997'

(Leach and Pratchett, 2005: 318). Here was a government that appeared to value local government. Was there to be a new 'golden age' of local democracy? It is true that the relationship witnessed its fair share of problems, with the local government policy of the Labour government being both contradictory and uncertain at times. Yet the mood music, notwithstanding the occasional discordant note, was softer in tone. There was, it appeared, the potential for a more vibrant local politics.

In this context, the chapter focuses on nine key aspects of the reform of local democracy over the last fifteen years: local democracy and the New Labour reform agenda; the constitutional position of local government; double devolution; the citizen engagement, neighbourhood and empowerment agenda; civic engagement, neighbourhood, empowerment and the role of elected local government; partnership working; policy autonomy and the role of elected local government; creative autonomy and the need for a cultural shift; and finally the fiscal autonomy of local government.

The analysis will draw on the views of policy think tanks, government-commissioned enquiries, pressure groups, and parliamentary reports. There will also be a focus on the emerging policy towards local government and local politics of the Conservative/Liberal Democratic coalition government that came to power in May 2010.

Local democracy and the New Labour reform agenda

In its election manifesto for the 1997 General Election the Labour Party spoke in grand terms of giving power back to local people and of revitalising local democracy. Tony Blair himself talked of creating a 'reborn and energised local government' (quoted in *Guardian*, 3 November 1997). Such language seemed a world away from Thatcherism. Yet even early on, uncertainties and contradictions were apparent in New Labour's stance in respect of elected local government.

Writing in a pamphlet for the Institute for Public Policy Research (IPPR), a left-of-centre think tank, Tony Blair made it clear that, should local authorities fail to carry out their role effectively, central government would not hesitate to intervene (Blair, 1998). The clear suspicion remained that the Labour government did not quite trust local government. Tabloid newspaper headlines with their vivid portrayals of 'loony left' Labour-controlled local councils in the 1980s, such as the Greater London Council (GLC) and Liverpool, remained burned in the hearts and minds of Labour strategists.

In the very early days of the Labour government local government reform was not an obvious priority. Broader constitutional matters dominated the government's policy agenda with its programme of devolution to the nations of the UK. In 1999 there were elections for the first Scottish Parliament since the Act of Union of Union in 1707 and a National Assembly for Wales. The search for a constitutional settlement in Northern

Ireland culminated in the so-called Good Friday Agreement in 1998 and the eventual restoration of devolved government to Northern Ireland.

Yet reform of local democracy did emerge as an important element in the government's policy agenda. It is important to note that Labour's early plans for local democracy did not develop in a vacuum but drew on a number of sources. The 1995 Commission for Local Democracy (CLD) report, *Taking Charge: The Rebirth of Local Democracy*, was an important source for some of Labour's early thinking on local democracy and the direction it should take. The government drew on the experiences on the ground of a number of Labour-controlled councils and also sought the views of the associations representing local government. Despite the broad welcome from the local government community, it is fair to say that the Labour government's policies came in for criticism, some of it quite stinging.

A number of local government initiatives soon started to emerge from central government from 1997 onwards. The broad policy vision contained in the 1997 General Election manifesto was given more detailed shape in the 1998 white paper, *Modernising Local Government: In Touch with Local People*. The Local Government Acts of 1999 and 2000 followed. We can identify four broad elements of Labour's emerging local government strategy which continued to shape its thinking over the following decade, albeit refined, revisioned and reformulated. First, there was a strong emphasis on the efficacy and performance of local services with particular reference to the policy of Best Value and the Beacon Council strategy. Second, there was a strong focus on the community leadership role of local councils. They were to have broad responsibility for the well being of their local communities. Other important elements here included community strategies (such as New Deal for Communities) and the development of Local Strategic Partnerships (LSPs).

Third, New Labour talked of the need for what it termed 'democratic renewal', with reform of the processes of local political decision making. This included the replacement of the long-established local committee system. In the majority of local councils (in England and Wales) this has meant a council leader supported by a cabinet of senior councillors, a kind of mini-version of central government. Also included was the big idea of directly elected mayors, a radical departure from the broadly collectivist decision making of British local government. Yet in only a small number of councils (thirteen in 2010) have we witnessed the arrival of directly elected executive mayors. The reasons for this and the arguments for and against directed elected mayors, including the current proposals of the coalition government, will be analysed in Chapter 4 when I look at formal democracy at the local level.

Fourth, and directly related to the democratic renewal agenda itself, was the focus on boosting electoral turnout (see Chapter 4), but also broader forms of public and civic engagement. This has taken a variety of forms including the introduction of different forms of neighbourhood governance and an increasing emphasis on the so-called 'empowerment' of individuals and communities at the local level.

Leach and Pratchett have argued that in its first term there was a real clarity in Labour's strategy to revitalise local democracy but that this turned to policy drift after the 2001 general election (Leach and Pratchett, 2005: 319). 'It soon became clear', Leach and Pratchett argue, 'that the momentum of the 1997 agenda [to revitalise local democracy] had been lost' (Leach and Pratchett, 2005: 319). Indeed Stoker has spoken of the lack of coherence in New Labour's policy approach towards local government (Stoker, 2003: 227).

In December 2001, a white paper was published entitled *Strong Leadership: Quality Public Services.* For Leach and Pratchett, this was a 'flawed and unconvincing document' that offered 'little in the way of long term vision' (Leach and Pratchett, 2005: 319). Criticism in the local government press was widespread.

A brief analysis of the white paper illustrates why it met such a critical response. Although the central elements of New Labour's local government modernisation strategy (discussed above) remained formally in place, there was a distinct change of emphasis, with a more instrumentalist approach. Public service improvements were becoming central to the strategy with the introduction of such measures as comprehensive performance assessments and local public service agreements. Promoting democratic renewal slipped down the agenda. As an illustration of this, directly elected mayors no longer seemed the big idea they once were. Stephen Byers, the Secretary of State, ruled out central government intervention to force local authorities to hold local referenda to establish elected mayors (Leach and Pratchett, 2005: 319). For Leach and Pratchett, central government policy towards local government became 'increasingly piecemeal and disconnected' Leach and Pratchett, 2005: 320).

In July 2004, the Office of the Deputy Prime Minister (ODPM), which had taken on responsibility for local government, set out its thinking for the long term in the document *The Future of Local Government: Developing a 10 Year Vision.* It appeared to signal a strategic shift in the so-called policy of democratic renewal. Sustainability now entered the lexicon of the Labour government and its strategy of local democratic renewal and the reform of the local space.

As the document put it:

> One of the government's key priorities is to create sustainable communities – places where people want to live and that promote opportunity and a better quality of life. Local government has a vital role [to play] in this. Sustainable communities require an environment of good governance, public participation, partnership working and civic pride. A new approach to local government could ... increase public engagement in the decisions that affect them and lead to better outcomes for people and places. (ODPM, 2004:8)

With no little hubris, the document goes on to state that 'This is a big prize and one that makes the project worthwhile' (ODPM, 2004: 8). It is to this project that I now turn.

It would not be a misinterpretation to describe the Labour government's attempts to reform the local space over the last decade as a mesmerising miasma of white papers, green papers, pre-policy announcements, press releases, symposiums, consultations, parliamentary Bills and Acts of Parliament.

The policy process became overloaded with an endless stream of initiatives: double devolution, directly elected mayors, community em-powerment action packs, local assemblies, LSPs, multi-area agreements and so on. The list seemed to get longer and longer. Added up, such a stream of initiatives puts the Heinz fifty-seven varieties to shame. Just as you think you might have got to grips with the agenda, there is yet another policy announcement. It brings to mind those ubiquitous fairground ducks. As fast as you shoot them down, more simply pop up!

In evidence to the CLG House of Commons select committee, Warwickshire County Council referred to the tortuous nature of some of the legislation affecting local government (House of Commons, 2009a: 27). The titles of parliamentary Bills and Acts of Parliament seemed to get longer and longer. In 2007, the Local Government and Public Involvement in Health Act was passed. In 2009, the Local Democracy, Economic Development and Construction Bill was put before parliament. Debating the Bill in the House of Commons on 1 June 2009, the then Shadow CLG Secretary of State Caroline Spellman, a woman not best known for her witticisms, exclaimed that the longer the title of a parliamentary Bill was 'the more Delphic was the content'. This is a reference to the Oracle at Delphi whose utterances became less and less comprehensible the more they went on!

Yet out of this miasma of complexity some discernible themes did emerge and it is to these that I now turn.

The constitutional position of local government

In Britain, local government has historically operated under the doctrine of *ultra vires*. In effect, local authorities are only allowed to act in such areas as are expressly permitted by various Acts of Parliament. Any actions embarked on by local authorities that do not have specific statutory backing can be struck down by the courts on the grounds that they are *ultra vires*, beyond their powers. The result has been a series of recurring tensions between local and central government, tensions only exacerbated by the failure of the formal doctrine of *ultra vires* to fully capture the real and substantive impact of local government on a day-to-day basis.

Within its first year of office (1998), the Labour government had signed the European Charter of Local Self Government. Drawn up under the auspices of the Council of Europe (as distinct from the European Union) the Charter only has a advisory status, but it does set out some key principles about the status and position of local government within the broader political system. Article 2, for example, states that 'the powers and responsibilities of local government must be recognised and laid down in the law'. Furthermore, article 4(2) states that local authorities shall within the 'limits of the law have the full discretion to exercise their initiative with regard to any matter which is not excluded from their competence nor assigned to any authority' (quoted in Scottish Parliament, 2002: 6). Though symbolic in nature, this might have been a cata-lyst for a revitalised British local democracy (Atkinson and Wilks-Heeg, 2000: 255). However, as the Power Inquiry has argued, that ratified charter 'seems to be growing mould on a shelf in Whitehall' with little substantive impact on increasing the policy autonomy of British local government (Power, 2006: 160). Jeremy Smith, Secretary General of the Council of European Municipalities, makes a similar point, arguing that the Charter 'has hardly been in the thinking of government since they ratified it' (House of Commons, 2009a: 55). A 2009 CLG select committee report argued that it is not clear 'how the prescriptive nature of the English system of local government complies with the Charter' (House of Commons, 2009a: 55). Beetham *et al.* go further by arguing that continuing central government 'controls over policy and finance and the absence of adequate tax raising powers contravene the standards of the charter itself' (Beetham *et al.*, 2008: 32).

Indeed, back in 1986 the Widdicombe Inquiry into the workings of local authorities spoke of the need for a system of local government that would provide 'political checks and balances and a restraint on arbitrary govern-ment' (Widdicombe, 1986).

The Power Inquiry called for a concordat between central and local government that should set out where the respective powers and responsi-bilities of the two tiers should lie. The aim should be to 'enshrine the process of decentralisation' (Power, 2006: 160). This would build on the principles outlined in the European Charter on Local Self Government.

Following on from this, on 12 December 2007 a concordat between central government and local government was launched. It was an agree-ment between central government and the Local Government Association (LGA), the body representing local government in England. It sought to establish a 'framework of principles for how central and local government work together to serve the public' (CLG, 2008a: 139). Separate arrangements exist in Wales under the terms of the devolution settlement.

The concordat was welcomed by some. In a letter to the *Guardian* in September 2007, Councillor Jeremy Beacham, the then Leader of the LGA Labour Group, welcomed the positive tone of Prime Minister Gordon Brown towards the work of local councils and councillors. He welcomed the idea of a concordat between central and local government, arguing that while it did not add up 'to a complete localist agenda' it was 'a clear and welcome start (*Guardian*, 26 September 2007). Others took a much more jaundiced view. The CLG House of Commons select committee took evidence on the impact of the concordat. Not one of the local councils that appeared before the committee felt that it had made any difference to central/local relations (House of Commons, 2009a: 54). Professor George Jones argued that the Concordat had 'disappeared without trace' (House of Commons, 2009a: 54). Councillor David Shakespeare, vice chair of the LGA, told the committee that 'the concordat was signed with a flourish, but if I got out my microscope and looked at the outcomes, they would be very tiny indeed' (House of Commons, 2009a: 54). In its conclusions the committee was less strident in its language but still critical, arguing that the concordat was a potentially useful document 'that ought to be guiding Government department's relationships with local government far more obviously than has been the case so far' (House of Commons, 2009a: 56).

The key criticism that can be levelled at the concordat is not so much what it says but what it does not say. It talks of how central and local government are partners in delivering improved services and in strengthening our democracy (CLG, 2008a: 140). The concordat stresses the general power that councils have to 'promote community well being of all citizens and a responsibility to do all they can to secure the social, economic and environmental well being of their areas' (CLG, 2008a: 140). It also talks of central/local relations being based on 'reciprocal rights and responsibilities' (CLG, 2008a: 141). This is all fine in so far as it goes but there is little in it to warm the cockles of those seeking a more localist agenda. The document is largely silent on the constitutional position of local government. It talks of how both central government and local government draw their legitimacy from parliament (CLG, 2008a: 139). Yet such a statement, though perhaps technically correct, is somewhat disingenuous. For in the Westminster system the workings and decisions of parliament are largely, though not exclusively, shaped by central government.

There is therefore an unequal relationship. For in reality local government is the creature of central government in broad constitutional terms. That does not mean that local government was nor is a mere agent of the centre, that it is involved in a master/servant relationship. Local government has over the years played an important role in the delivery and shaping of public services and in the broader political activity of the nation. Indeed, under the Thatcherite onslaught it sought to defend its position and responded in a number of positive and creative ways (Atkinson and Wilks-Heeg, 2000).

The current ambiguous constitutional position of local government does present a lopsided picture in terms of central/local power relations. It is too easy to forget how in 1986 at the height of the Thatcher government the GLC was abolished by virtue of an Act of Parliament. Many other European countries would simply not countenance such an arbitrary removal of part of their system of capital city local government. In Germany, for example, the position of local government is enshrined in the country's constitution or Basic Law. Article 28 of the Basic Law confers on local authorities the right to self-government (Council of Europe, 2007: 78). In Spain, local self-government has been guaranteed by the constitution since 1978 (Council of Europe, 2007: 8). In Hungary, local self-government is protected by the constitution and the relevant law. Restrictions on the rights of local self-government can only be passed by a two-thirds majority in parliament as laid out in article 44c (Council of Europe, 2007: 85). In France, under the terms of the constitution, the three levels of sub-national government – municipalities, departments and regions – are territorial authorities of the same legal nature (Council of Europe, 2007: 81). There is at present no such constitutional embodiment of British local government.

Now it might be argued that central government should have pre-eminence, for one of its roles is to take into account the broader national interest. Notwithstanding debates about the contested nature of the national interest, there is validity in this line of argument. But elected local government and a vibrant local democracy are key elements of a healthy polity. Giving local government some constitutional autonomy would contribute to a more sustainable politics at both local and national level. It would help local government to mature as it would not always have to look to its parents in Whitehall for permission.

A general power of competence for local government

One possible solution might be to move away from the current convention of *ultra vires* by giving a power of general competence to local government in line with European countries such as France. With a power of general competence, local authorities are able to pursue policy agendas so long as they are not in conflict with or forbidden by national legislation. The emphasis would be on local decision making, rather than on the imposition of limitations by central government.

A 2009 report by the House of Commons CLG select committee concluded that it had 'considerable sympathy with the case for local government to be given a power of general competence to provide greater recognition of the local leadership role that local government is asking it to play' (House of Commons, 2009a: 62). In evidence to the committee a number of local authorities expressed their support for local government to be given a power of general competence. Warwickshire County Council, for example, argued that such a move would put local authorities on a firm footing for moving into partnership 'with other agencies and organisations as well as strengthening its ability to respond and deal with local issues' (House of Commons, 2009a: 26). Similar submissions were made by Manchester City Council and the London Borough of Westminster (House of Commons, 2009a: 27).

However, the call for such a constitutional change is far from new. Back in 1995 the report of the CLD argued that 'Local authorities should be given some version of a power of general competence' (CLD, 1995: 37). A similar call was made by the Royal Commission for Local Government in England in 1969.

In opposition, the Conservative Party proposed the introduction of a new general power of competence which would give 'local authorities an explicit freedom to act in the best interests of their voters unhindered by the absence of specific legislation' (Conservative Party, 2009: 14). This on the surface seems a significant development, especially from a political party that when last in government seemed determined to throttle the life out of local government! Yet all is not quite what it seems. Whilst the policy proposes that 'no action will be beyond the powers of local government in England', there are important caveats for the policy document goes on to say that 'unless the local authority is prevented from taking that action by ... specific legislation or statutory guidance' (Conservative Party, 2009: 14).

Now whilst such caveats might be viewed as prudent, as central government always needs to leave itself some room for manoeuvre in the context of a turbulent political climate, there is potentially a gap big enough to drive a coach and horses through the principle of a power of general competence.

This apparent new freedom for local government is also undermined by the absence of any substantive boost to the fiscal autonomy of local authorities, such as the freedom to raise extra local taxes. Indeed a 1996 House of Lords select committee report on central/local relations argued that giving local authorities some kind of general competence power would be ineffective while current financial restrictions remained in place (quoted in Scottish Parliament, 2002: 6). Such a view still remains pertinent today.

A power of general competence has also been on the agenda for Scottish local government. Since the Scottish devolution settlement of 1999, local government has operated under the auspices of the Scottish Executive and the Scottish Parliament. Following devolution the Scottish Executive set up the Commission on Local Government and the Scottish Parliament (the so-called McIntosh Commission). The Commission recommended that legislation should be introduced to provide councils with a statutory power of general competence. The Scottish Executive carried out a consultation exercise on the McIntosh Commission's recommendation. It found widespread support for a statutory power of general competence from local authorities in Scotland and from the Convention of Scottish Local Authorities (CoSLA), the body representing Scottish local authorities. There was also overwhelming support from the Scottish Parliament's Local Government Committee (Scottish Parliament, 2002: 8).

The Scottish Executive had some reservations. These included the possibility of duplication of provision if local councils did not engage in a careful reassessment of priorities and the fact that a power of *ultra vires* might still be needed if some councils were thought to be using their powers irresponsibly. The Executive signalled its support for a change in the law to encourage flexibility and innovation at the local level. However, it shied away from the idea of a power of general competence and instead proposed a 'power of community initiative' (Scottish Parliament, 2002: 8). There followed the introduction of a parliamentary Bill that led to the Local Government in Scotland Act 2003. The legislation gives local authorities in Scotland a general power to advance well being in their areas (Scottish Parliament, 2002: 10).

Despite an endless steam of policy initiatives and legislation pouring out of Whitehall and Westminster since 1997, there had been up to the general election of 2010 no proposal emanating from central government for a general power of competence for local councils in England and Wales. However, there have been other developments that to some extent mirror the Scottish experience. The Local Government Act 2000 gave local authorities the power to promote community 'well being' in their areas. This power was further enshrined in the Sustainable Communities Act 2007. According to the CLG guidelines which accompanied the Act, 'The well being power enables local authorities to do anything they consider likely to promote or improve the economic, social or environmental well being of their area. The breadth of this power is such that councils can regard it as a power of first resort' (CLG, 2008c: 5).

At first reading, this legislative initiative seems to open up a space for greater autonomy for local authorities, even possibly approaching a power of general competence. However, the policy is wrapped up in a number of caveats. For example, local authorities can use the well being power as first resort as long as it 'does not involve raising money' (CLG, 2008c: 5). Without the financial clout to back it up, the well being power is somewhat weakened to say the least. In tortuous prose, the guidance continues 'And if what they propose is neither explicitly prohibited, nor explicitly subject to limitation and restriction on the face of other legislation then a council can proceed' (CLG, 2008c: 5). As one door opens another seems to close! Nonetheless, such a well being power, however circumscribed, might open up a space for imaginative local authorities to develop their leadership role and to address the needs and aspirations of their local communities. Let us consider the evidence.

In a submission to the House of Commons CLG select committee, Birmingham City Council argued that existing well being powers do not go far enough (House of Commons, 2009a: 26). Birmingham is not alone in its diffidence. Addressing the County Council Networks conference on 17 November 2008, John Healey, the then Local Government Minister, noted that local councils were not making the most effective use of what he described as the 'key tool' that is the well being power (CLG, 2009a).

Nonetheless, research carried out by academics at the Universities of Birmingham and the West of England showed that a number of local councils have used the well being power to develop and shape creative policy responses. For example, in 2003 the London Borough of Greenwich used the power to set up an employment agency, Gateway Employment, as a not-for-profit company. Greenwich has been faced with long-term economic problems and high levels of unemployment, a consequence of decades of deindustrialisation. Gateway Employment was set up to support the local community training agency Greenwich Local Labour in Business and the local community. Its key priorities were to sustain local jobs and use any surplus profits it made to support local good causes. In its first year it was notified of 204 job vacancies of which it filled 186. It had a turnover of around £1 million (CLG, 2008c: 13).

The House of Commons CLG select committee itself highlighted effective use of the well being power. Examples it gave included the decision by Essex County Council to open the first Council-run post office, the provision by North Yorkshire County Council of a broadband network and what the select committee described as the 'innovative restorative justice models of Lancashire County Council (House of Commons, 2009a: 29).

These and other case studies do reveal evidence of the take up of the well being power in a number of individual local councils. However, research by Kitchin *et al.* highlights a number of generalised problems with the application of the well being power. It was noted that potential use of the power was 'rarely discussed openly in authorities' but 'was restricted to specific groups of people involved in a particular issue'. Furthermore, the well being power was rarely the starting point in discussions, only emerging as a way of 'facilitating a solution that had already been proposed'. In addition elected councillors were rarely involved in discussions about utilising the power (Kitchin *et al.*, 2007: 49).

The research also focused on the efficacy of the well being power in the context of central/local relations. Many local authorities argued that the priority given to the large number of centrally imposed targets and initiatives was an important factor in the limited impact and take up of the well being power. Central government needed to be less prescriptive in its relationship with local government and should 'recognise the need for risk taking at the local level'. More resources needed to be made available for innovation by local authorities (Kitchin *et al.*, 2007: 52).

This brings us to a broader point. If local government and democracy is to flourish, if it is to be responsive to the needs and aspirations of local communities, then it needs to be able to operate in its own space free from the overweening presence of central government. In other words, the power of well being cannot be separated from the well being of elected local government.

The same applies to any power of general competence for local government. In opposition, the Conservatives set a policy to introduce a power of general competence to local councils 'so that they have explicit authority to improve their communities' (Conservative Party, 2009: 75). This policy commitment has been carried through into office with the publication in December 2010 of the Conservative/Liberal Democrat coalition government's Decentralisation and Localism Bill. This might suggest considerable opportunities for local councils to operate in creative ways. For Andrew Stunell, a junior minister in the CLG department, it opens up a space for local government. In his view, before the proposals set out in the Decentralisation and Localism Bill, all activity in the world of local government was either mandatory or prohibited. In this new policy context, Stunell argues, local government will have much more room for manoeuvre in the shaping and delivery of local services (LGA, 2010).

There might be some validity in this point of view. However, such a proposed change to the constitutional position of local government needs to be set in the context of major cuts in the budgets of local authorities, some 30 per cent in the period 2011–15. Such cuts will have a significant impact on the capacity of local councils and militate against any potential benefits that a power of general competence might bring. Andrew Sawford, Chief Executive of the Local Government Information Unit (LGiU), raises a more specific point. Whilst acknowledging that the proposed new general power of competence is a 'bold statement in law', Sawford notes that a close examination of the Bill throws up 'many qualifications and limitations on how councils may use the power'. Thus the impact on local government of the proposed general power of competence remains unclear. Indeed as Sawford observes 'It may be that the big test [of the power] comes in the courts' (*Guardian* online, 22 December 2010).

Double devolution

Any analysis of the well being of local government has to be seen in the context of the government's stated aim to both promote the leadership role of local government and to empower and engage people at the local level; what has been referred to as 'double devolution'.

As part of an apparent attempt break with the Thatcherite past, the Labour government set out a strategy that it described as double devolution. Central government was to relax its centralising grip, allowing more autonomy for both elected local authorities and the communities and neighbourhoods within them. David Miliband, the then Minister for Communities and Local Government, outlined his thinking on this new localism in a speech to the National Council of Voluntary Organisations (NCVO) on 21 February 2006. He spoke of the need to tackle a 'power gap' by giving local people more control over their own lives.

In his speech Miliband spoke of his support for initiatives such as citizens' juries. He had previously spoken about giving local communities the right to purchase local facilities such as disused local spaces. For Miliband the phrase 'double devolution' best summed up this policy approach. It was 'not just devolution that takes power from central government and gives it local government, but power that goes from local government down to local people, providing a critical role for individuals and neighbourhoods, often through the voluntary sector'. He called for a 'double devolution of power from Whitehall to town hall and from the town hall to citizens and local communities (*Guardian* online, 21 February 2006).

This theme was also taken up by the former Health Secretary, Alan Milburn, in an article in the *Guardian*. He spoke of a 'new politics' that 'goes beyond structures and committees to policies that empower the individual citizen to take greater control of their lives' (*Guardian*, 26 February 2006). In a speech to the LGA on 5 July 2008, the then Secretary of State for Communities and Local Government, Hazel Blears, took the argument further. She argued that 'Devolving power from Whitehall to the Town Hall, and from the town hall to local communities is not just the right thing to do, it is the most effective way to build places where people are proud to live, work and raise their family' (CLG online , 5 July 2007).

Mulgan and Bury argue that 'At root, double devolution offers a vision for a different governing philosophy, and a significant change in the relationships between the tiers of government' (Mulgan and Bury, 2006: 19). For Mulgan and Bury it offered the potential for a more strategic approach at both central and local government levels, moving away from constant interference and micro management to 'bring power closer to where it belongs – the people' (Mulgan and Bury, 2006: 19).

But how substantive has the double devolution strategy been? On a general level, there is a real sense that it has been somewhat overengineered, with a stream of specifications, modifications, and new product launches which have left the public dazed and confused. Launches, re-launches and the use of public relations have become at various times a substitute for real policy change. Indeed Hazel Blears recognised the problem herself when addressing the LGA Conference on 5 July 2007: 'We have been debating localism for many years now', said Blears, 'but I am sick and tired of talking about it. I want to get on with it' (CLG online, 5 July 2007). So what has been done? It is to this question that I now turn.

The citizen engagement, neighbourhood and empowerment agenda

Earlier on in this chapter, reference was made to the Labour government's ten-year vision plan that was published in 2004. Addressing the issue of citizen engagement the plan identifies the problem in terms of traditional concerns about low electoral turnout. It speaks of new initiatives, such as all-postal voting, which have helped boost turnout. But it goes beyond this and talks of the need for more 'opportunities for citizens to participate and exert influence on local issues and decisions'. One approach put forward by the plan is the development of neighbourhood arrangements which involve local people and which also exercise some governance functions. Various local authorities across the country have subsequently put in place such arrangements that exist alongside the more traditional forms of local representation. The assumption underpinning such a policy is that it will boost citizen participation and engagement, which in turn will help develop sustainable and cohesive communities and build the social capital that I referred to in Chapter 1. The prescription for the problems of engagement is to give citizens the appropriate skills to build citizen capacity in order that they can participate more in local affairs (ODPM, 2004: 13).

In 2005 the ODPM brought out a consultative green paper, entitled *Citizen Engagement and Public Services: Why Neighbourhoods Matter* (ODPM, 2005). An analysis of the green paper highlights a number of key themes. Amongst other things, it aimed to reverse the alleged decline in civic engagement at the local level. There was also going to be greater involvement by local groups in the shaping and delivery of local services.

A raft of policy proposals and legislative measures has followed promoting this civic engagement agenda. These have included citizens' juries, local referenda, participatory budgeting, citizen initiatives, enhanced petition powers for local people and community ownerships of assets, to name but a few! These will be the focus of more detailed analysis when I look at democracy beyond the formal realm in Chapter 5. Furthermore, in a key development, a range of local authorities has set in place local political arrangements that seek to move part of the locus of decision making away from the traditional representative structures of the town hall and into the neighbourhoods. Such neighbourhood arrangements are in line with the expressed wish of central government that local people should have a more direct say in local decisions that impact on their daily lives. They operate under a number of guises, such as neighbourhood partnerships in Croydon, local assemblies in Lewisham and community forums in Leicestershire.

This neighbourhood agenda emanating from central government over the last decade raises fundamental issues about the nature and future shape of local democracy. These include the representative nature of such neighbourhood bodies and the lines of accountability to local people. Indeed the government itself talked of the need to ensure that all voices were heard at the local level and 'not just the most vociferous' (DLTR, 2001: 14). Cynics might suggest that the focus of New Labour was more about giving nebulous and unaccountable power in the form of various neighbourhood arrangements than giving real power to elected local government. Yet central government has been in no doubt that 'the majority of citizens are attracted by such direct mechanisms and that many are willing to engage with them' (CLG, 2008a: 28). I shall return to some of the specifics of the neighbourhood agenda in Chapter 5.

Empowerment

Over the last few years 'empowerment' has become part and parcel of the lexicon of public policy and of strategies to boost civic engagement at the local level. It has become ever-more omnipresent in the policy initiatives coming out of the CLG. We have seen things such as community empowerment networks, empowerment champions and community empowerment packs. The list of initiatives seems endless. The CLG even kindly produced its own community power pack, setting out how communities can empower themselves! However, the empowerment agenda should not be summarily dismissed. It does present an analytical challenge, as it can come across as a somewhat vague and nebulous concept. There is perhaps a danger of being overpowered by empowerment, but it does have a substantive core and it is to this that I now turn.

The 2006 white paper, *Strong and Prosperous Communities*, spoke of the need to empower citizens and communities. It spoke of the need to give local people more say in the running and shaping of local services and encouraging the further expansion of neighbourhood governance arrangements (CLG, 2006b: 26). It also set out plans to facilitate community ownership of local assets and facilities (CLG, 2006b: 27). Building on this, the Local Government and Public Involvement in Health Act 2007 paves the way for a network of eighteen local authorities whose brief is to act as 'empowerment champions'. The stated purpose of such 'champions' is to spearhead a reinvigoration of local democracy.

In July 2008, the so-called empowerment white paper, *Communities in Control: Real People, Real Power*, was launched. It sets out what it calls the principles of empowerment. In particular, it stresses the need to shift 'power, influence and responsibility away from existing centres of power and into the hands of communities and individual citizens' (CLG, 2008a: 12). In the words of the white paper, 'democratic reforms must be focused on the role of the citizen, acting alone or with others, to influence decisions, hold politicians and officials to account, seek redress or take control of local services' (CLG, 2008a: 12). In something of a rhetorical flourish, the white paper argues that the answer to the problem of civic disengagement lies in 'passing more and more political power to more and more people'. By such methods, 'democracy becomes, not a system of occasional voting or an imperfect method of selecting who governs us, but something that infuses our way of life' (CLG, 2008a: 21). This is a noble if somewhat inflated aim.

Such a tendency to hyperbole is found in other aspects of the white paper. For example, it speaks of plans to introduce a new 'duty to promote democracy' that is designed to help local authorities to promote community involvement (CLG, 2008b: 3). This again sounds all well and good but how are local authorities to be judged in respect of their performance and what sanctions, if any, will central government bring to bear on local authorities who do not live up to the duty?

As part of the so-called empowerment agenda, a *duty to involve* has been placed on local authorities in England. This duty requires local authorities 'to take those steps they consider appropriate to involve representatives of local persons in the exercise of any of their functions'. This on first viewing does seem a significant development. Indeed in its deliberations, Power supported the idea of such a local authority duty of involvement. However, the report made the case that if such a duty was to make inroads into the problems of disengagement, then it needed to go beyond mere consultation (Power, 2006: 233). Backing up this point, Cornwall has argued that if there is to be a real boost to civic engagement, 'the public sector is going to need to push beyond the comfort zone of consultation culture' (Cornwall, 2008: 12). In the view of the Power Inquiry, there had to be genuine involvement whereby 'the public can clearly recognise that their participation has led to their views being taken into account when a final decision is made' (Power, 2006: 233).

To what extent does the duty to involve meet the criteria as set out by Power? The new duty does contain the usual suspects, namely an emphasis on information giving and consultation. But it appears to go beyond them. For example, there is a focus on the need for representatives of local people to influence decisions through mechanisms such as participatory budgeting and citizens' juries. There is also reference to involvement in the commissioning of local services. There is no doubting the long list of initiatives, but assessing their substantive impact is quite another matter.

A critique of the civic engagement, neighbourhood and empowerment agenda

The Labour government's civic engagement, neighbourhood and empowerment agenda met with a mixed response. On the positive side, Geoff Mulgan, then the Chief Executive of the Young Foundation, welcomed 'the commitment to supporting real shifts of power within communities across the country – and to moving the field of community empowerment from words to action' (CLG, 2007a: 48). The conclusions of the Power Inquiry also offered some support to the Labour government strategy to boost civic engagement. Power argued that citizens should have a 'much more direct and focused say over political decision making and policies' (Power, 2006: 20). It called for the creation of 'democracy hubs' in each local authority. These would be resource centres based in the community where people could access information and advice to help them navigate their way through the democratic system (Power, 2006: 24).

The evidence gleaned by Power found that many citizens felt that they had little say over political decisions. The Commission on Urban Life and Faith expressed concern at the 'democratic deficit' evident in public policy making (Commission on Urban Life and Faith, 2006: 45). Power found that the majority of citizens were 'attracted' by mechanisms that gave citizens a 'more direct say' over specific policy areas (Power, 2006: 220). It commissioned a study by Dr Graham Smith of Southampton University into the various methods of such direct citizen engagement (Smith, 2005). I shall look at some of these methods in more detail in Chapter 5.

To test public support for more direct citizen involvement, Power sought the views of a citizens' panel based in Newcastle–Gateshead. The findings show that there was broad support within the panel for more opportunities for direct citizen involvement at the local level. However, there were important caveats. For example, 'there was no sense on the panel that power should be handed over without qualification to ordinary citizens' (Power, 2006: 222). In addition, the panel took the view that 'final decisions over most aspects of policy should be left to elected representatives, once the public had their say' (Power, 2006: 222). Just how local councillors fit into the government's civic engagement and empowerment agenda is a question I shall deal with shortly.

Power received many submissions from interested parties. There was broad support here for more opportunities for direct citizen engagement. However, there was a widespread view that such opportunities should be about more than consultations, which politicians might chose to ignore. It was also important that engagement went beyond the realm of the 'usual suspects' (Power, 2006: 223).

There is also a broader point that one could make. Despite the criticisms levelled at representative forms of government they do, at their best, provide a forum for collective deliberation about policy responses to societal and economic challenges. Whilst it is certainly true that more direct forms of citizen engagement can complement and enhance this process, there is also the possibility that they can lead to fragmentation and a stronger emphasis on individual preferences and choices. The government's empowerment agenda over the last few years is a case in point. In the conclusion to the white paper, *Communities in Control: Real People, Real Power*, it talks of the modern citizen being 'empowered to make real choices … across a huge range of services, from their finances, food clothes, holidays and music to the big decisions' such as 'how their parents are cared for and how their children are educated' (CLG, 2008a: 128). There is a danger here that empowerment becomes just a sub-set of the market mechanism with such apparent comparisons between choices over music and clothes, on the one hand, and social care and education on the other. Public services are then viewed as commodities to be exchanged in the market place rather than services with an intrinsic public value (see Chapter 1).

Civic engagement and the one per cent solution

One insightful approach to the whole issue of civic engagement is the so-called 'one per cent solution'. This is set out in a publication written by Skidmore *et al.* in 2006. Its findings draw on case studies of Ely in Cardiff,

South Wales, and Wythenshawe, Manchester, two areas with high levels of social exclusion.

In Chapter 1 I talked about the importance of social capital in sustaining and shaping local communities and individuals. Skidmore *et al.* argue that 'One of the most important ways governance can influence social capital is through creating institutions and opportunities for public engagement and participation' (Skidmore *et al.*, 2006: 9). The argument goes like this. If we involve 'people in the governance of services, participants build relationships with public institutions or officials that give their community access to valuable external resources like money, support or political leverage' (Skidmore *et al.*, 2006: 9). Such relationships between local communities and those with key positions in the formal decision making process are an example of the linking social capital that we discussed in Chapter 1. For Skidmore *et al.*, 'It is linking social capital that policies to promote community participation have the best chance of influencing' (Skidmore *et al.*, 2006: 9). Yet herein lies a potential dilemma for, as Skidmore *et al.* note, such policies have the tendency to concentrate this linking social capital in the hands of what they describe as 'the usual suspects ... a small, very active group of insiders who are disproportionately involved in a large number of governance activities' (Skidmore *et al.*, 2006: 47).

For Skidmore *et al.*, the key to the matter does not lie in the problematic practices of particular institutions 'but at the level of the system as a whole'. For the authors the problem 'emerges from properties of the social networks through which community participation arrangements operate' (Skidmore *et al.*, 2006: 47). Skidmore *et al.* argue, however, that the existence of a community elite network is not in itself a barrier to the diffusion of political, economic and social benefits to the wider community. What is crucial is the extent to which such networks 'overlap and combine with the more informal, bonding and bridging social capital that grows out of every day involvement in local community groups, associations and activities' (Skidmore *et al.*, 2006: 48).

In a side swipe at the new localism of empowerment and neighbourhood pushed by the Labour government, Skidmore *et al.* argue that because of the properties of social networks identified above 'simply encouraging more people to participate seems a forlorn hope, and creating more structures wrong-headed' (Skidmore *et al.*, 2006: 48). Or as Michael Walzer succinctly puts it, 'You don't engage people by trying to engage them' (Walzer, 2007). However, it is clear that a new policy approach is needed if we are to 'strengthen the relationship between community participation in governance and social capital' (Skidmore *et al.*, 2006: 48).

In this context, Skidmore *et al.* put forward the following thoughts. First, they argue that 'More direct participation by citizens in decision making is the *only* credible basis on which democratic renewal will take place'. However, it is not a requirement for 'all citizens to be equally involved for this participation to be legitimate'. Second, it is important to recognise that elites have always played an important role in shaping and pushing social change. Third, and this is central to the process of democratic renewal and civic engagement, 'Elites are only undemocratic if they are disconnected from processes by which they can be influenced and held to account by the communities they purport to serve' (Skidmore *et al.*, 2006: 8).

Could it be that in seeking to develop strategies to boost community participation in local governance structures, policy makers have been looking through a distorted lens? Skidmore *et al.* certainly think so. They raise concerns about the emphasis on building formal structures at the local level which they feel are likely only to 'be inhabited by the committed few' whilst at the same time policy makers have paid insufficient regard 'to ensuring that these structures interact with, and are embedded in, the places and organisations in and through which people actually live their lives' (Skidmore *et al.*, 2006: 49).

For Skidmore *et al.*, the solution is to set out an agenda 'which is simultaneously more radical and more realistic than that which is presently on offer' (Skidmore *et al.*, 2006: 50). They call this the 'one per cent solution'. Their argument is persuasive. First, the focus should not be about getting everyone to participate. 'The trick is to ensure that everyone's participation counts towards making the system as a whole more effective and legitimate, even if it cannot count equally.' Second, attention must given to how 'formal structures [can] plug into the everyday social networks people do choose to inhabit'. For example, local governance structures need to link up with youth clubs or mothers in a play group, not the other way round. Third, creating ever-more structures for participation is the easy option, but this misses the point. The key priority should be to 'invest in changing cultures of participation in the long term' (Skidmore *et al.* 2006: 50). Fourth, building on these ideas, the authors propose the 'one per cent solution'. They call for an end to the government rhetoric of empowerment. This should be replaced by a more 'coherent goal for community participation – at least one per cent of people should participate in governance' (Skidmore *et al.*, 2006: 51). The authors acknowledge that such a prescription could be viewed simultaneously as optimistic and pessimistic depending on which side of the fence you are on (Skidmore *et al.*, 2006: 51). But their research shows that strategies to boost community participation in local governance 'will only ever mobilise a small group of people'. 'Rather than fight against this reality, the solution lies in maximising the value from the existing group' (Skidmore *et al.*, 2006: 54).

There are other question marks over the empowerment agenda. Do communities have sufficient capacity in terms of financial resources, a critical mass of political and policy knowledge and access to decision makers? Do they have sufficient social capital to take advantage of the purported desire of central government to devolve more power to local communities?

The answer to these questions is, of course, clearly contingent on a variety of factors, and outcomes vary from locality to locality. And indeed there are countless examples of local communities engaged in a wide variety of activities, whether it be promoting and sustaining local sustainability projects, running community schools or local credit unions. I shall return to these issues in subsequent chapters.

Civic engagement, neighbourhood, empowerment and the role of elected local government

Any analysis of the neighbourhood and empowerment agenda needs to be carried out in the context of its potential impact on the role of elected local government. Such 'bottom-up' local initiatives are to be welcomed, but they should not be seen as a replacement for our long-established system of local democracy. Rather both levels of activity should be seen as complementary, as a relationship of reciprocity and mutual benefits. Civic engagement and empowerment can best be nurtured within the context of a vibrant system of elected local government. As Beetham *et al.* argue, 'the less autonomous local authorities are, the smaller is the scope for meaningful public participation' (Beetham *et al.*, 2008: 32).

Even the strongest supporters of the British system of elected local government, and I include myself firmly in this camp, acknowledge its many weaknesses. The local town hall is often seen as remote and too bureaucratic. People are not sure what goes on beyond its doors. At best there is not always a real sense of what is does and at worst it can viewed as interfering. It often attracts a bad press, ranging from relatively trivial stories on the lines of 'Council fine family for putting recycling in the wrong box' to the more serious and traumatic headlines of 'social workers breaking up families' by taking children into care. Yet at its best local government has the knowledge base and strategic capacity to support local communities. Elected local government can act as an arbiter between competing community groups. Amidst the myriad arguments and conflicting claims, where there is a danger of not being able to see the wood for the trees, the distance of the town hall can itself be an asset, putting matters into perspective and providing a balanced view. It can provide financial resources, advice and strategic support to community groups within the context of the democratic accountability, imperfect as it may be, that elected local government can provide.

Local government can act as a point of reference for local groups providing a flow of information and advice. It can play the role of a community hub allowing local groups to contact each other, talk about experiences, support each other and share good ideas and practices. On a broader level, it can act as an advocate on behalf of the community. The challenge in all of this for local government is to support local groups and act as the arbiter of competing demands whilst not undermining the autonomy and independent voice of local groups and organisations.

However, the strong suspicion remains that the Labour government did not over the last decade share this vision of elected local government as a strategic enabler promoting and supporting community engagement. Despite its narrative of local democratic renewal, it had a tendency to view local government through a 1980s lens, albeit recalibrated, seeing it as an adolescent on the verge of adulthood but still not quite ready to strike out on its own. Stories of the 'loony left' may no longer feature on the front pages of the tabloid press but they lingered on in the collective memory of New Labour strategists.

The double devolution strategy of the Labour government over the last decade was presented as the forward march of local democracy. But was it a march at the double? Note has already been made of the strong government focus on the civic engagement, neighbourhood and empowerment agenda, but how does elected local government fit into this agenda?

Various commentators have stressed the role that local government has to play. Barry Quirk, chairman of SOLACE, argued in 2007 that 'Local government is indispensable to the effective empowerment of local communities' (CLG, 2007a: 48). In the same year Stephen Bubb, Chief Executive of ACEVO, stated that 'A vibrant local democracy requires a partnership between local authorities, citizens and communities, and the broader third sector' (CLG, October 2007a: 48). The Power Inquiry argued that participatory and representative systems of democracy can complement each other (Power, 2006: 229).

Central government seemed to share this view. For example, in one policy document it argues that 'participatory and representative forms of government are complementary and we think that it is vital that elected representatives are at the heart of the empowerment agenda' (CLG, 2007a: 44). Elsewhere, it argues that 'Councils remain at the heart of local democracy' (CLG, 2008a: 2). So on the surface all seems rosy for the world of local government.

Yet the suspicion remains that central government initiatives at the local level over the last decade have sought in many aspects to bypass elected local government. Government statements add to this suspicion. For example, the government in 2008 stated that 'our reforms are designed to shift power, influence and responsibility away from existing centres of power and into the hands of communities and citizens' (CLG, 2008d: 12). This does not appear to bode well for elected local government.

Localism and the 'big society'

The notion of community empowerment has been taken up the Conservative/Liberal Democrat coalition government since it came to power in May 2010. In many ways the rhetoric of the coalition government is remarkably similar to that of the previous Labour government. One publication states 'Our ambition is localism – Real change driven by local people working together in the community' (CLG, 2010d: 2). Such a statement would not have been out of place in the countless policy papers produced by the Labour government. Under the coalition government, localism and the 'big society' have become the new mantras.

But what will be the impact on local government of this emerging agenda? The government argues that 'The fundamental building block of the Big Society is decentralisation and the redistribution of power. This means turning central government on its head ... and handing power to local authorities and the communities they serve' (CLG online, accessed 8 December 2010). Eric Pickles, the Secretary of State responsible for local government, argues that 'The Localism Bill will herald a ground breaking shift in power to councils and communities overturning decades of central government control' (CLG online, accessed 13 December 2010). The government also talks of 'a radical shift of power from Westminster to local people' (CLG, 2010d: 2). All of this appears to presage a bright future for elected local government. But a word of caution is needed here. A closer reading of government policy reveals a more complex picture. Reference has been made by the government to the need for a 'smaller state' where the default position 'is no longer big government but big society' (CLG, 2010d: 2). This reflects Conservative Party notions of a post-bureaucratic age that I referred to earlier in this chapter (Conservative Party, 2009). If this means a smaller state at local as well as central government level, and recent local authority budget cuts might suggest this, then the future for local government is less positive.

The coalition government's proposals on localism have met with a mixed response. The LGA, for example, welcomed the 'thrust of the [Localism] Bill and the Government's aims to decentralise power and decision making' (LGA, 2011). Yet the Bill also contains 142 powers for central government to issue guidance, lay down regulations and 'otherwise direct how localism will work' in local areas (LGA, 2011: 4). For, as the LGA notes, this 'is contrary to the policies put forward by ministers and demonstrates the difficulty it has had in legislating for the post bureaucratic age' (LGA, 2011: 4). Mike Freer, former Conservative Leader of Barnet Council and now MP for Finchley, has reservations about the government's agenda. He does not doubt the good intentions of CLG ministers, but for him localism is a nebulous concept. He also expresses uncertainty about how localism interacts with notions of a 'big society' (LGA, 2010). Andy Sawford, Chief Executive of LGiU, feels there are 'some reasons for optimism'. For him, the Bill contains a number of measures that local councils should welcome. But this needs to be set in the context of the 'huge cut in funding for local government' (*Guardian* online, 22 December 2010).

Partnership working

In office, the Labour government put great emphasis on the importance of 'partnership working'. The arena of local government was no exception. For the government, shaping places and creating vibrant communities needed strong local leadership. This required a partnership approach that fully engaged local communities in planning for the future of their area (H.M. Government, 2007: 17).

Local Strategic Partnerships (LSPs) constituted a 'collection of organisations and representatives coming together voluntarily to work in partnership' (H.M. Government, 2007: 17). One of the key roles of LSPs was to identify and articulate the requirements and aspirations within local communities and to reconcile and arbitrate between competing interests (H.M. Government, 2007: 17). LSPs have become a very visible aspect of the local political landscape. The North East Lincolnshire LSP, for example, was founded on the principle that more could be achieved 'by working together and with the community, than any single partnership or organisation could [achieve] working on its own' (North East Lincolnshire Council, 2011).

In the London Borough of Lewisham, the LSP seeks to develop 'New ways of working together to improve the quality of life for Lewisham's citizens' (Lewisham, 2011). In the area covering Cheshire East Council, the LSP brings together various parts of the public sector 'so that different initiatives and services support each other' (Cheshire East, 2011). These are just a few examples of LSPs that came to represent an important element of the Labour government's strategy to improve the effectiveness of local services and strengthen local communities.

The Conservative/Liberal Democrat coalition government that came into office in May 2010 has sought to adopt a different approach to policy making at the local level with its focus on localism and the 'big society'. This has consequences for LSPs, as key aspects of their role disappeared and downward pressure on local authority budgets continued to build (IDeA, 2011).

Policy autonomy and the role of elected local government

One good test of the health of elected local government is the level of policy autonomy that it has enjoyed over the last decade. It is to this that I now turn.

The Labour government's 10 Year Vision Plan, published in 2004, stated that 'Local government should be at the heart of our communities in the years ahead' (ODPM, 2004: 3). Taken at face value such a statement might suggest greater autonomy for local government and a departure from the centralising agenda of the 1980s and the 1990s. Nick Raynsford, the then Local Government Minister, developed this theme in a speech to the Local

Government Policy Forum on 15 March 2004. He talked about the need 'To take forward the principles of decentralisation ... and turn them into reality across the range of locally delivered services'.

In his speech to the special Labour Party Conference on 24 June 2007, Gordon Brown, as the newly elected Leader of the Labour Party, talked about giving more power to local government and local communities. This seemed to be good news for those who believe that a vibrant local democracy is an essential ingredient for the political health of Britain. The 2006 white paper, *Strong and Prosperous Communities*, seemed to be singing from the same hymn sheet. For example, it talked about providing local councils with the 'freedom and space 'to respond flexibly to local needs and demands' (CLG, 2006b: 4).

There is, however, an alternative view that sees the relationship between central and local government in a different light. One of the most trenchant critics of the Labour government's policy on local government since 1997 is Simon Jenkins, the *Guardian* journalist. In something of rhetorical flourish, he has argued that 'Pronouncements with such ironic titles as empowerment, organic change and strong and prosperous communities ... have reduced English local government to agency status' (*Guardian*, 18 June 2008). However, the notion that local government is a mere agent of the centre is open to challenge, for central/local relations follow a complex pattern in which both tiers of government have resources and powers that they bring to the table. Thus central/local relations can best be described as one of power dependency. Just as central government has policy ideas and resources, so does local government (Rhodes, 1981).

However, Jenkins' argument does have an underlying truth. For it can be argued that what we have been witnessing over the last decade is some 'hollowing out' of the role of elected local government. It has been subject, one might say, to a pincer movement from above and below. Central government control, far from diminishing, has in fact gone in the other direction. Local authorities have seen their room for manoeuvre limited in a number of policy areas. In education, for example, the introduction of 'independent' city academies dilutes the role of local education authorities. Initiatives such as the national literacy hour and the national numeracy hour point to a lack of confidence on the part of central government about local government's capacity to deliver effective public services. Indeed, the 2007 white paper implicitly acknowledged such centralising tendencies with its acknowledgment that there was a need to 'reduce the amount of top down control from central government' (CLG, 2006b: 7). In housing, the policy of housing stock transfer has resulted in some 1.3 million former authority run homes being transferred to housing associations over the last two decades. This represents a significant reduction in the role of local authorities in the provision of social housing.

It is in this context that there have been calls from various quarters for an increase in the policy autonomy afforded to local government. In other words, local authorities should have more flexibility to shape and deliver local services that best suit the needs and requirements of the local communities they serve. The Power Inquiry, for example, called for a 'rebalancing of power between the constituent elements of the political system' (Power, 2006: 21). In particular, it called for an 'unambiguous process of decentralisation of powers from central government to local government' (Power, 2006: 22). Chandler has argued that most other European countries 'appear to strike a far better balance between local and central power' than has been the case in Britain (Chandler, 2009: 185). In December 2007, the then Chairman of the LGA, Sir Simon Milton, called for greater powers for local councils (LGA, 1 May 2008). The Lyons Inquiry into the role and funding of local authorities was of the view that 'the weight of central controls ... can lead to local choices being crowded out'. This could stifle policy innovation (Lyons, 2007: 5).

In evidence to the CLG House of Commons select committee in 2009, Anna Turley, Deputy Director of the New Local Government Network, argued that 'by allowing local authorities much more ability to tailor and focus their resources and their powers to provide services in a way people need they would be much more likely to have substantially better outcomes than through a top down restrictive framework'. The select committee concurred with this view (House of Commons, 2009a: 25).

The select committee did, though, strike a positive tone about the autonomy of local government. It was of the view that 'however slowly and imperfectly, the balance of power is tilting back towards local government' (House of Commons, 2009a: 38). The committee noted that several new powers had been given to local government since 1997. These include the power of well being which I discussed earlier in this chapter. Under the provisions of the Local Government Act 2003, local authorities that have been rated as excellent, good, or fair are now able to trade commercially through a company. In addition, the Sustainable Communities Act 2007 contains a provision for local authorities to request greater powers to promote the sustainability of their areas (House of Commons, 2009a: 28).

Some witnesses before the committee were sceptical of these new powers. For example, Sir Richard Leese, Leader of Manchester City Council, argued that the Sustainable Communities Act 'is a rather clumsy way of us being able to ask to do things that we ought to be able to decide in our own right to do'. Warwickshire County Council said that 'local authorities would use charging and trading more if the legislation was simplified' (House of Commons, 2009a: 28). The committee noted the frustration of local authorities who 'regardless of their track record ... remain subject to invasive central government scrutiny and interference' (House of Commons, 2009a: 63). It urged the government 'to take a more flexible view of decentralisation' and 'to deliver on its promises' in respect of its policy of earned autonomy' (House of Commons, 2009a: 63). In evidence to the committee, Paul Carter, Leader of Kent County Council, was broadly supportive of the idea of earned autonomy that recognised the complex nature of the local government landscape. He questioned the efficacy of a 'one size fits all' policy. Instead he argued that 'Government could say to us, there you are, Kent, we like your ideas, we like your innovation, let us try it for five or three years and review whether the outcomes for the residents of Kent are better or worse than they would be from a centrally managed, centrally administered direction' (House of Commons, 2009a: 27).

It should be noted that the Power Inquiry explicitly rejected the idea that greater powers for local councils 'must be earned and very gradually devolved' (Power, 2006: 159). For Power, greater decentralisation and policy autonomy for local government were an important element in dealing with problems of public engagement (Power, 2006: 159). Those who remain sceptical of the empowerment agenda argue that the only really effective way to reinvigorate local democracy is to grant elected local government real and substantive policy autonomy (Wilks-Heeg and Clayton, 2006: 190).

The strategic role of local authorities

Policy makers have in recent times laid emphasis on what has become known as the 'place shaping' role of local authorities. Lyons set out the broad outline of such a place shaping role in his inquiry into the purpose and financing of local government. Lyons defined place shaping as the 'creative use of powers and influence to promote the general well being of a community and its citizens'. It is made up of a number of components. For Lyons, these include: building and shaping local identity, representing the community, understanding local needs and preferences, maintaining the cohesiveness of the community, working to strengthen the local economy but within the context of environmental sustainability, and working in partnership with other bodies to meet complex challenges (Lyons, 2007: 3).

None of these ideas is particularly new. Many local authorities have been involved in much of this activity for a number of years, but taken together they do provide us with an important analytical framework to consider the role of local government. Lyons rightly points out that, too often, the focus has been on what services local government is responsible, for as if 'this were the true measure, of the importance and worth of local representative government'. The focus needs to be much wider to embrace the place shaping role, a role that Lyons argues local government is 'well placed to play' (Lyons, 2007: 3). This notion of the place shaping role has been taken up by government. For example, it talks of how local authorities need 'to consider what should happen to ensure that their *place* has a viable economic future' (CLG, 2006b: 94). It talks of the need for local authorities to assess and mitigate the impact of climate change in their localities as well as adapting to demographic shifts and build cohesive communities (CLG, 2006b: 94).

This is a big challenge, to say the least, especially in the context of the centralising agenda of the last decade. Not surprisingly, central government strikes an optimistic chord, noting that 'a growing number of local authorities' have used initiatives such as the power of well being, LSPs and Local Area Agreements (LAAs) 'to seize this place making agenda' (CLG, 2006b: 94). However, as noted earlier, research evidence points to a mixed picture, for example in relation to local authority use of the well being power. The House of Commons CLG select committee has noted a number of examples of local councils proactively involved in this place shaping role (House of Commons, 2009a: 39). However, in evidence to the committee various local authority leaders expressed frustration. For example, Richard Leese, Leader of Manchester City Council, was of the view that insufficient powers for local authorities hindered their efforts to effect the place shaping role. In similar vein, Stephen Hughes, Chief Executive of Birmingham City Council, was of the view that there was a 'particular role for cities' in the place making agenda but 'we can contribute more if we are able to have more powers at the local level' (House of Commons, 2009a: 27).

Lyons, however, comes at the matter from a different perspective, arguing that 'Local government needs to think widely and creatively about how to use its existing powers to the full and take a more entrepreneurial approach to problem solving, as part of the place shaping role' (Lyons, 2007: 366). One might describe this as the need for a cultural shift.

Creative autonomy and the need for a cultural shift

Despite the reservations of many in the local government community about the general thrust of central government policy over the last decade, a potential space has opened up for local authorities to take policy action. It has been argued elsewhere that even in the darkest days of the 1980s and 1980s, when Thatcherism seemed to threaten the very existence of local government, it stood its ground and responded in imaginative ways carving out a creative autonomy in a number of policy areas (Atkinson and Wilks-Heeg, 2000).

In evidence to the House of Commons CLG select committee, the government argued that local government should be making better use of existing powers, such as the power of well being and the power to trade commercially (discussed above) instead of seeking new ones (House of Commons, 2009a: 27). Such a view is perhaps not surprising coming from where it does. What is perhaps more surprising is that not dissimilar views are also found in sections of the local government community. For example, in evidence to the CLG select committee, Andy Sawford, Chief Executive of the LGiU, observed that 'local government I think would accept, and we certainly would acknowledge, that has not been as ambitious as we would like it to be'. Anna Turley of the New Local Government Network (NLGN) said there was 'a bit of a culture of pleading and wanting' in local government (House of Commons, 2009a: 38). Assessing the available evidence, the select committee stated that it had 'encountered examples of local government already undertaking a very proactive leadership role'. However, it went on to note that 'local government has become so used to existing in a culture of central control' that it has at times lacked the lacked the ambition to take on new powers and responsibilities in an enterprising way. In the view of the committee local councils need 'to keep testing the boundaries' (House of Commons, 2009a: 39).

But the need for cultural change is not limited to local government. For example, the LGA argued strongly for 'cultural change in the way that central government and its organisations relate to the LGA and to our member councils'. It called for greater clarity in respect of the well being power 'which sounds fine in theory' but in fact, if you try to do anything of significance utilising the power it would become 'an accountants' and solicitors' charter' (House of Commons, 2009a: 29). The select committee concurred with this view, arguing that it is incumbent on central government to 'promote cultural change at every tier of government, and hence sow the seeds for a growth of local government ambitions' (House of Commons, 2009a: 39).

Changing laws, regulations and structures is relatively easy; changing culture is more complex. It requires mental agility and a psychological adjustment. Yet local government has shown its resilience and creativity in the part. It has without doubt the potential to meet the cultural challenge but realising it is the difficult bit!

The problems with the target culture

A key criticism levelled at central government over the last decade has been the imposition of a multitude of targets on local government. Ostensibly designed to monitor and improve performance and efficiency, they have been described as part of 'The spider's web of central control' (Mason and McMahon, 2008: 6). Getting a handle on the exact number of targets is not easy for, as the *Lifting the Burdens Task Force* has noted, there is no consensus as to what exactly defines a target. Nonetheless, 'there is a recognition that the system has gone too far' (LGA, 2007a: 3). Even by the government's own admission, the number of Whitehall targets in place in 2007 was 1,200. The House of Commons Public Administration Committee argued in 2003 that this target or measurement culture 'had failed to give a clear enough statement of the government's aims and priorities' (House of Commons, 2003: 13). It went on to argue that 'Where centrally imposed targets differ widely from what local people judge to be sensible aspirations, tensions can arise making it difficult to keep a sense of direction and ambition' (House of Commons, 2003: 14).

In opposition, the Conservative Party talked of substantially reducing the number of these central targets. Sweet music, it would appear, to the world of local government! But they went on to argue that instead local authorities would be required 'to publish comprehensible and standardised information about the quality and quantity of frontline services' (Conservative Party, 2009: 18). This information would be published online. This seems very much a case of replacing one set of burdens with another!

In response to criticism of the target culture, the Labour government set out a number of proposals. For example, in 2006 the white paper, *Strong and Prosperous Communities*, was published. Its stated aim was to 'provide freedom and space for local councils to respond with flexibility to local needs and demands. It radically reduces national targets, tailors others to local circumstances and introduces a lighter touch inspection system' (CLG, 2006b: 4). Following on from the white paper we saw the passing into law of the Local Government and Public Involvement in Health Act 2007 that, in the words of the then Local Government Minister John Healey, reduced the number of central targets from 1,200 to 198 (CLG online, 30 October 2007).

The *Lifting the Burden Task Force* broadly welcomed the government's policy thrust but argued that it would need an on going dialogue between all interested parties if it was to be effective (LGA, 2007a: 3). In particular, it argued that a new generation of LAAs must allow local councils the space and opportunity to determine local priorities 'free from continuous central interference' (LGA, 2007a: 10).

The Lyons Inquiry was also supportive of central government proposals, as set out in the 2006 white paper, *Strong and Prosperous Communities*, to reduce the number of targets and performance indicators in the revised performance framework (Lyons, 2007: 362). But it argued that government needed to go further by, for example, reducing the wider data burdens and reporting requirements that are imposed on local councils. The *Lifting the Burden Task Force* has also made this point.

More recently, the discourse around public services has switched from targets to one of entitlements. In June 2009, the Labour government launched its policy document, *Building Britain's Future*. Whilst there were few new ideas, the government sought to shift the terms of the debate around public services. Central to this was the introduction 'of clear entitlements to public services' (H.M. Government, 2009: 61). For example, in respect of education, every pupil at secondary school would have a personal tutor. There would be one-to-one tuition for those who needed it. In health care, patients would have access to a cancer specialist in two weeks and there would be free health checks on the NHS for people aged forty to seventy-four (H.M. Government, 2009: 61). This is a return to the choice agenda in respect of public services, a theme I shall return to in Chapter 6.

Setting aside the debate about how these entitlements are to be paid given the credit crunch and the parlous state of the public finances, a point made by the Public Administration select committee (House of Commons, 2009b:

33), are not entitlements, albeit dressed up in the language of consumer choice, targets by another name? Giving each secondary school pupil the right to a personal tutor is also a target set for every school and local education authority regardless of local circumstances and local priorities.

However, on a positive note the Public Administration Committee has welcomed government efforts to 'set out people's entitlements to minimum standards of public service provision' (House of Commons, 2009b: 32). However, it does sound a note of caution, noting that there is the danger of 'unintended consequences or perverse circumstances' (House of Commons, 2009b: 31), a problem often identified with targets themselves.

Looking at the role of central government on a broader level, debate has focused on calls for the smaller, smarter state (House of Commons 2009c: 50). The Conservative Party, in opposition, spoke of a 'post-bureaucratic age' (Conservative Party, 2009: 5). What implications this debate has for the role of local government is not clear for, as the Public Administration Committee has acknowledged, notions of a smarter state and a post-bureaucratic age 'suffer from a degree of imprecision in their formulation' (House of Commons, 2009b: 50).

The implications for local government in the context of such talk are far from clear, especially given the imprecise nature of these concepts. Yet past evidence has shown that political parties, once in power, despite the rhetoric of opposition, are not averse to utilising the power of the bureaucracy and the state to achieve their policy aims. The coalition government is a case in point. In line with the government's localism agenda, Greg Clark, Minister of State at the CLG, told an LGA conference on 8 July 2010, 'Quite simply we are rebooting Whitehall. We are prising the micro managers' fingers from the leavers of control' (CLG online, accessed 6 July 2010). But despite the rhetoric there is evidence that the micromanagers are still at work. Let us take some examples. In its first year in office, the coalition government issued advice on how many resits A level students could take, increased the targets for schools in respect of grade A to C GCSE passes and wrote to local councils about the frequency of bin collections!

That central government will continue to intervene at the local level in various ways to stamp its authority is as sure as night follows day. The challenge for local authorities is to be as certain and assertive in their own role.

Fiscal autonomy

One way to assess the relative degree of autonomy in the local government system is to assess the level of fiscal freedom that local councils enjoy. This includes the scope for levying local taxes.

The 1980s saw an increasing centralisation in the area of local government finance and a concomitant reduction in the fiscal autonomy of local authorities. Rate capping, the nationalisation of the local business rate, council tax capping, the increased ring fencing of central government grants and limits on local authority spending were just some of the elements in this process. The Private Finance Initiative (PFI), central government's preferred choice for the financing of capital projects such as the building of new schools, has further weakened the financial autonomy of local authorities. Whilst it is fair to point that there have been some attempts to free up the local government finance regime since 1997 – for example, the end of universal council tax capping – local government's room for financial manoeuvre remains constrained, with central government still keeping a watchful eye.

The outcome of all of this is that local government is dependent on central government for some 75 per cent of all its income. This, as the CLG select committee notes put it, 'at one extreme of the European spectrum' (House of Commons, 2009a: 46). Local authorities in Denmark and Sweden, by contrast, raise around 70 per cent of their own revenue.

What are the implications for local government of such financial dependency? In 1976 the Layfield Committee was set up to look into the whole question of local government finance and central/local relations It is regarded by many as the definitive analysis of local government finance (see Butler *et al.*, 1994). It expressed concern at the muddled way in which local authorities were financed. For Layfield, local government had become too dependent on central government funding with local autonomy being severely undermined. Layfield argued that local authorities should be responsible for raising a higher proportion of their own revenue in the form of local taxes (Layfield, 1976: 300–301).

Striking a similar note, Professor George Jones, a member of the Layfield Committee, stated in evidence to the CLG select committee that 'There can be no local government responsive and accountable to its local voters, if a local authority simply spends money given to it by central government' (House of Commons, 2009a: 46). The select committee itself agreed that there needed to be a shift in the balance of funding (House of Commons, 2009a: 46).

The Power Inquiry also pursued the agenda of local fiscal autonomy, arguing that local councils should have enhanced powers to raise taxes and administer their own finances (Power, 2006: 22). For Power, it was crucial for the 'independence of local authorities' that they had the freedom to raise the 'great majority of their income locally' (Power, 2006: 160). It was particularly critical of the practice of ring fencing central government grants to local authorities that it regarded as 'the surreptitious erosion' of local government powers (Power, 2006: 160).

Central government has countered this view arguing that local councils 'remain at the heart of local democracy' (CLG, 2008b: 3). This notwithstanding, a number of specific proposals have been put forward in respect of local government finance. For example, the CLG select committee has endorsed the view that local authorities should have control of at least 50 per cent of their income (House of Commons, 2009a: 46). In addition, the committee has called for the relocalisation of the business rate, removed from the control of local authorities with the introduction of the community charge in Scotland in 1989 and a year later in England and Wales.

The CLG select committee, based on the evidence it took, said that there appeared 'to be a general consensus' that such a policy approach 'would greatly increase [councils'] flexibility' (House of Commons, 2009a: 48). Indeed such a move would increase the amount of income controlled by local councils from 25 per cent to around 45 per cent (House of Commons, 2009a: 48).

The Lyons Inquiry, which reported in 2007, made a number of recommendations and observations in respect of local government finance. For example, it called for 'significant further reductions in the amount of conditional ring fenced and specific grants to local government' (Lyons, 2007: 362). However, its overall approach to the reform of local government finance was cautious. For example, it did call on government to give up its capping powers but with the caveat of only 'as pressures on council tax reduce' (Lyons, 2007: 362). The views of the CLG select committee were less equivocal. It noted how such capping powers undermine local accountability (House of Commons, 2009a: 49), arguing that 'the continued use, and threat of capping are emblematic of the Government's ultra cautious approach to devolution' (House of Commons, 2009a: 50).

In contrast to the CLG select committee, the Lyons Inquiry rejected the idea of a relocalisation of the business rate, arguing instead that a 'new local flexibility to set a supplement on the current national business rate should be introduced' (Lyons, 2007: 368). In another recommendation, Lyons called on government to consider the benefits of a permissive power for local authorities to levy a tourism tax, as is the case in parts of the USA (Lyons, 2007: 369).

What was the response of the last Labour government to these various proposals? In evidence to the select committee the then CLG Secretary of State, Hazel Blears, specifically rejected the idea of relocalising the business rate (House of Commons 2009a: 49). However, the Business Rates Supplement Act 2009 contains provision for a supplementary business rate, as suggested by Lyons, subject to various safeguards. The government also resisted calls for the removing of its capping powers in respect of council tax, arguing that it had a responsibility to protect tax payers' (House of Commons, 2009a: 50).

There have been some developments in local government finance since the Conservative/Liberal Democratic coalition government came to power in May 2010. There has, for example, been a reduction in the amount of ring fenced central government grant given to local councils. This, argues the government, gives local councils more autonomy with regard to spending decisions at the local level. However, this has to be viewed in the context of cuts to local budgets of some 30 per cent in the period 2011–15. In opposition, the Conservative Party put forward proposals to end the council tax capping regime. At first glance this might suggest increased local fiscal autonomy. However, under the terms of the Decentralisation and Localism Bill, proposals for council tax rises are subject to referenda and a possible veto. Whilst such a proposal, it might be argued, boosts accountability to local communities, it makes local authority financial planning difficult to say the least.

There have been some outline proposals made by the coalition government in respect of relocalising the business rate. Indeed, the Communities Secretary, Eric Pickles, announced a review of the future of the business rate in March 2011 (CLG online, 17 March 2011). However, the impact of this review on local government finance remains uncertain. There are also, it would seem, no immediate plans for new sources of local revenue for local councils, such as the idea of a tourism tax as suggested by the Lyons Inquiry. Local government needs greater financial autonomy with access to its own revenue streams that are not at the whim of central controls, which do not help the development of a vibrant and innovative local government. As Mulgan and Bury argue, 'There is no prospect of significant political autonomy without fiscal autonomy' (Mulgan and Bury, 2006: 14). As things stand, central government may not able to tell the local government pipers the exact tune to play but it does have significant control over the quality of their instruments.

Conclusion

If a constant array of government initiatives, announcements, policy proposals and legislation were a guarantee of a revitalised local politics and an engaged local citizenry, then we would indeed have reached the promised land. Alas, things are never quite that simple. Whilst the energy and activity devoted to the matter by respective secretaries of state responsible for local government and local civic engagement is not in doubt, the substantive impact of this energy and activity is far from clear. One gets a real sense that what we have witnessed to a considerable degree is legislation for legislation's sake, the duty placed on local authorities in the Local Democracy, Economic Development and Construction Act 2009 being a case in point.

Central government's agenda to reinvigorate local democracy and civic engagement needs less of a prescriptive hue. What is needed is a more permissive framework, building to some extent on the power of local councils to promote community well being and the proposed new general competence power, which sets broad parameters but then allows local councils and communities to build on their own experiences and shape the agenda to suit local needs and local variations. Lessons learned and ideas developed could then be shared. This would be in the best tradition of local democracy. Whether the self-proclaimed localist agenda of the current coalition government helps us towards this end is a matter only time and future policy developments will determine. However, past experience does not bode well.

4

Local democracy at the formal level

Introduction

This chapter will focus on the so-called 'crisis of formal democracy' at the local level. First, the decline of political parties in terms of membership, activism, resources and public regard will be considered. The factors in this decline will be analysed, together with possible solutions for a reinvigorated local party politics and the key role this might play in boosting civic engagement and democracy.

Second, attention will be given to the perceived problem of declining electoral turnout at the local level, together with a focus on potential remedies, including the introduction of proportional representation, all-postal ballots and electronic voting, together with other policy initiatives. Third, the potential for directly elected mayors to reinvigorate local politics and democracy will be a focus of attention.

Fourth, the broader role of local authorities and local councillors in shaping the agenda at the local level and supporting and facilitating civic engagement will be analysed.

Political parties

Few aspects of the political system investigated by Power received more hostile comment than the main political parties (Power, 2006: 181). Wilks-Heeg and Clayton, in their study of local politics in Burnley and Harrogate, noted that the local political parties were finding it increasingly difficult to fight effective local election campaign campaigns. As a consequence, they argued, there is 'a clear danger that relations between the electorate and local politicians' would weaken further' (Wilks-Heeg and Clayton, 2006: 12).

The decline of political party membership in Britain is well evidenced (Seyd and Whiteley, 2004: Bogdanor, 2006). For the Power Inquiry, 'the extent of this decline' was clearly supported by qualitative and anecdotal evidence that it received (Power, 2006: 46).

In the 1950s it is estimated that 1 in 11 voters was a member of a political party. Yet, fifty years on, this figure has declined to just 1 in 88 (Bogdanor, 2006). The combined membership of the three main parties has declined from 3.2 million in 1964 to just over 0.5 million in 2006 (Wilks-Heeg, 2010a: 383). Labour Party membership stood at some 800,000 in 1964 but had dropped to around 300,000 by 1992. In 1997, however, membership had gone up to 405,000. This year was, one might argue, the high water mark of New Labour. By 2008, however, membership stood at around 166,000 (House of Commons Library, 2009).

Wilks-Heeg argues that the 'decline in Conservative Party membership has been the most dramatic' (Wilks-Heeg, 2010a: 383). Figures produced by Democratic Audit show that Conservative Party membership had fallen from a high water mark of 2.2 million members in 1964 to 300,000 members in 2001 (Power, 2006: 47). The most recently available figures put Conservative Party membership in the region of 250,000 (Wilks-Heeg, 2010a: 383; House of Commons Library, 2009). The Liberal Democrats have 60,000, well down on the figure of 135,000 that its forerunner the Liberal Party recorded in the early 1980s.

It is also important to point out the difficulties in obtaining accurate membership figures. All the main political parties seem reticent to give accurate details. Therefore, as Beetham *et al.* note, 'The true figure is almost certainly' lower than official figures suggest (Beetham *et al.*, 2008: 42).

Indeed, Wilks-Heeg and Clayton have argued that the 'erosion of local political parties has reached such an advanced state that meaningful party competition is increasingly difficult to sustain at the local level' (Wilks-Heeg and Clayton, 2006: 102). Their specific research, conducted on behalf of the JRT, focused on the northern towns of Burnley and Harrogate. It found that there were 540 members of political parties in Burnley and 1,220 in Harrogate, which would seem on the surface to be relatively high. However, when it came to the actual number of party activists – that is, those members actively involved on the ground canvassing, those delivering leaflets and attending meetings – the total numbers were 89 in Burnley and 118 in Harrogate (Wilks-Heeg and Clayton, 2006: 111). This represented 0.1 per cent of the total population in both towns. Interviews with local party leaders suggested that the number of activists had fallen over recent years (Wilks-Heeg and Clayton, 2006: 110). The authors found that party activists in both towns were ageing 'with little recruitment of younger members or activists taking place'. This low level of political activism has broader implications for the democratic process. For, as Wilks-Heeg and Clayton observe, research 'constantly shows' that strong party competition, involving door-to-door campaigning, 'has a strongly positive impact on local electoral turnout' (Wilks-Heeg and Clayton, 2006: 111). Copus and van der Kolk make a similar point, arguing that 'there has been, in many countries, a decline in electoral participation which has gone hand in with a decline in local party organisation' (Copus and van der Kolk, 2007: 2).

The role of political parties

But should such a decline in political party membership and electoral activity concern us? Indeed there is a view that representational politics is reaching the end of its life. This taps into the argument that we are now in what might be termed a 'post-political world' in which the kind of broader forms of civic engagement that I discussed in Chapter 2 have overtaken traditional forms of engagement, such as political party membership. 'In many ways', Wilks-Heeg argues, 'politics has simply become more pluralist with representative democracy existing alongside a myriad of forms of participatory democracy' (Wilks-Heeg, 2010a: 382). 'Yet at the same time' he contends 'it seems difficult to imagine how political affairs could be managed without political parties' (Wilks-Heeg, 2010a: 382). Indeed the problems of accountability, effectiveness and legitimacy that are prevalent in participatory politics highlight the important role of representation. Political parties, it is argued, are a key element of this role of representation.

I made reference to the role of political parties in our theoretical discussion in Chapter 1, and how they are a key agency in driving social and political change. In liberal democracies political parties are central to the process of government and decision making, but their role goes well beyond this. Political parties can be defined as associations of generally like-minded people that seek to gain political power to further their common goals. Liberal democratic theory argues that political parties help the process of political integration, bringing together diverse policy interests via broad policy streams. This in turn helps promote political and social stability. Political parties, it is argued, also encourage participation in the political process, a view somewhat undermined perhaps by evidence of declining voter turnout and party membership.

Copus, in his study of local party politics, has argued that 'Parties touch every facet of political life and are involved, to one degree or another, in guiding and influencing the shape, nature and direction of our local communities' (Copus, 2004: 1). Yet he takes issue with the liberal democratic notion of the party as representative, arguing instead that the 'party group [on the local council] is less about representing citizens' views in the council, and more about filtering the views, preferences and needs of citizens which do not accord with its own political frame of reference'. The consequence of this for Copus 'is less a democracy and more a partyocracy – rule for and by the party on behalf of the party' (Copus, 2004: 3).

Yet whilst this critique of the functioning of particular party systems may well be valid, it does not invalidate the potential broader value of political parties to the democratic process. For, as Beetham cogently argues, 'pressing social problems cannot be solved by individual action alone, but only through collective social action'. But what is the agent of change required for such collective social action? For Beetham, the answer lies in the political party 'which belongs to both civil society and the state, and hence is uniquely placed to link democratic initiatives between the two' (Beetham, 1996: 47). Thus the political party has the potential capacity to shape and invigorate local democracy. Realising this potential is, of course, another matter.

The resource base of local political parties

One of the consequences of reduced membership of political parties is a declining resource base. If we accept the premise that political parties have a key role to play in a healthy democratic polity, then this is a concern.

The Power Inquiry recommended state funding to support local activity by political parties. In fact, political parties do already receive some public funds – for example, to resource government and opposition at Westminster. At the local level councillors receive allowances to perform their duties. However, Power's proposals go beyond this. At a General Election, voters would tick a box allocating a £3 donation per year to a party of their choice. This would be paid for out of public funds (Power, 2006: 24). In 2007, an enquiry chaired by the senior civil servant, Sir Hayden Phillips, proposed some extra £25 million of state funding for political parties, based on their electoral support (Phillips, 2007). The Councillors' Commission recommended that a ring fenced fund should be established to provide public money for political parties with the specific aim of the recruitment, selection and training of local council candidates (Councillors' Commission, 2007: 64).

These are interesting ideas but whether voters would be willing to pay extra taxes to fund political parties, given the public perception of them, is a moot point. The pressure on public services and the reduction in the tax base in the aftermath of the credit crunch make such a proposal even more problematic.

Research by Wilks-Heeg and Clayton in Burnley and Harrogate highlighted the paucity of funds and resources available to local parties. In an interview, one party leader spoke of leaflets being produced on an ink duplicator in his kitchen! Another party leader said that he paid for the production of leaflets out of his own pocket (Wilks-Heeg and Clayton, 2006: 112). As Runswick has noted, 'if local parties cannot even afford to print campaign leaflets then we cease to have a competitive party system' (Runswick, 2004:9).

There was a clear imbalance in Harrogate and Burnley between the resources available to the political parties and the myriad of non-elected local bodies in the two towns with their glossy information and other publicity materials. 'Unless such resource imbalances can be addressed',

Wilks-Heeg and Clayton argued, 'it is difficult to see how effective local elections campaigns can be sustained in the short to medium term' (Wilks-Heeg and Clayton, 2006: 112). The implications of this are clear, not just for formal political participation but broader forms of civic engagement since, as I noted earlier, there is a symbiotic relationship between the two that is mutually reinforcing.

Electoral turnout at the local level

The Power Inquiry, as I noted in Chapter 2, found evidence of a 'declining willingness to get involved in the formal political system' (Power, 2006: 59). As part of this process, attention has been drawn to the low turnout in local elections over recent years. Let us consider the evidence. One of the key liberal democratic arguments put forward in favour of elected local government is that it helps foster democracy by providing opportunities for participation in the political process. Yet such an argument would appear weakened by the fact that Britain 'has by far the lowest rates of turnout in local elections of all European Union countries', with turnout in British local elections some 30 per cent below the European average (Wilks-Heeg and Clayton, 2006: 175).

Wilson and Game have noted that historically local electoral turnout has rarely exceeded 45 per cent but by the same token it has rarely dipped below 40 per cent (Wilson and Game, 1998: 204). On average, local election turnout between 1979 and 1996 was 41 per cent (LGA, 2008a); in 1994, it stood at 43 per cent. However, the picture changed significantly in 1996 with turnout dropping sharply to 34 per cent. By 1997, it had fallen as low as 30 per cent. In the years from 1998 to 2000, turnout stood at around 30 per cent. Figures from the *Local Government Chronicle* Elections' Centre show that turnout in local elections in the period from 2002 to 2009 ranged from 33 per cent to 39 per cent. (See Figure 3.)

Looking at this data, there is no evidence of a linear decline in voter turnout at the local level over the last decade or so. Whilst voter turnout in Britain may not stand comparison with its EU counterparts, the picture is more complex than some of the headlines suggest. It is much more a question of ebbs and flows. Indeed some local authority turnouts go against the stream, like the journey of the salmon as it makes its way upstream against the current of the river to its spawning grounds. Take for example the 2008 elections for the GLA. In the constituency of Bexley and Bromley turnout reached the dizzying heights of 49 per cent! Barnet and Camden had a turnout of just over 46 per cent (*Guardian*, 3 May, 2008).

In the 2008 London Mayoral Election that was held on the same day, the turnout was just over 45 per cent, up 4 per cent on the previous election. This was a high-profile contest between two well-known and controversial figures: Labour's Ken Livingstone and the Conservative Boris Johnson. As Tony Travers observed, 'Boris Johnson's victory made the front page of

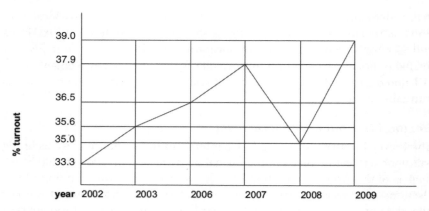

3 Turnout in English local elections: 2002–9

virtually all the British and overseas papers' (*Local Government Chronicle*, 8 May 2008).

The Power Inquiry noted during its investigations (Power, 2006: 60) how occasionally it would hear the claim that the problems of voter turnout, at both local and national level, were due to the fact that most citizens were broadly content both economically and socially. Power's findings did of course pre-date the 2008 credit crunch and its aftermath. More significantly it was a view that tended to come largely from politicians.

Power cast significant doubt on this explanation, based on the evidence it heard (Power, 2006: 61). It made a number of observations. First, contentment was suggested very infrequently as a cause of low voter turnout. Second, if the contentment theory holds true one would expect to see a decline in all aspects of political involvement, but the evidence from Power and other sources that I looked at in Chapter 2 does not back this up. Third, Power noted that there was no empirical research to substantiate the contentment theory and no support in the academic literature. Indeed the Labour government itself from 1997 onwards expressed its concern about the state of local democracy and low voter turnout in a number of consultation documents and policy announcements. Fourth, in all the evidence gathered by Power as an explanation for voter disengagement, the argument of contentment paled into insignificance compared to the most often-expressed explanation, that of 'frustration and alienation' amongst the voting public. So what might be done to tackle such frustration and alienation?

Boosting electoral turnout

Under the terms of the Representation of the Peoples Act 2000, local authorities in England and Wales can submit proposals to the Secretary of State for Justice to carry out electoral pilot schemes. In Scotland, local councils can apply to the Scottish Executive. The outcome has been a number of studies that sought to examine the impact of technical changes to local voting systems. These have included voting at local supermarkets, extending polling hours, remote e-voting, all-postal ballots and advance voting. For the purposes of this chapter, the focus here will be on the last three of these initiatives.

Remote e-voting

One possible solution put forward to deal with low turnout at local elections is the introduction of various forms of electronic voting. Various methods can be employed here including voting via the internet, the use of touch tone phones and text messaging. This, so the argument goes, will help increase turnout especially amongst the media-savvy eighteen- to twenty-four-year-olds who, as I noted in Chapter 1, are the least likely to vote in elections (whether they be national or local). Norris notes that the UK has been at the forefront of testing the impact of a wide variety of e-voting technologies in local elections (Norris, 2004: 45).

A number of e-voting pilot studies have been set up since 2002 under the auspices of CLG. Detailed analysis by the BBC's political research editor, David Cowling, suggests a mixed outcome. Residents of the town of Swindon have been able to vote electronically since 2002. Overall turnout increased from 29.5 per cent in 2003 to 33.8 per cent in 2007, with 24 per cent of Swindon residents voting online or by phone in 2007. This might suggest a link between increased voter turnout and e-voting. Yet correlation is one thing but the link between cause and effect is another, and the BBC research does not establish such a link.

Indeed, in English local elections in 2003, the majority of local government areas offering e-voting actually saw a lower turnout than in the previous election. Of the fourteen pilot studies analysed by the BBC only four saw an increase in voting. In 2007 five local authorities took part in e-voting pilot studies. Voter turnout went up in four, namely Swindon, Sheffield, Rushmoor and South Bucks. But the BBC analysis could not attribute this to e-voting. Indeed in one local authority, Shrewsbury and Atcham, turnout actually fell by 12 per cent.

What about the argument that e-voting could boost turnout amongst eighteen- to twenty-four-year-olds? Some available evidence appears to be counterintuitive. For example, data for the 2003 local elections in Ipswich shows that only 5–7 per cent of eighteen- to twenty-four-year-olds who voted did so online. This was the lowest figure in any age group including the sixty-five-plus cohort! However the 2007 local elections showed that the average age of an internet voter was forty-five years, as compared to an average of fifty-two years for all voters (Electoral Commission, 2007a: 32). According to BBC research, low-tech methods of voting remained the most popular method of voting. In fourteen 2003 pilot studies studied by the BBC just under 98,000 people voted by telephone, internet, text message, or digital television. This compares with 368,809 who voted by post or at a polling station. For David Cowling, 'There seems to be no evidence that e-voting increases participation in elections'. Indeed, he argues that evidence from the pilots suggests that those who opted for the e-voting alternative would have voted anyway (BBC News online, 5 July 2007).

In other research Norris has argued that claims that electronic voting could increase voter turnout, especially amongst the young, 'should be regarded with considerable scepticism' (Norris, 2004: 41). For Norris evidence shows that e-voting only marginally increases voting amongst the young.

Norris analysed the outcomes of the seventeen e-voting pilot studies in the May 2003 English local elections and the impact this had on turnout. Overall turnout in local elections in England was 37 per cent. This was an increase of 3 per cent on 2002 and of 5 per cent on 1999. What then was the link between e-voting and increased voter turnout? Drawing on data from MORI, Norris highlights the fact that only 9 per cent of voters opted for e-voting in areas where pilot studies were being carried out. Overall, two-thirds of the areas experimenting with e-voting actually recorded a small fall in turnout, 'disappointing the hopes of the reformers' (Norris, 2004: 47). Based on such evidence, Norris concludes that 'there are few grounds to believe that remote e-voting would radically improve turnout' (Norris, 2004: 48).

In 2007, the Electoral Commission carried out a number of evaluations into e-voting pilots. Sheffield City Council, for example, made remote internet touch tone telephone voting available to its electors for a period of four days prior to polling day. The Commission found that this pilot had only a marginal impact on turnout (Electoral Commission, 2007d). The same was also true of e-voting pilots in Swindon (Electoral Commission, 2007b) and Shrewsbury (Electoral Commission, 2007c).

Overall turnout at the May 2007 Sheffield elections was 36 per cent, an increase of 1.5 per cent compared to the previous year. Indeed research found that of the relatively small number of electors who opted for e-voting, 'a significant proportion indicated that they were predisposed to vote in any case' (Electoral Commission, 2007d). In all, the May 2007 local elections saw five local councils pilot a number of e-voting methods. On the positive side the Commission was of the view that 'In broad terms the remote e-voting elements of the May 2007 pilot schemes proved successful and facilitated voting'. However, it recommended that no further e-voting should take place until key changes had been made to the electoral process, including greater transparency and more time for effective planning (Electoral Commission, 2007a). In June 2007 the Open Rights Group raised concerns about the legitimacy of e-voting. It was concerned about oversight of such voting and the possibility of fraud since the people were not able to see how their votes were recorded or counted (BBC News online, 5 July 2007).

All-postal ballots

Until 2000, postal votes were only available for those could give a valid reason as to why they could not vote at the local polling station, such as those with a medical condition or people away on holiday on polling day. The Representation of the People Act 2000 changed this position by introducing postal voting on demand. Building on this, a number of local councils have carried out all-postal ballot pilots to test their impact on electoral turnout.

For example, in the local elections for England in 2002, all-postal ballots were held in a number of areas. Analysis by Norris shows that in areas where all-postal ballots were held 'the results illustrate its outstanding success'. On average turnout increased by 34 per cent to 49 per cent compared to the previous election. Norris conceded that the increase in turnout could in part be attributed to the publicity generated and also the novelty value but noted that the rise was consistent across a range of different electoral areas. For Norris, this suggested that the benefits of all-postal ballots would be enduring if they were used more widely (Norris, 2004: 47). The Electoral Reform Society (ERS) has noted that postal voting is a proven way to boost local electoral turnout (ERS, 2009).

On the back of this, the Electoral Commission in its 2003 report, *The Shape of Things to Come*, recommended all-postal ballots as standard for all local elections (Electoral Commission, 2003). The Independent Commission on Alternative Voting Methods concluded in 2002 that universal postal voting offered 'increased convenience to the voter' and had the 'potential to increase turnout at a manageable cost' (Independent Commission on Alternative Voting Methods, 2002: 9). However, by 2005 the Electoral Commission had appeared to shift its position on all-postal ballots. Whilst supportive of the idea that electors should be given a choice in how they cast their vote, it was of the view that the 'polling station should remain the foundation of our voting system for the present' (Electoral Commission, 2005: 3). It went on to argue that:

> All postal voting should not be pursued for use at statutory elections or referendums in the UK, and the option of sending ballot papers automatically to every registered voter should not be pursued. (Electoral Commission, 2005: 3)

What explains this change of policy? The ERS has talked of the 'widespread evidence of fraud' associated with all-postal voting which leads it to the conclusion that it is not ready for wider use (ERS, 2009). The Independent Commission on Alternative Voting Methods spoke of the problems of voter identity in respect of postal ballots (Independent Commission on Alternative Voting Methods, 2002: 9). In an April 2009 report, the Electoral Commission expressed concern at the incidence of fraudulent applications for postal votes (Electoral Commission, 2009: 17). Indeed there have been no all-postal ballots since 2005; due to problems with voter identification, the government has 'At present ... no plans to invite local authorities to apply to pilot all postal voting methods in elections or to hold all postal elections at statutory elections' (Ministry of Justice, 2009).

The use of advance voting

Advanced or early voting, casting a vote before the actual polling day, has long been part of the electoral landscape in the USA with a number of states adopting such a method. It played a relatively significant role in the 2008 Presidential election with states such as Nevada recording over 60 per cent advanced voting.

A number of pilot studies have been carried out at the local level in England in attempt to analyse the potential impact on voter turnout. Sheffield City Council, for example, located a polling station in the town hall that allowed for advance voting at the May 2007 local elections. The impact on turnout was very limited Analysis shows that 909 people took up this option; this represented fewer than 1 per cent of those who voted! In testing the pilot study, the Electoral Commission found that feedback from voters was in the main positive, but many of them said that they would have voted anyway at their local polling station on 3 May (polling day). In the same year Bedford Borough Council carried out a similar pilot study. Overall, despite some benefits, the Electoral Commission concluded that the 'impact on turnout was negligible' (Electoral Commission, 2007e: 18).

The nature of the electoral system

The debate on how to boost local voter turnout has also focused on the broader issue of the nature of the electoral system itself. Some commentators have argued that a change to the electoral system used for local elections would be one important element in boosting voter turnout (Adonis and Twigg, 1997: 12). The Power Inquiry called for what it denoted a 'more responsive electoral system' to be introduced for local elections in England and Wales (Power, 2006: 189).

At present the electoral system used for the vast majority of local elections in England and Wales is that used for parliamentary elections: namely, first past the post (FPTP). The one exception is London where a system of proportional representation, known as the additional member system (AMS), is used for elections for the Greater London Authority (GLA). The proportional single transferable vote system (STV) has been used in local elections in Northern Ireland since 1973 and was introduced into Scottish local elections in May 2007.

The continuing use of FPTP at the local level is open to challenge. Proponents of FPTP have long argued that for British general elections it produces strong and effective government. If such a view is increasingly open to challenge at the national level, then it is looking increasingly irrelevant in the complex and multi-faceted world of local politics. Analysis by the

ERS of the results of the May 2006 English local elections illustrates this point well (ERS, 2006). It found many anomalies. For example, twelve councils in England ended up being controlled by the 'wrong' party, with the party with the highest percentage of the vote not winning the most council seats. In six of the thirty-two London boroughs the party receiving the most votes did not win the most seats. In two of these boroughs (Haringey and Kingston) the party that came second in the overall share of the vote actually won enough seats to take overall control of the council (ERS, 2006: 23). In Barking and Dagenham, the far-right British National Party (BNP) won twelve seats on the councils with 17 per cent of the vote. Yet the Conservative Party, with nearly 19 percent of the vote, only gained one seat (ERS, 2006: 25). In Croydon, the Labour Party won three successive elections from 1994 to 2002 even though in each of these elections the Conservatives won the higher share of the vote. This was, as the ERS study points out, due to the fact that there are a number of very safe Conservatives seats in the leafy south of the borough where turnout has traditionally been relatively high. The Labour Party, by contrast, won a number of key wards in the centre and north of the borough on a lower turnout and with a lower share of the overall vote. In 2006, the Conservatives did actually gain control of the council but with a share of the vote lower than that in 2002 (ERS, 2006: 31).

Moving outside London a number of similar oddities can be observed. In six of the thirty-six metropolitan boroughs there was, in the words of the ERS, a 'wrong winner', with a party winning the most council seats even though it did not have the largest share of the vote (ERS, 2006: 75). There were also examples of highly exaggerated majorities. For example, in Rotherham Labour actually won 90 per cent of the seats based on only 43 per cent of the vote. By contrast, the Liberal Democrats won nearly 24 per cent of the vote, the second highest in Rotherham, but they failed to win a single seat on the council. Such are the vagaries of FPTP at the local level!

Critics of the FPTP system argue that a more proportional system is needed if we want to attain fairness and appropriate representation. To this end the ERS advocates the STV system. STV uses preferential voting in multi-member constituencies. The seats gained by parties are broadly proportional to the votes gained. The ERS argues that where candidates are elected to multiple vacancies, as is the case in local elections (council wards are represented by two or three councillors), STV offers voters the best and most effective choice (ERS, 2009).

The ERS argues that STV has a number of distinct advantages over FPTP. First, it gives accurate representation on party lines. Second, it encourages parties to select a more representative group of candidates. Third, it eliminates safe seats and makes more votes count, giving the potential for increased voter turnout (ERS, *Firm Foundations: Building Strong Local Democracy for Wales*, accessed 29 July 2009). In similar vein, Dungey has argued that STV 'would reflect the spread of public opinion more accurately' (Dungey, 2007: 14).

What substantive impact might the introduction of STV have on local election turnout in England and Wales? Events in Scotland may offer some pointers here. In May 2007 local elections in Scotland moved from FPTP to STV. Did this change have any impact on voter turnout? Analysis shows that 177,817 more votes were cast compared to 2003 when local elections were last held under FPTP. This represented a turnout of 52 per cent, up 2.5 per cent on the 2003 local elections. It should be noted that that in both cases local elections were held on the same day as elections for the Scottish Parliament (Dungey, 2007: 10). Such an increase, though relatively small, might suggest that more voters were engaged with the electoral process due to the move to the proportional STV system. However, there is the thorny issue of causation and correlation. For it is important to highlight the broader political context in which these local elections took place. On the same day voters also cast their ballots for the newly created Scottish Parliament, part of the UK devolution settlement. An unpopular Scottish Labour Party was up against a resurgent Scottish National Party (SNP) that eventually emerged as the largest party in the parliament and formed a minority administration, breaking the Labour dominance of Scottish politics that had lasted for over fifty years.

A number of observers are in no doubt about the impact of STV. Ken Ritchie, Chief Executive of the Electoral Reform Society, has argued that the new STV system redefined the landscape of Scottish local government. It had given greater opportunity to voters to remove unpopular local political administrations, opened up the landscape of local political representation through the election of independents and produced elected local councils reflecting the votes that the people of Scotland actually cast (Ritchie, 2008).

The ERS paper by Baston on local authority elections in Scotland has argued that the STV system has 'resulted in a dramatic redistribution of power between the parties in Scottish local government' (Baston, 2007: 9), with many local councils under no overall political control (Baston, 2007: 17). The report also argues that 'most votes mattered in the sense that they contributed to the election of councillors' (Baston, 2007: 10). This is in itself significant (in respect of turnout) for if we accept the argument that significant numbers of people are put off voting because they feel their vote does not matter then the corollary applies. If votes count for more, more people may vote, thus strengthening the local formal democratic politics.

Just as important for Baston, proportional systems such as STV 'not only produce results that more accurately reflect the spread of political opinion but also social diversity' (Baston, 2007: 12). Baston argues that under the STV system parties have to nominate a team of candidates. Therefore, parties will have an incentive to put forward candidates with an appeal to all parts of society. This will increase the number of candidates from underrepresented groups such as women ethnic minorities and the young (Baston, 2007: 12). STV can over time, Baston argues, 'change the way we do our politics (Baston, 2007: 15). The Councillors' Commission also echoes the view that STV could lead to an increase in the diversity of councillors (Councillors' Commission, 2007: 61).

Critics of proportional systems such as STV argue that, given the nature of the system, the outcome of elections is often not clear cut, with parties only infrequently receiving an overall majority and generally having to form coalitions with other parties. Indeed, one of the outcomes of the 2007 Scottish local elections was that twenty-seven of the thirty-two councils had no overall control. Critics would argue that such an outcome produces weak and unstable government. By the same token, it is possible to argue that such an outcome results in local councils that are more representative of the wishes of local people. Coalition politics at the local level may also result in more considered decisions, with parties having to consult and compromise. The result can be more effective policy outcomes.

Looking beyond Scotland, the Commission on Local Government Electoral Arrangements, chaired by Professor Eric Sunderland, recommended the introduction of STV for local elections in Wales in its report published in July 2002 (Sutherland, 2002). The ERS has also expressed this view. However, these proposals have not been taken up by the Welsh Assembly government; as a consequence, FPTP still remains in place for Welsh local elections even though a system of proportional representation (AMS) is in place for the Welsh Assembly!

At present CLG has no plans to introduce a proportional system such as STV for English local elections outside London. This creates a (potentially) lopsided system in the nations of the UK, with English and Welsh local democracy very much the odd ones out. Whether this situation can be sustained in the medium to long term is questionable, should pressure for change grow. The Councillors' Commission, for example, argued that in principle local councils should be entitled to pilot STV if they wanted to (Councillors' Commission, 2007: 61). Peter Facey, the director of Unlock Democracy, believes that moves towards localism and electoral reform are inextricably linked. He argues that:

> A localist who argues that local authorities should remain elective dictatorships in hock to single party hegemonies, which failed to command a majority of the vote, is as lamentable as someone who thinks that electoral reform should be introduced for local government, but only if it remains a glorified talking shop. (*Guardian*, 10 May 2007)

More autonomy for local government

Norris has argued that 'Technological quick fixes cannot solve long term and deep rooted civic ills' (Norris, 2004: 48). Indeed, a number of commentators has argued the case that greater autonomy at the local level would heighten voter interest and, as a consequence, boost electoral turnout. For example, Sir Simon Milton, a former Chair of the LGA, has argued that 'The best way to boost turnout at local elections would be to give councils greater powers genuinely to improve people's lives. More people would vote at council elections if local authorities had power to raise and retain more money locally' (LGA, 2008a: 2). In similar vein, the Power Inquiry expressed the clear view, based on the evidence it received, that the 'dilution of the powers of local government has had a major impact on engagement with formal democracy' (Power, 2006: 153). Furthermore, Wilks-Heeg and Clayton, in research for the JRT, have argued that in order to boost electoral turnout action is needed so that 'elections have a meaningful impact upon local service provision'. For Wilks-Heeg and Clayton, the answer lies in a 'significant increase in local political autonomy' and 'greater [local] democratic control over the full range of public services'. In their view, 'experience suggests that, where voters understand that there are major local issues at stake, and where they can see that their votes count, turnout rises sharply' (Wilks-Heeg and Clayton, 2006: 190).

These are all strong arguments but do they stack up with the evidence? Here the picture is complex. The increased turnout in the high-profile 2008 London mayoral elections discussed above lends credence to the Wilks-Heeg and Clayton thesis. However, if we go back to the early 1970s, a period when local government enjoyed more fiscal and policy autonomy than is the case today, turnout showed patterns little different from today. For example, turnout for English county council elections in 1973 was 42 per cent. By contrast, in 1974 turnout for local government elections in London was only 36 per cent (Source: *Local Government Chronicle* Elections' Centre). This is an example of the ebb and flow of local turnout that was discussed above.

Directly elected mayors

Unlike countries such as France, Germany and the USA, there has been no tradition in British local government of directly elected executive mayors with policy responsibilities. Rather the mayor, with his or her chain of office and official dress, has been more of ceremonial figure projecting the image of their town, city, or county.

Decision making at the local level was traditionally organised through a series of council committees focused on particular service areas. Unlike central government, there was no formal separate executive. Upon taking office in 1997, the Labour government set out its plans for change. It argued that the traditional committee structure led to inefficient and unclear decision making. New structures were needed to create a clear and well-understood focus for local leadership. There was to be a separation of powers and a change in the role of councillors. An executive group of councillors would take the lead role in policy making with backbench councillors performing a scrutinising role. Such ideas became enshrined in the Local Government Act 2000. Two models of local government decision making emerged:

- A directly elected executive mayor with a cabinet. The mayor is directly elected by local people and appoints a cabinet of senior councillors.
- A council leader with a cabinet. The leader is elected by the council and forms the executive with a cabinet of senior councillors.

Supporters of directly elected mayors argued strongly they would enhance local democracy. For the CLD, they would be 'highly visible and thus highly accountable' (CLD, 1995: 22). As Copus has noted, the experiment of elected local mayors was predicated on three broad assumptions. First, they would help deal with the 'perceived problem of a disconnection' between local communities and the councils that served them. Second, they would help tackle the issue of declining turnout in local elections. Third, they would provide for more 'visible and clearly identifiable local leadership' that in turn would strengthen local democratic accountability (Copus, 2006: 191). Elected mayors would 'provide stronger political leadership for their localities' and 'increase the levels of popular engagement' (Curtice *et al.*, 2008: 53).

The discourse of elected mayors was one of big hitters doing big things. Cities such as New York and Barcelona were held up as examples of what high-profile mayors could do to boost the standing of their localities and get things done. Michael Heseltine, as Secretary of State for the Environment in the Conservative government from 1990 to 1992, had been an advocate for elected mayors (House of Commons, 1998). The former Prime Minister, Tony Blair, was also known to be a keen supporter of elected mayors (Blair, 1998). There was a view that the position of mayor would attract high-profile individuals outside the world of politics with key figures in the world of business such as Alan Sugar and Richard Branson rushing to the fore!

However, despite the rhetoric, elected local mayors have failed to set the world of local government alight, being more akin to a damp squib. As of January 2011 only thirteen local councils in England, including London, are running the executive mayor model, with none in Wales. Copus has argued that the outcome of a number of referenda on the question of bringing in an elected mayor indicates that 'the experiment has a long way to go to stimulate the public' (Copus, 2006: 191). To date there have been thirty-eight such referenda in England and Wales. In only fourteen of these was there a 'yes' vote. Indeed the people of Stoke, having voted for an elected mayor in May 2002, actually overturned this decision in 2008 and opted instead for the council leader and cabinet system. The introduction of the elected mayor of London was not subject to a local referendum, it being a Labour

Party manifesto commitment in 1997. It should be noted that in Scotland, where local government is a devolved responsibility of the Scottish Parliament, there are no arrangements for executive mayors. Indeed the 1998 McIntosh Commission on local government in Scotland ruled out elected mayors as there was little if any demand for them.

There has been vocal opposition from a number of leading Labour Party figures in the world of local government concerned about the threat elected mayors might pose to its local government base and the dangers of maverick independents being elected. One could point to examples such a as Ray Mallon, first elected mayor of Middlesbrough in 2002. Known as 'Robocop' for his support of zero tolerance policing when a senior police officer in Middlesbrough, he has attracted much controversy during his time in office (*Independent on Sunday*, 5 March 2002). In nearby Hartlepool, voters opted for a candidate called H'Angus. Dressed in a monkey suit, he was the official mascot of Hartlepool football club! Not long after his election, he emerged from his monkey suit, put on a formal suit and became plain Stuart Drummond, very much a case of maverick to mainstream!

Concerns over extremist capture have also been raised. For example, the candidate for the English Democrats was elected as mayor of Doncaster in May 2009. A little-known party, the English Democrats put forward a forthright English nationalist agenda criticising the emphasis on minority rights which they claim undermines the English way of life.

Copus has cogently argued that the mayoral agenda was a policy experiment that 'was set up to fail' (Copus, 2006: 191). For Copus, to make a real difference to local politics the executive needs to be more than just a directly elected council leader, which is in effect what current arrangements give us. He argues that elected mayors need a great deal more political power and influence over policy if the quality and effectiveness of local political leadership are to be enhanced (Copus, 2006: 214). Yet, as he notes, elected mayors were given no extra powers or responsibilities than similar councils with an indirectly elected leader (Copus, 2009: 5). In addition, despite the argument that elected mayors could lead to the revitalisation of local democracy and help tackle the perceived problem of political disengagement, there was, as Copus notes, 'no fundamental re-assessment of the constitutional position of local government' nor crucially any 'consideration of enhanced local autonomy or local self government' (Copus, 2009: 9).

Elected mayors do have the power to appoint and dismiss cabinet members. In addition, to overturn or amend a mayoral budget, a two-thirds majority in the council chamber is needed. However, they do not have the power to appoint or remove council officers. Elected mayors are also limited by their general lack of powers over the world outside the council and instead have to use their direct electoral mandate as 'leverage and as a moral and political tool for influence' (Copus, 2009: 26).

Notwithstanding Copus' well-argued critique of the mayoral agenda, it is still possible to hold that elected mayors can carve out a creative autonomy using the political space that the office of mayor provides. Elected as Mayor of London in 2008, Boris Johnson has certainly pushed the boundaries of his office. For example, in 2008 he effectively forced the removal of the then Metropolitan Police commissioner, Sir Ian Blair, even though such a move was outside his formal powers (*Guardian*, 2 October 2008). (In constitutional terms, it is the Home Secretary who is vested with this power.)

Indeed the issue of elected local mayors has come back onto the policy agenda more recently. In opposition, the Conservative Party talked up the role of elected mayors, arguing that they could bring more accountability and strong political leadership (Conservative Party, 2009: 21). The Conservative/Liberal Democrat coalition has brought this agenda into government with proposals to strengthen and extend the role of elected mayors. Under the terms of the Decentralisation and Localism Bill, referenda are to be held in England's twelve largest cities including Birmingham, Leeds, Liverpool and Manchester. A positive vote in the referenda would see the establishment of directly elected mayors. This has the potential to change the local political landscape since the whole mayoral experiment seemed to have gone on the back burner. Yet there is little available evidence suggesting widespread public support for elected mayors. Sawford has argued that 'People will only say yes to mayors if they can see clear advantages' (Sawford, 2010). Indeed, results from the majority of referenda held on the subject suggest a distinct lack of enthusiasm amongst the public. Granting new powers and responsibilities to elected mayors might just change public perceptions. In this regard, the Conservatives in opposition spoke of the 'strong case' for giving 'new powers' to elected mayors (Conservative Party, 2009: 21). Ideas about such new powers are in the Decentralisation and Localism Bill but, as Sawford notes, there are still major political battles ahead if they are to become a reality (Sawford, 2010).

The role of elected local government and local councillors

Amidst all the talk of localism and local democratic renewal, (including debates about the 'big society'), there is a real danger that we overlook what is regarded in some circles as a 'seemingly endangered species in the ecology of local politics, the beast that is the local councillor' (Atkinson, 2008: 328). At a conference in 2008 on neighbourhood democracy, Norwich city councillor Alan Waters spoke of the role of councillors and their near-'superhero' status in respect of the wide range of skills that were needed to perform the role effectively. Whilst there were many threats to the role of councillors, for example in the form of neighbourhood arrangements (see Chapter 5), Waters voiced the strong opinion that councillors should not simply sit back and complain. Rather, councillors should seize the initiative. They should get involved, for example, at the earliest stage in the shaping and formulation of such neighbourhood arrangements. Councillors should not be seen as somehow apart from the local community. They were genuine community activists who could act as an important link between the needs and demands of local neighbourhoods and the broader responsibilities of the town hall (Atkinson, 2008: 329).

It might be argued that non-executant backbench councillors, freed from the responsibilities of day-to-day decision making associated with cabinet members, might be best placed to liaise with local communities and to champion their interests. This of course begs the question as to whether such councillors have the appropriate resources, status and leverage within the council. The introduction of area committees of local councillors may in part be seen as a way to facilitate the role of councillors as community champions. Sullivan *et al.* argue that decentralisation to such area committees helps to support and develop the councillor's community championship role by 'giving local councillors the opportunity to bring local stakeholders together to plan for the needs of their community' (Sullivan *et al.*, 2001: 2).

Oxford City Council has implemented a system of area committees based on local wards. These committees usually meet once a month and are open to the public. According to the Council's web site these area committees work in partnership with residents, the police, NHS representatives and other organisations to 'drive forward local projects' such as young people's drop-in centres and grid-tied solar power lights. Kirklees Council is another local authority that has adopted the area committee model. According to the Council, such area committees work with local communities to identify local priorities. A number of common themes for action have been identified including community engagement, the environment and young people. On the surface such developments would appear to have value. However, as Sullivan *et al.* point out, such 'sub local level councillors will only have credibility as community leaders if they are able to influence partners such as the council and other service providers to address and take on and address local priorities' (Sullivan *et al.*, 2001: 4).

But how realistic is this view of local councillors as in effect community champions? The role of councillors is complex and multi-faceted, with incumbents bringing a variety of skills and experiences to the office. A local councillor's status as leader, cabinet member, or backbencher will clearly impact on their role and their perspective on local politics. A variety of typologies has been put forward over the years to try and capture how councillors perceive their role. Heclo, for example, saw the role of councillors as falling into three categories. For some councillors the key focus was as a *committee member,* specialising in the business of the council. Others laid stress on the role of *constituency representative,* with an emphasis on dealing with local concerns. The final category was the *party activist* who viewed their principal role as promoting the interests of their party (Heclo, 1969). For Jones, in addition to representing a defined territorial constituency, a councillor could act for particular organised groups, individual citizens as well as broader sections of the community (Jones, 1973).

The role of local councillor needs to be viewed, as Copus argues, in the context of normative arguments about local democracy. They can be summed up as follows. Elected local government results in decision making by local elected representatives. There is, therefore, a local democratic mandate. Furthermore, as local government is more immediate to local communities it can be more responsive to local wishes than national government. As a consequence local people can be assured that the views they express will be listened to and acted upon by their local councillors. However, for Copus, such normative views do not take sufficient regard of how local party groups operate on local councils. Party groups, he argues, 'act as a filter between the views of the citizen and the councillor'. In addition, the party group system 'serves to ensure' that the councillor's primary loyalty is focused on the group and the party rather than the electorate as a whole (Copus, 2004: 180). Copus argues, however, that party group discipline and cohesion has increased significantly over the last thirty years and as a consequence there is 'less space for councillors to develop a relationship with the group that may rest on their own terms' (Copus, 2004: 183). Of course this is a generalisation since councillor motivations vary as does their perception of the job, but this does not deny the key role of local party groups as outlined by Copus.

Finally, if local councillors are to be effective community champions it seems axiomatic that they should be broadly representative of the people they purport to represent. On a general level all political parties report difficulties in getting local people to stand in local elections. Angus Johnson, chief executive of Clapham Park New Deal for Communities (NDC) in South London, has spoken of the high level of community activity within the NDC but made the telling point that very few community activists were keen to become councillors (Atkinson, 2008: 330). The Councillors' Commission drew a similar conclusion (Councillors' Commission, 2007).

On a general level as Lepine observes, 'Councillors have generally been seen as unrepresentative of those they represent in terms of age, class, race and gender (Lepine, 2009: 2). Wilks-Heeg and Clayton's study of Burnley and Harrogate noted the preponderance of older-age councillors in the two towns (Wilks-Heeg and Clayton, 2006). In recognition of this representative imbalance, the Councillors' Commission made a number of recommendations. For example, it called for specific legislation to be brought forward to include specific requirements for councillor equality and diversity targets (Councillors' Commission, 2007: 62). The Commission also recommended that the Equality and Human Rights Commission (EHRC) should be asked to assess local authority compliance with such targets and to work with those councils who are 'least reflective of their communities in order to address the situation' (Councillors' Commission, 2007: 27). In addition it called on local authorities to be given a 'clear responsibility to promote equality of opportunity in terms of opportunities for participation as elected representatives' (Councillors' Commission, 2007: 63).

The size of local authorities and democratic vitality

Various commentators have noted that, measured by population, Britain has the largest units of local government in Europe. In addition, the ratio of people to elected local councillors is the highest in Europe (Beetham *et al.*, 2008: 267; Wilks-Heeg and Clayton, 2006: 173).

The debate about the relationship between democratic vitality and the size of political units has been with us for many years, ever since democracy flowered in ancient Greece. As Dearlove notes, the idea that democracy truly flowers in communities and in small areas came originally from ancient Greece where 'Plato calculated the optimal number of citizens as 5,040 and Aristotle thought even this number too large' (Dearlove, 1979: 32). This idea that small is beautiful for democracy has received much attention. Indeed, as Wilks-Heeg and Clayton observe, 'national and international research evidence points consistently to a strongly negative relationship between size and democracy' (Wilks-Heeg and Clayton, 2006: 11). At the same time, other studies have looked at the issue of economies of scale as justification for large-scale local authorities. Yet, they 'have generally failed to uncover any positive relationship between size and efficiency' (Wilks-Heeg and Clayton, 2006: 11). Yet even in the face of such evidence, there has grown up a conventional wisdom in Britain that the trade off between democracy and efficiency is a key factor to be taken into account when considering the size and shape of local authority units. This, as Wilks-Heeg and Clayton observe, has provided a 'powerful justification for larger units of local government' over the last four decades (Wilks-Heeg and Clayton, 2006: 11). The Local Government Act 1972, for example, reduced the number of county councils in England and Wales from fifty-eight to forty-seven and replaced 1,250 municipal boroughs, urban districts and rural districts with 333 district councils.

This strong appetite for 'bigger is best' is well reflected in the Local Government Review (LGR) that took place from 2006 to 2008. It introduced unitary local government in the former county councils of Bedfordshire, Cheshire, Cornwall, Durham, Northumberland, Shropshire and Wiltshire. These changes, argued the CLG, would 'engage and empower local people' (CLG, *Local Government Restructuring*, accessed online, 15 April 2009). However, it is difficult to see how reducing the number of councils from forty-four to just nine will somehow further the cause of community empowerment. This is especially so as according to the CLG's own figures, the number of local councillors has been reduced from 2,290 to 744 in the reorganised areas, hardly a move calculated to bring local elected representatives closer to local people! Indeed the outcome of the LGR seems to fly in the face of stated government policy in the white paper, *Strong and Prosperous Communities*, that local councillors should be regarded as 'democratic champions' (CLG, 2006b: 48) and 'the bedrock of local democracy' (CLG, 2006b: 52).

Indeed the LGR has come in for some potent criticism. Game notes wryly that the new arrangements came in on April Fool's Day 2009! These new unitary authorities have average populations of some 350,000 people. For Game, this begs the question as to whether these new authorities are 'seriously recognisable as local government at all '(Game, 2009: 3). Altogether the whole process has potentially significant consequences for local democracy.

Chisholm and Leach are very critical of the community engagement aspect of the LGR noting the 'contrast between the rhetoric of involving citizens [in the process] and the reality that citizens voices' were not heeded if the message was antagonistic' to official proposals. On a more general level Chisholm and Leach are highly critical of the absence of clear goals in the LGR process and the lack of any definable blueprint. There were, as a consequence, many inconsistencies with those involved in the process not knowing where they stood (Chisholm and Leach, 2008: 148).

Conclusion

In this chapter, I have looked at formal aspects of democracy at the local level. Standard measures of political participation, including electoral turnout, membership of political parties and the level of political party activism, lend credence to the argument that we really do have a crisis of local democracy. I also focused on a number of policy initiatives designed to deal with this crisis. These involved innovations in voting (such as all-postal voting), the introduction of proportional representation for local elections and directly elected executive mayors. Despite some evidence of positive effects on the local democratic process, the overall impact of such measures has been relatively limited.

However, as I noted in Chapters 2 and 3, there are broader forms of participation and civic engagement that go beyond voting and political party membership. It is this activity, beyond the formal realm of politics, which is the focus of Chapter 5.

5

Opening up local democracy beyond the formal realm

Introduction

I noted in Chapter 4 how the Labour government after 1997 tried to stimulate formal local democracy by various initiatives to boost electoral turnout. But it was, as Wilson notes, 'particularly keen to emphasise innovation in participatory democracy' (Wilson, 1999: 248). Attempts to encourage local public participation are by no means new. They enjoyed prominence on the public policy agenda in the 1960s with such initiatives as the Skeffington Report and the establishment of community development projects.

In the 1980s and 1990s, successive Conservative governments promoted public participation in relation to the delivery and shaping of local public services. This took various forms. Customer satisfaction surveys were increasingly used to gauge the public view on the quality of public services. There were also attempts to bring the public into the domain of local service management. In education, local school governing bodies (with representatives from the local community including parents) were given more power. In health, patients were given more influence over policy with the creation of primary care trusts (PCTs). Market forces were brought into public services.

With the election of the Labour government in 1997, the focus on public participation did not diminish but its ideological underpinnings were somewhat different. As Wilson notes, whilst the new government recognised the importance of 'public participation in relation to service quality', extending public participation was 'also part of an explicitly political agenda incorporating broader issues of democratic renewal'. This new localism as discussed in Chapter 3, was part of a strategy to broaden civic engagement and to take forward the so-called 'empowerment agenda'. It reflected New Labour concerns about the malaise afflicting (formal) representative democracy, an issue I discussed in Chapter 4 (Wilson, 1999: 247).

This chapter looks at recent democratic developments beyond the formal realm of elections, political parties and local political institutions. First, there will be an analysis of three local initiatives beyond the ballot, namely citizens' panels, local referenda and participatory budgeting. The effectiveness of these measures in boosting political participation and civic engagement will be analysed. Second, there will be a focus on the growing trend towards neighbourhood governance at the local level over the last decade. Third, there will be a focus on town and parish councils. Town and parish councils have been a traditional feature on the local government landscape since the latter part of the nineteenth century. Although they are technically part of the formal institutional structures, their relative small size, immediacy, and closeness to the local community give them a character that sets them aside from what we traditionally understand to be local authorities. One might argue that they are informal in their formality. In essence they reflect both the representative and participatory forms of democracy that I discussed in Chapter 1. Fourth, consideration will be given to the potential of utilising technology such as high-speed community broadband, in enhancing civic engagement, building communities and developing social capital.

Finally, there will be an examination of what one could term the new forms of democracy. Examples here include the increasing role of parents in the running of local schools and more direct influence for patients on decision making in the NHS. This reflected a new attitude to public services. The emphasis moved from the public as service users to consumers of services. The underlying ethos was of the consumer as sovereign.

Local initiatives beyond the ballot

I will first focus on a series of initiatives outside the traditional formal democratic process that we can collectively term 'beyond the ballot'. Since the mid 1990s more innovative methods of consultation and public participation have taken root in the local political ecology. These have ranged from citizens' panels with a relatively large 'representative' sample of local people (usually about 1,000) who put forward their views on a particular local service or policy idea, through to local referenda where the entire electorate can vote. As I noted in Chapter 4, referenda have been carried out in a number of local councils to decide whether executive mayors should be introduced. They have also been used to determine the level of local council tax.

Participation has also come to be expressed through the market mechanism. There has been an increasing emphasis on local citizens as consumers with the ability to make choices about what kind of local public services they want and how they would like them delivered. This became one of the more controversial aspects of the last Labour government's reform agenda. I shall look at this in more detail in Chapter 6.

As Wilson has noted, such approaches to wider civic engagement and participation have become part of a 'complex web, reflecting new forms of citizenship and representation' (Wilson, 1999: 246). I will look at three aspects of this complex web, namely citizens' panels, local referenda and participatory budgeting.

Citizens' panels

Standing citizens' panels are relatively large and representative samples of citizens. As a rule they contain 1,000 or more people. As Smith notes 'A panel is recruited to act as a sounding board for public authorities' (Smith, 2005: 33). Panel members are polled on a regular basis as to their views on local services and new policy ideas. A proportion of the panel membership is changed periodically.

Citizens' panels operate in a number of local authority areas. In Brighton and Hove, for example, the local panel (called Xchange) covers the work of not only the local council but also the local primary care trust (PCT) and the local police service. There are 1500 local residents on the panel. According to the Council's web site, panel members are asked to give their views on a range of local issues by either online or postal questionnaires. Over the past four years panel members have been consulted on neighbourhood management, crime and community, changes to the local PCT and the level of council tax as well as local public transport. Such consultations, claim the council, have helped to shape strategies to tackle crime and disorder (including a visible police foot presence on Friday and Saturday nights) and to develop initiatives for young and old people. Panel views have also fed into the local public transport plan (Brighton and Hove Council, 2009).

Corby Borough Council also operates a citizens' panel; consultation takes place in the form of focus groups, questionnaires and surveys. Bristol City Council was one of the first local authorities in 1998 to set up such a panel, which currently has a membership in the region of 2,000. The council claims that the panel has proved 'invaluable' in finding out how local 'people feel on issues and as a sounding board for future policies and decisions' (Bristol City Council, 2009).

Watford Borough Council set up its citizens' panel in 2002. Each year panel members complete a questionnaire about key local policy issues. The panel has responded to surveys on issues such the local community plan, community safety and improving Watford town centre. According to the Council's official web site, the panel makes a real difference. It says that the findings of all the surveys are used by its political leadership to help them make decisions and plan services. If we look at some newsletters produced by the citizens' panel we can see some possible evidence of this. For example, 45 per cent of panel correspondents identified improving Watford town centre as their top priority. The executive mayor made this one of the key policy priorities with outline proposals to tackle traffic congestion and to redevelop Watford market. It is of course difficult to establish a causal link but the very fact that the panel puts this issue into the spotlight makes it harder for the local political leadership to ignore it. In an introduction to the citizen panel newsletter, the then mayor of Watford, Dorothy Thornhill, states that she believes 'in real consultation, which means asking you [panel members] about live issues and things where we are genuinely wanting your views' (Watford Borough Council, 2009).

What conclusions can we draw about the role of citizens' panels in enhancing civic engagement and allowing local people an opportunity to shape local services and impact on policy making? They can introduce important elements of accountability to the community and boost public participation. Smith has argued that citizen panels have a number of strengths. For example, with their relatively high membership and the fact that they operate on a regular basis, they 'can provide trend data' (Smith, 2005: 33). In other words, they provide local councils with the 'opportunity to track the impact of local services and policies over time'. Another strength, argues Smith, is that the findings of panel surveys can be used to analyse the views of a variety of groups, 'including those that are hard to reach'. This helps militate against the 'usual suspects' argument – that is, those that shout loudest (often the educated and articulate) get their voice heard more often. Furthermore, whilst it is difficult to gauge the direct impact of such panels on the decision making process, their very existence opens up a space for potential influence. In terms of resourcing, Smith makes the point that although the initial set up costs of panels can be high, in the long run they are relatively cost effective when compared to a series of one-off public opinion surveys (Smith, 2005: 33).

Yet there are also problems with the system of citizens' panels. Pratchett has written about the problem of 'recalcitrant groups' (Pratchett, 2004), a reference to politically marginalised groups such as young people. He argues that 'there are real concerns that those who are recruited from some recalcitrant groups may well not be typical and are thus not qualified to express the interests of the category that they are recruited to represent' (Pratchett, 2004). There is also the issue of what one might term 'panel member capture'. Pratchett talks of how membership of a citizens' panel might make people more sympathetic to the activities of local authorities and other public bodies and as a consequence less representative of the wider public (Pratchett, 2004). Despite such potential problems, citizens' panels do have a broader benefit. For as the Power Inquiry notes, the evidence that it received 'confirmed that the majority of citizens are attracted by such direct mechanisms and that many are willing to engage with them' (Power, 2006: 220).

Local referenda

Another mechanism employed by local councils to gauge public opinion that sits outside traditional representative formal democracy is the referendum. Unlike citizens' panels, all locally registered voters can have a say in referenda. They are an example of the direct democracy that I looked at in Chapter 1.

Unlike a number of political systems across Europe, the referendum has not traditionally been part of the British political scene. The 1975 referendum on Britain's continued membership of the European Union was the first time it was employed here to gauge national public opinion. It seemed to be a constitutional one-off. However, with the election of the Labour government in 1997, the referendum seems to have come into its own. There have been referenda on whether to set up a Scottish Parliament (1997) and Welsh Assembly (1997) and a referendum to set up a devolved Northern Ireland Assembly (1998), all of which were passed. By contrast, in 2004 voters in the north east region of England were asked in a referendum if they wanted an elected regional assembly. The result was a 'no' vote.

This increasing pattern in the use of referenda has been repeated in varying degrees at the local government level. In 1998 London-wide local government was restored after a 'yes' vote in a referendum proposal to create an executive mayor and set up the GLA. At the more local level, local councils have used referenda to gauge public opinion on a number of issues. Indeed, the Local Government Act 2000 gives local people the right to secure a referendum on directly elected mayors, should a minimum of 5 per cent of electors call for it. In Chapter 4, reference was made to the thirty-eight local areas (including London) that have held referenda on whether to introduce directly elected executive mayors. One local authority, Stoke, even had two referenda on the matter. In 2002 local people voted yes to a mayor, only to overturn their decision in 2008 and abolish the post! Local referenda have been used in other contexts. For example, in the last wave of local government reorganisation (the Local Government Review from 2006 to 2008), referenda were held in a number of local authority areas which asked local people their views on replacing the two-tier structure of county and district councils with single all-purpose authorities (Chisholm and Leach, 2008). A number of local authorities over the past decade have also used referenda to make decisions about raising the level of local council tax. Local councils that have gone down this route include the London Borough of Croydon, Bristol City Council and Milton Keynes Council.

Indeed, whilst in opposition the Conservative Party set out proposals to extend the use of local referenda in respect of local council tax (Conservative Party, 2009). These are now being taken forward in the coalition government with the Liberal Democrats. For example, the Coalition programme for government stated, 'We will give residents the power to veto excessive council tax increases' (H.M. Government, 2010a: 28). As part of this process, the coalition government issued a consultation paper in July 2010.

Eric Pickles, the Communities Secretary, called the plan 'a radical extension of direct democracy' (CLG online, 30 July 2011). These proposals were subsequently set out in the 2010 Decentralisation and Localism Bill.

They have met with a mixed response. Colin Barrow, Leader of the London Borough of Westminster, seemed to welcome the proposal, arguing that 'This measure is an important step towards a grown up debate about the size of the public sector' (*The Times*, 30 July 2010). However, the plan was criticised by David Monks of the Society of Local Authority Chief Executives (SOLACE). In an interview with the *Municipal Journal*, he said that 'The idea of spending more than £100,000 on a referendum to put council tax up by X% is not a particularly good use of public money' (*Municipal Journal*, 15 July 2010: 3).

Jones and Stewart have been very critical of the proposal. They argue that:

> The local budget is the result of a process of balancing expenditure priorities, which cannot be expressed in a simple yes/no question. It damages representative democracy since it destroys the whole point of local elections, if elected councillors see their judgments based on their electoral promises overturned in a referendum called by a minister. (*Local Government Chronicle*, 5 August 2009: 9)

Other commentators have expressed broader doubts about the use of referenda. Wilks-Heeg accepts that 'The appeal of referenda as an instrument that will encourage a more participatory politics is understandable'. Yet for Wilks-Heeg 'they must not be seen as a magic bullet' (Wilks-Heeg, 2010b: 8). One has to view the use of referenda in the context of broader debates about reforms to the constitution that, amongst other things, requires 'wider steps to fashion a more deliberative and participatory democracy' (Wilks-Heeg, 2010: 8).

Despite such criticisms, some commentators would like to see the use of local referenda extended. Vernon Bogdanor, for example, asks 'Why should not voters be able to secure a referendum on the organisation of schools in their area, on the size of their local authority budget or even the organisation of the National Health Service?' (*New Statesman*, 1 June 2009).

Indeed, the current Conservative/Liberal Democratic coalition government is pushing forward this agenda under the localism banner. Under the terms of the Decentralisation and Localism Bill, 5 per cent of the electorate can trigger a referendum on any local issue. However, there are important caveats. Such referenda are not binding and it falls to the Secretary of State to determine what is a local issue.

Participatory budgeting

Participatory budgeting is an emerging concept in Britain. It first came to prominence in the city of Porto Alegre, Brazil, in 1989. It established itself as an effective mechanism for engaging citizens and subsequently spread to another 180 Brazilian municipalities. In principle, participatory budgeting directly involves local people in making decisions on the spending priorities for a defined local budget. 'This means engaging residents and community groups representative of all parts of the community' (CLG, 2010c: 12).

On 5 July 2007, the then Communities Secretary Hazel Blears, announced the setting up of a number of pilot projects on participatory budgeting. Her stated aim was in that within five years every neighbourhood would have control of 'a community kitty' (CLG online, 5 July 2007). In total, there were eighteen pilot projects.

Drawing conclusions from the Porto Alegre experience, Marquetti has argued that participatory budgeting 'is capable of empowering segments of the population, particularly poor sectors of society that traditionally never had an active role in the definition of State policies' (Marquetti, 2004: 18). But what conclusions can we make from the British experiment with participatory budgeting?

One of the earliest pilot projects was in Bradford and Keighley in west Yorkshire. Here participatory budgeting was driven by the LSP, Bradford Vision. As part of its neighbourhood renewal strategy, the LSP consulted local people about what they would like to be incorporated into the action plan. Concerns were expressed by local people that their views would not be taken seriously: 'The acid test for local people was whether politicians would trust them with some public funding to carry out the action planning' (IDeA, 2008). The Council Leader responded to this challenge by setting aside £1.5 million of the local Neighbourhood Renewal grant. This was to be used by local communities that, in partnership with public, private and voluntary sector organisations, could make decisions as to how the money was spent (IDeA, 2008).

A number of findings resulted from the Bradford and Keighley experience. First, it became clear that communities have knowledge and ideas that if utilised by public agencies can make a positive difference. Second, such a participatory approach 'strengthens community cohesion and encourages people to see what they have in common with each other' (IDeA, 2008). Third, given good information local communities 'make sensible decisions'. Finally, participatory budgeting introduces people to the political realities councils face in making decisions about scarce resources' (IDeA, 2008).

Such points are echoed in a national evaluation report on participatory budgeting which highlights the role that it can play in developing and strengthening social capital (CLG, 2010c: 4). The evaluation, carried out by a number of private consultancies for CLG, including Cambridge Economic Associates, highlighted a number of positive aspects of participatory budgeting. It gave local people a sense that they could influence local decision making as well as boosting their self-confidence. Local people also gained an important insight into the local budget setting procedure, together with a broader understanding of the local democratic process. Participatory budgeting also helped to build local community capacity and resulted in decisions that better reflected the views of local people. In particular it helped to strengthen linking social capital, a theme I looked at in the theoretical discussion in Chapter 1. However, the CLG report did sound a note of caution. The case examined in the report 'emphasised outcomes could not be expected on a significant scale, given the relatively limited scale of expenditure involved'. Any outcomes would also take some time to become apparent given that many of the projects examined had only `been running since 2008 (CLG, 2010c: 7).

One variant of the participatory budgeting model was the Harrow Open Budget process that was designed and managed by the Power Inquiry in association with the London Borough of Harrow. As Power notes, the process 'was designed to give Harrow residents a more direct and detailed say over their local councils 2006/7 budget' (Power, 2006: 225). This was done by setting up a large deliberative assembly. The Open Budget assembly attracted some 300 participants who took part in six hours of deliberation one October day in 2005.

Before the assembly started its deliberations, there was a period of consultation between the local council and community groups that sought to identify the types of budget choices that should be put to the assembly. In addition, 'A proactive recruitment campaign was launched to encourage people to attend the assembly'. Concerted efforts were made to ensure that the assembly reflected the social composition of Harrow so that 'not only the usual suspects took part' (Power, 2006: 226). In addition to choosing budgetary priorities the assembly elected an open budget panel from amongst its members. The principle role of the panel was to produce a report which analysed the extent to which the local council's final budget was in line with the priorities set out by the assembly (Power, 2006: 226–227).

Participants gave a positive response to the process: 90 per cent, for example, said that the event was good or very good. 74 per cent said the process should be repeated and 80 per cent said they would now be more interested in Council decisions. For Power, this indicated 'how effective deliberative political events can be' (Power, 2006: 226), and that such approaches could have wider public appeal (Power, 2006: 225).

A number of local councils have adopted elements of participatory budgeting. I will look at some other specific examples of these in the following section on neighbourhood governance.

Neighbourhood governance and the new localism

Over the last decade community involvement in governance became a key component of government policy. A variety of local authorities have put in place political arrangements that aim to move part of the locus of decision making from the town tall down into neighbourhoods. This new localism has been fostered and encouraged by central government as part of its strategy to reinvigorate local democracy and boost civic engagement and empowerment. How effective has this been? Let us consider some examples.

The model adopted in the London Borough of Croydon has been one of neighbourhood partnerships. These were first set up in 2000. There are ten in total and each partnership covers two or three wards. There are approximately 30,000 residents within each of the partnerships. The purpose of the partnerships, as laid out on the Council's own web site, 'is to consult, encourage comment on the provision of services locally and influence the policies of the Council and its partner agencies' (Croydon, 2009). Partnerships are allocated a budget, known as a community capital funding. According to Michael Fisher, Conservative Leader of Croydon Council, spending priorities for the budget were agreed locally. A range of local stakeholders is represented including tenants' and residents' groups, NHS professionals and police officers (Atkinson, 2008).

To get a flavour of these neighbourhood partnerships, I attended a meeting of the Fairfield, Heathfield, and Shirley neighbourhood partnership in early April 2009. Despite the alternative attraction of an England football World Cup qualifying match, fifty-five local people and representatives of community groups attended the meeting. In attendance were key local political figures such as the local MP and the Leader of the Council. Their presence could be taken as an indication of how important they thought the partnership meeting was. Local ward councillors, council officers and the local police were also present.

The overall impression gained was that it had a role to play. It provided a useful forum for local people to 'get stuff off their chests'. Whilst it did not appear to have any executive decision making powers, it went beyond being a mere talking shop. The key here was that the voices of local people and community groups could be heard. Local people have the opportunity to propose agenda items. The meeting gave a very helpful insight into some of the principal concerns and worries of local people. Road safety, in particular the issue of speeding cars along residential roads, featured strongly at the meeting. Arising out of these concerns, the council, in partnership with the local safer neighbourhood team (SNT), set up a scheme called Road Watch. Its purpose was to gather information with the use of tools such as speed guns. Such a development suggests some policy influence on the part of the neighbourhood partnership.

There was further evidence of some policy influence in respect of the recycling of garden waste. Croydon Council operates a kerbside collection scheme for garden waste in the borough. A council officer present reported that as a result of calls at a previous meeting of the partnership for an extension of this service, six bags of garden waste would now be collected on a fortnightly basis, up from the previous two. This may on the surface seem a trivial matter (though not in environmental terms) but to local residents such issues do matter. Such micro decisions can add up to something bigger, building confidence amongst local people and helping to shape and strengthen social capital.

The partnership meeting also served a helpful report-back role, especially in the area of crime. An officer from the local SNT set out a number of priorities for the year ahead, including a targeted approach to dealing with burglaries and car crime. These were welcomed by those present at the meeting. Local residents had expressed concerns about anti-social behaviour as children left a local secondary school on their way home at the end of the school day. As a response, police and local community support officers were now patrolling local buses and trams. The meeting was told how local residents appreciated such action.

Albeit only a snapshot, the experience from the meeting showed that such neighbourhood partnerships provided added value. They provided a regular forum for local people to raise their concerns. They do not seem to undermine the role of local elected councillors but to complement it. They also feed into current discourse about the so-called 'big society'.

The London Borough of Lewisham also operates a system of neighbourhood governance but it differs in a number of respects from the arrangements in Croydon. Unlike Croydon, Lewisham has a directly elected mayor, the Labour politician Sir Steve Bullock. This in itself raises interesting questions. At a conference on neighbourhood governance in London in 2008, Bullock told the audience that in his first term as mayor he had asked himself the question: what is my neighbourhood as mayor? This is a key question in a borough as diverse as Lewisham. In 2006 a mayoral commission was set up to look at what type of local political arrangements might best suit this diversity and how empowerment and local democracy might be developed and strengthened (Atkinson, 2008).

The result was the setting up of eighteen local assemblies that are based on the geography of existing electoral wards. Each local assembly has a small budget at its disposal that contains elements of participatory budgeting. This is called a locality fund. The Council's own web site states that the assemblies are a 'new way of working in which you [local residents] and others will decide how to improve your area'. At a meeting of the Downham local assembly on 14 March 2009 there was a discussion on the priorities for spending the £10,000 locality fund. A key policy priority for the assembly was youth provision. A grant in the region of £2,000 was awarded to the youth diversity challenge education support project and a smaller sum of £739 was awarded to the local Wesley Halls youth club (Lewisham, 2009).

Moving outside London we find other examples of such neighbourhood arrangements. In Thurrock (in Essex), for example, there are bodies called community forums. There are twenty such community forums; membership includes individual residents, community groups, local businesses and local service providers. They are described officially as 'independent community groups' one of whose key roles is to establish a link between Thurrock Council and other service providers such as the police and health services. They should not be viewed as mere talking shops. Such forums, should 'give residents a real chance of being involved in decisions that affect their local community' (Thurrock, 2009). There is an element of participatory budgeting as community forums are allocated a budget to spend on local projects.

An analysis of the minutes of a meeting of the Tilbury community forum held in February 2009 gives us a useful insight into how the structure works. There were a number of report-backs by various service providers and several residents expressed their views on matters such as crime, anti-social behaviour, employment and the local environment. One major issue discussed was that of the Port of Tilbury, which provided in the region of 45,000 jobs, 55 per cent of which were taken by Thurrock residents. Discussing the future of the Port, a representative of the company said they were hoping to create a further 3,000 jobs, some as a result of the 2012 London Olympics. The minutes show that a useful dialogue took place between representatives of the Port, local residents and local councillors. As such, the community forum played a valuable role.

There was also evidence of the community forum's role in participatory budgeting. It approved an application for £4,200 for three metal benches to be placed outside Tilbury health clinic. A local children's centre was awarded a grant of £500 towards the cost of a sensory garden. Though the figures involved are relatively small they do reflect some ownership by local people of the budgetary and policy process and as a consequence they help strengthen social capital (Thurrock, 2009).

Leicestershire County Council has a community forum structure. There are twenty-seven forums in total and they cover the whole of the County Council area. According to the official web site, these forums 'play an important role in ensuring that services provided in your area match the needs and wants of your local community' (Leicestershire, 2009).

A reading of the minutes of the Blaby central community forum in April 2009 again show participatory budgeting in play. The forum had a devolved budget of £20,000. There was a discussion on how to allocate this money, and various priorities were discussed and a broad agreement reached, reflecting perhaps some of the priorities of the local community. Yet attendance at the meeting was made up almost entirely of council members and officers, not a very broad section of the community. However, an analysis of the minutes of the Shepshed, Hathern and Dishley community forum in January gives us quite a different picture, with a high proportion of local residents in attendance. A variety of matters were discussed including plans to close the local fire station. This met with strong opposition from the meeting. The minutes record a voting exercise in a previous meeting about future local policy priorities. The overall theme that emerged was that priority should be given to measures that would make the local area a safer and more attractive place to live. In the wake of this, the County Council provided an additional allocation of £200,000 in the 2009/10 budget in four pilot areas (Leicestershire, 2009).

Leeds City Council has also adopted a community forum structure. The minutes of the Bramley and Stanningley community forum held on 27 November 2008 show that initiatives to combat crime featured strongly in the meeting. Representatives from the local police force were there to answer residents' questions. The forum seemed to act as a helpful conduit through which local people could express their views to elected councillors. Indeed, this is one of the strengths of such governance structures that provide a regular opportunity for interested residents to quiz their councillors and hold them to account. It is by no means perfect, but it is a useful addition to the local democratic process. For example, in the Bramley and Stanningley forum residents put forward ideas in respect of local traffic-calming measures. The local councillor present said that he was committed to supporting the views of the community and any agreed schemes would take into account their suggestions (Leeds, 2009).

Various issues arise out of these neighbourhood governance initiatives. First, there is the issue of how such neighbourhood governance bodies are constituted and how are they brought into the process of local decision making. Bacon *et al.* argue that the 'closer to the ground you get the less structures matter and the more approaches to work become important. Conversely, it is true that for neighbourhood working to be effective the further away from the ground you get the more structures matter.' This is due to the fact that 'Successful neighbourhood working needs to be driven from the centre of the local authority and embedded within the different departments' business plans' (Bacon *et al.*, 2007: 4).

Second, there are substantive issues around about the legitimacy and accountability of such bodies and the extent to which they speak for the wider community (Atkinson, 2008: 329).

Third, there remain concerns about the implications for local government of such new arrangements. To what extent do such participatory forms of local democracy sit with more traditional methods of local democracy or are they part of an attempt to 'hollow out' the role of elected local government? However, for commentators such as Pike, participatory and representative forms of local democracy are and should be complementary (Atkinson, 2008: 329). This is a view shared by Councillor Alan Waters of the LGiU (Atkinson, 2008: 329).

On a final note, the 'big society' agenda has, somewhat ironically, prompted some local authorities to consider withdrawing funding for such neighbourhood arrangements. What, if any alternative arrangements might be put in their place is not clear.

The role of town and parish councils

Town and parish councils are the most immediate level of democratic local government. They are often referred to collectively as 'local councils', in an attempt to draw a distinction with the other tiers of local government – county, district, or unitary – which are generally referred to as 'principal authorities'. Confusingly as, Jones notes, principal authorities themselves are sometimes referred to as local councils (Jones, 2007: 230). For the purposes of analysis I will use the term 'town and parish council'. There is very little legal difference between town and parish councils. However, town councils tend to be larger and better resourced than their predominantly rural parish council counterparts. Town councils are also broader in their policy scope. The majority of town and parish councils have populations of fewer than 5,000. However, Weston-Super-Mare and Shrewsbury have populations of around 72,000. This is significantly more than some so-called principal authorities.

The history of town and parish councils can be broadly traced back to the Local Government Act 1894. Originally focused on rural areas, their reach spread to some urban areas. They still remain, however, a largely rural phenomenon. Their role and influence have waxed and waned throughout various reforms of local government. There are currently 8,550 parish councils in England covering some 15 million people with 80,000 local councillors and 25,000 staff. Their total annual budget is in the region of £500 million (Source: National Association of Local Councils). Under the provisions of the Local Government and Rating Act 1997, a community at the level of a village, neighbourhood, or town beneath a district or borough council in England was given the right to demand its own elected town and parish council, either in partnership with the principal local authority or by means of a petition of local electors. New town and parish councils continue to come into existence, with over 200 added to the list in the last ten years. As Jones notes, this 'suggests an appeal to this form of government' (Jones, 2007: 231). Bevan has spoken of the growth of town councils in urban areas in recent times indicating that this trend will continue (Bevan, quoted in Jones, 2007: 231). Yet, as Jones argues, town councils have no significant presence in the large cities of England (Jones, 2007: 231).

One potential area of growth might be in London. With the creation of the Greater London Council (GLC) in 1965, there has been a constitutional impediment on the creation of town and parish councils in London. The reasons for this appear lost in the mists of time. However, with the passing of the Local Government and Public Involvement in Health Act 2007, there is now a legal provision for town and parish councils to be set up. Under the provisions of the Act, an area of London seeking to set up a town or parish council has to present a petition signed by 10 per cent of local electors to the relevant London Borough who will then have to carry out a community governance audit to assess the proposal.

Simon Jenkins, the distinguished *Guardian* columnist, took up the issue of town and parish councils at a conference on 'Local Democracy and Empowerment in London's Neighbourhoods' held in 2008. Jenkins was very sceptical of the whole New Localism agenda of New Labour. When set against our European counterparts, he argued, local democratic arrangements in the UK are weak (Atkinson, 2008: 326). He was critical of the recent fad for neighbourhood governance, which simply in his view produced another layer of consultation. What was needed were elected local bodies that had real responsibilities and substantive powers. For him, the vehicle of choice was the town or parish council. In his view they were 'the rock to fasten onto in the quest to reinvigorate local democracy'. For Jenkins, Londoners defined themselves by the neighbourhood in which they lived. So why not grant these neighbourhoods real powers and democratic legitimacy in the shape of parish councils (Atkinson, 2008: 326)?

Also speaking at the conference was Justin Griggs, Head of Development at the National Association of Local Councils (NALC, the representative body for parish councils). For Griggs, one of the major plus points for parish councils was their flexibility and responsiveness. But to be effective, he argued, they had to work in partnership with principal local authorities and other agencies (Atkinson, 2008: 326).

Alan Pike, a journalist and well-known expert on local government, had some concerns about introducing parish councils into the London local government scene. They were not a priority for Londoners. The use of petition powers (to set up town and parish councils) might well result in a disparity of local arrangements across London. This might put neighbourhoods in conflict with each other and possibly undermine community cohesion. He was also concerned about the possibility that parish councils might be hijacked by certain groups and individuals, who would use their position simply to 'bash the borough'. The Conservative Leader of Croydon Council, Michael Fisher, was worried that parishes could be the subject of extremist capture (Atkinson, 2008: 327).

But there are some potentially strong arguments in favour of the introduction of parishes into London. There are real challenges with the current structure of local government in London. Covering a population of over 7 million people, the GLA and the Mayor have a broad strategic responsibility for the running of London, with key responsibilities in policy areas such as transport and planning (GLA, 2010). The role of primary service delivery in areas such as education, social services and community safety falls to the boroughs. Yet these boroughs are large units both in terms of population area covered. The Borough of Croydon has a population of some 342,000, which in effect makes it the eleventh largest city in the UK. The neighbouring Borough of Bromley covers an area of some 58 square miles and has a population of 302,000. At the very least, such factors raise questions about the capacity of some London boroughs to be responsive to the needs of local people and indeed to be accountable. Town and parish councils, by dint of their relatively small size and more local representatives, are by definition closer to the local community certainly in physical terms and offer the real potential for a greater immediacy and accountability in terms of decision making and policy outcomes.

There are already a variety of systems of local neighbourhood governance sitting below the formal structures of London local government. I have already looked at some examples of these. Such experiences could be built upon with the introduction of town and parish councils whilst at the same time providing those extra elements of accountability and legitimacy which are for some lacking in the neighbourhood arrangements rolled out over the last few years. One could argue that there is little to lose in experimenting with town and parish councils in London. The start up costs would be relatively low as evidenced by experience outside of London. Why not just see where the experiment takes us? Viewed from a democratic perspective, town and parish councils can be regarded as a good thing in themselves, offering opportunities for local people to participate in the political process and to have an impact on decisions that shape their lives.

Finally, let us consider the argument that town and parish councils are at risk of extremist capture. This could be viewed as a counsel of despair. There is always a risk that in any system of democracy views inimical to many people may find expression as a result of the democratic process. What matters is the level of vibrancy in local politics and the extent to which people feel that decisions at the council level are relevant to their lives and aspirations. Town and parish councils that met such exigencies might well militate against the danger of extremist capture.

Town and parish councils in London

So far, there is little evidence so far of support for town and parish councils in formal London local government circles. Jones makes a good point when he argues that a 'tradition or culture of [town] and parish councils appears to be a precondition of their coming into existence, but this is largely lacking in urban areas' (Jones, 2007: 231). Whilst this may be true, proposals to set up town and parish councils in London came on to the agenda in 2011. Indeed, Stevens further argues that the 2007 Act creates 'the opportunity for more relevant community governance' in London (Stevens, 2008: 4).

The Queen's Park Community Council (a variant on the town council model) was launched on 22 January 2011. Queen's Park is near Paddington in the London borough of Westminster. The campaign to create the community council came about as a result of the closure of the Paddington Development Trust (a social enterprise). At a meeting organised by London Civic Forum in February 2011, Fabian Sharp, one of the local organisers behind the idea, said that in the beginning there was scepticism amongst local people about the idea but support was now growing. The campaign was made easier, Sharpe said, by the fact that it was backed by ten years' experience of running services and lobbying under the auspices of the Paddington Development Trust (London Civic Forum, 2011).

There have also been campaigns to set up a community council in London Fields (in the borough of Hackney) and a town council in Wapping (in the borough of Tower Hamlets). We are talking about small numbers so far and it is too early to say whether it is an agenda that will take off. Time alone will tell.

Town and parish councils and public participation

On 18 November 2008, the then Communities Secretary, Hazel Blears, set out plans to encourage new town and parish councils to be created with the expressed purpose of devolving more local decision making powers to local people. The Secretary of State praised the contribution of town and parish councils: 'As the smallest unit of electoral democracy, they play a vital and effective role in putting power in the hands of local people, to make the key decisions that affect their local communities' (CLG online, 18 November 2008).

These are fine words but what is the impact of town and parish councils on political participation and broader forms of civic engagement? The research in this area is limited but the available evidence suggests a mixed picture. For example, Edwards *et al.* found that only 28 per cent of town and parish council elections were contested in England and Wales between 1998 and 2001 (see Jones, 2007: 237). Research by Woods et al covering 1998 to 2000 found that electoral turnout is generally highest in small rural parishes and lowest in urban wards. The turnout for parish and town councils was between 30 and 45 per cent (Woods *et al.*, 2011: 5). Such figures bare reasonable comparison with those from so-called principal authorities.

Other evidence suggests some grounds for optimism. One local authority with a great deal of experience of the effects of parish councils on civic engagement and the shaping of public policy is Milton Keynes Council, which has an estimated population of 227,000. About 70 per cent of the Council's area is rural in nature with a number of historic towns and villages. The remaining 30 per cent is urbanised and is centred on the city of Milton Keynes. The Council has been fully parished since 2001 and has 45 town and parish councils.

Its community liaison officer manager is Caroline Godfrey, who argues that the parish councils are central in encouraging wider political and civic engagement (Atkinson, 2008: 327). In 2004, a 'Council and Parish and Town Council Charter' was launched by Milton Keynes. Its central premise is that parish and town councils are the grass roots level of local government and are a central element if partnership working with the community is to be effective and productive (Atkinson, 2008: 327). The parish councils hold regular community cohesion events such as local fun days. They attract broad community participation that simply would not be the case if they were held at the town hall.

Broadband and local communities

The link between community broadband and wider forms of local democracy and political activity may not at first sight seem obvious. Indeed, Hampton notes that critics of such 'new communication technologies' argue that as a consequence of their increased use, 'we will become increasingly home centred and disconnected from our friends, family, and communities' (Hampton, 2001: 301). Yet on closer examination the link becomes apparent. In broad terms, local community broadband has the potential to tackle social isolation, providing the opportunity for social interaction. But it also has a broader function. Far from reducing community feeling, the virtual communities that it helps shape can build social capital. It can act as a forum to discuss local issues, giving local people the opportunity to express their opinions and potentially have an impact on local policy. It can help build local campaigns. Those involved may come into contact with local decision makers helping to create the kind of linking social capital that I discussed in Chapter 1. It can build self-confidence and encourage local people to become more involved in the type of local formal democracy that we discussed in Chapter 4. For, as I noted earlier, there is a clear reciprocal relationship between such broader forms of civic engagement and more formal local democracy.

Former US Vice President Al Gore has argued that the internet (with related technologies such as community broadband) has the potential to re engage the electorate with politics on both sides of the Atlantic (*Guardian*, 28 August 2006). Jonathan Freedland has also argued that 'the internet has facilitated action locally' with local residents' associations, for example, being able to communicate through a web site as an option to having constant meetings (*Guardian*, 30 May 2007).

But where is the evidence to back up such broad propositions? Writing in a North American context, Gillett *et al.* refer to just a few case studies of local government community broadband projects but argue that 'there is little systematic data or research ... assessing the effectiveness of these efforts' (Gillett *et al.*, 2003: 1). That said, there are case studies that do at the very least provide interesting insights into the role of community broadband. Netville is a small neighbourhood in the outer suburbs of Toronto, Canada. It is a relatively new suburban development and, as Hampton notes, 'was one of the first developments in the world to be built from the ground up with a series of advanced communication technologies supplied across a broadband high speed local network' (Hampton, 2001: 301). At the time of the study, of the 109 homes that made up Netville, sixty-four were connected to the broadband network and forty-five were not. As such the latter group 'provided a natural comparison group for studying the effects of living in a wired environment' (Hampton, 2001: 301).

A sample survey of 'wired' and 'non-wired' residents was carried out to ascertain the degree of neighbourhood social networks. The findings were revealing, possibly even counterintuitive. In comparison to their unwired neighbours, wired residents recognised three times as many of their neighbours and spoke to them twice as often. They also visited them 50 per cent more often (Hampton, 2001: 302). This evidence seems to corroborate the observation made earlier that the use of community broadband can help mitigate against social isolation. In terms of broader civic engagement, wired residents used their neighbourhood networks to build social capital by organising local events and as a platform to mobilise around community issues. These included housing concerns (Hampton, 2001: 301).

The results of this study, albeit a small-scale study, provide some evidence that internet use does not inhibit interpersonal communication. For, as Hampton cogently points out, 'Social ties do not exist only face to face, they are a mixture of online and in person encounters'. As such, at the local level, 'the increasing use and availability of community broadband will increasingly be used to expand neighbourhood social capital' (Hampton, 2001: 302).

In the UK context, the Community Broadband Network (CBN) was launched by the then Rural Affairs Minister, Alun Michael, back in 2004. The CBN is a social enterprise that supports and helps develop community-led broadband initiatives. CBN works with a range of clients. Its stated aim is to 'help them realise the benefits' of what it calls 'Next Generation broadband networks'. The nature and expectations of such clients differ. Some see the opportunity to delivery public services, others are more concerned by digital and rural inclusion and strengthening social capital. For others the imperative is more commercial (CBN, 2010).

In 2009, the Department of Culture, Media and Sport (DCMS) House of Commons select committee launched its report, *Digital Britain*. Whilst much of the thrust of the report is about the economic opportunities to Britain of new digital technologies (DCMS, 2009a: 1), there are also references in the report to the broader societal benefits. In the foreword, there is talk of the need to ensure that all people 'can participate in digital society' (DCMS, 2009a: 1). Implicit in this is the worry that any 'digital divide' will simply reinforce social exclusion. In the report, Steve Ballmer, Chief Executive of Microsoft, argues that 'The number one benefit of information technology is that it empowers people to do what they want to do' (DCMS, 2009a: 27), allowing people to learn and to be creative. This can feed into individual success and fulfilment but there are also potential benefits for the broader community. For example, the report argues that the internet 'is a participative generative network promoting interactivity, collaboration and conversation' (DCMS, 2009a: 22). As such, it offers up a number of possibilities at both the global, national and local level. The report identifies potential benefits in what it terms 'democratic engagement' by means of increased opportunities to participate in and discuss the democratic process' (DCMS, 2009a: 29). It talks of how people are using digital technology to engage with their local communities through the use of things such as e-mail (DCMS, 2009a: 28).

There are in Britain currently in the region of forty locally organised projects to install high-speed broadband networks (CBN, 2010). Though there is perhaps a tendency to over-focus on technical aspects, analysis of some of these projects does highlight the potential for innovation in community social networking, civic engagement, service delivery and the building and strengthening of social capital.

One such project is Angus Glens, an area on the edge of the Scottish Highlands with limited access to telecommunications of any sort. CBN is working with other specialists to bring super-broadband services to the area. The aim is not just for fast internet and digital television but to develop ways of working which support and enhance the community. One such initiative is that of e-Health. Members of the local community have been working with Dundee University on projects for independent living for those subject to chronic ill health and for the introduction of so-called tele-medicine. A fast and reliable community broadband network is key to this (CBN, 2011).

The town of Alston in Cumbria in is one of the most sparsely populated areas in England. As such, it was considered by some industry experts not to be a viable site for deploying first-generation broadband. Cybermoor, one of the first community-run broadband projects in the UK, challenged this view. Today they are the main provider of first-generation broadband services in the area, providing connectivity for isolated communities and the potential for social interaction. But there is also an important local public service dimension to Cybermoor. In conjunction with CBN it has been exploring the possibility of using fibre optic broadband technology to deliver improved local health care to isolated communities 'at a reduced cost to taxpayers' (CBN, 2011).

The Conservative/Liberal Democratic coalition government is taking forward the community broadband agenda. On 6 December 2010, the Culture Secretary, Jeremy Hunt, announced that every community in the UK would have access to the new generation of super-fast broadband by 2015 (BBC online, 6 December 2010).

Public participation and consumer choice

There has been a growing trend amongst policy makers, not only over the last fifteen years but going back to the politics of Thatcherism in the 1980s, to look at public participation through the lens of the market. Local citizens have become viewed as consumers of services with the market the forum for participation. It is a controversial approach, which some commentators argue fundamentally changes the nature of local democracy and accountability. For Wilks-Heeg and Clayton, it marks a shift in traditional notions of accountability and democracy as a collective process to a more individualistic one that is designed to make service providers more responsive to their clients (Wilks-Heeg and Clayton, 2006: 4). This can take a number of forms including direct involvement in local services and representation on partnerships such as LSPs. There has also been an array of new consultation procedures brought in. Some of these we have already discussed in the section above including participatory budgeting and citizens' panels. Another important component of what Wilks-Heeg call the 'consumerist conception of user democracy' is the widespread use by local bodies 'of mechanisms to respond to customer complaints' (Wilks-Heeg and Clayton, 2006: 129). These include customer satisfaction surveys and consumer focus groups.

The idea of the direct involvement of local people in service provision is not a new one. New forms of participatory democracy were introduced in a number of policy areas from the late 1960s onwards. 1974, for example, saw the creation of Community Health Councils (CHCs) with a specific mission to represent patients in the NHS. CHCs were abolished in 2003, to be replaced by Patient Forums. In 2007, Patient Forums themselves were abolished and replaced by Local Involvement Networks (LINks). LINks sit within the PCTs, the bodies responsible for the commissioning of local health services. They have a number of roles. These include representing the views of patients and the public to the NHS, monitoring how well NHS bodies perform in taking account of these views. However, radical changes to the NHS are afoot. In September 2010, the coalition government launched the white paper, *Equity and Excellence: Liberating the NHS* (Department of Health, 2010). Amongst other things, it proposed the abolition of PCTs, to be replaced by GP commissioning consortia. How this will affect the patient voice is a matter for future debate.

In education, parents were given the statutory right to be represented on school governing bodies in 1980. Furthermore, the general role of school governors was strengthened in the 1980s with a series of reforms implemented by the then Conservative government. Today, there are in the region of 350,000 people serving as school governors (Wilks-Heeg and Clayton, 2006: 125), representing broader elements of the local community together with parents, teachers and elected local councillors. A report in 2010 published by the then Department for Children, Schools and Families (DCSF) noted that the majority of governing bodies carry out an effective role. However, it did argue that there needed to be greater clarity concerning the strategic management role of governing bodies and the day-to-day management role of head teachers (DCSF, 2010).

More recent proposals have sought to shift the emphasis of public participation beyond citizens as mere consumers. The so-called 'John Lewis' council model, for example, puts forward the idea of cooperative ownership of local services, with local people and service providers working in partnership. It is most clearly associated with the Labour-controlled London Borough of Lambeth. More surprisingly, perhaps, the Conservative Party has put forward proposals for a form of cooperative local service delivery. I shall return to these issues in Chapter 6.

Partnership working has become a key part of the lexicon of local government reform over the last three decades. LSPs were set up in 1999 to promote joint working between key local stakeholders such as local public agencies, the voluntary sector and the private sector. The aim of such LSPs was to tackle what was seen as the fragmented nature of local services and provide more joined-up provision. Such stakeholder involvement has been described by Wilks-Heeg and Clayton as a 'form of network democracy' that, Wilks-Heeg and Clayton argue, 'appears to be an increasingly powerful element of the democratic mix' (Wilks-Heeg and Clayton, 2006: 68). Yet questions have been raised about the democratic accountability of such bodies and their representative nature. Wilks-Heeg and Clayton, for example, talk of the lack of transparency in LSP decision making and their tenuous links to local communities (Wilks-Heeg and Clayton, 2006: 68).

Conclusion

In this chapter I have focused on a number of aspects of participation and civic engagement that go beyond the realm of traditional local politics. Indeed over the last fifteen years there has been an increasing policy emphasis on new forms of community participation and community empowerment. 'Such participatory methods abound but do they actually broaden the base of decision making?' (Wilson, 1999: 52). For Wilks-Heeg and Clayton 'it is possible that broadening the scope for citizen input will increase overall levels of participation in local democracy' (Wilks-Heeg and Clayton, 2006: 131). Yet as they note the available evidence is limited.

However, research carried out by the Power Inquiry showed significant public support for wider forms of participation. Broadening community participation can help strengthen the local polity but only in the context of a vibrant elected local government. Indeed a mixture of traditional forms of political participation and broader forms of civic engagement can be mutually reinforcing. In some ways the local political landscape resembles a jigsaw puzzle. If you lose any one of the pieces, you do not get the full picture.

6

Local services, community and civic engagement

Introduction

In Chapter 6 the focus is on local services and their impact on strengthening civic engagement and local communities.

First, there will be a focus on central government policy. There will be an analysis of some initiatives of the last Labour government as well as an initial assessment of the emerging policy agenda of the current Conservative/ Liberal Democrat coalition. Local public service reform will also be looked at in the context of the role of markets and the increasing emphasis on the choice agenda, with citizens seen more and more as consumers.

Second, there will be an analysis of new approaches by local authorities to service delivery. This will include an analysis of innovative approaches adopted by local providers in the delivery of services. New and emerging paradigms will also come under scrutiny, such as the 'John Lewis' model, the 'Easy Council' model and the 'Virtual Council' model.

Third, the role of the private sector and the part it plays in providing local services will be analysed. There will be a focus on banks and building societies, local post offices (which operate as quasi-market organisations) and community pubs.

Fourth, there will be an examination of various local service initiatives that have developed out of the social enterprise and voluntary sectors and the local community. These include credit unions and community-run shops.

Central government policy and local services

First, let us consider some attempts by central government to reform local public services over the last fifteen years. The way public services are delivered and shaped offers the potential for effective civic engagement and the concomitant development of social capital. The empowerment agenda, notwithstanding its limitations and contradictions (see Chapter 3), was framed in terms that sought to develop such potential. I will now analyse the extent to which such potential was realised by focusing on three important policy areas: crime and community safety; privatisation, marketisation and the choice agenda; and finally the emerging concept of the 'big society' and localism.

Crime and community safety

Involvement by local people in the fight against crime is by no means a new phenomenon. Projects such as Neighbourhood Watch and the voluntary special constables' scheme are well-established examples of civic engagement in crime prevention and community safety. But it is true to say that that crime has had a higher policy profile in recent times. Over the last decade and a half partnership working has been one of the key mantras of public service reforms. The argument goes like this. Complex, multi-faceted problems require a multi-faceted response, involving a number of local agencies organisations and the local community. Crime and community safety policy is no exemption.

Originally piloted in London but subsequently rolled out across England and Wales, safer neighbourhood teams (SNTs) were seen as part of a strategy whose expressed aim was to bring policing closer to the community. Based on local electoral wards, they are made up of police officers and police community support officers. Introduced in part due to public demand, these teams aim to work with communities and partner organisations to identify and address local concerns. In addition local community forums (their precise title varies from area to area) provide the opportunity, for local residents to raise issues and concerns.

Such an initiative appears on the surface to be a good example of a service devolved closer to the community. Underpinning this policy initiative was a belief in government that local people must be encouraged to win back their communities and be supported by local and central government to do so. More specifically, government was 'determined to give people more control over the fight against crime' (H.M. Government, 2009: 76). From the perspective of government, there was a 'need for citizens to be active in helping to identify community safety priorities for their neighbourhood' (H.M. Government, 2006: 23). It is by means of such 'effective community engagement' that 'stronger and sustainable communities' can be developed (H.M. Government, 2006: 23).

However, some academic commentators have raised doubts about such an approach. Gordon Hughes, for example, argues that 'there are no simple answers nor technical fixes to community based crime prevention' (HMSO, 2006: ii). Atkinson and Flint go further, questioning whether it is the right approach to 'involve local residents more centrally in crime reduction plans' and whether this is an 'empowering or worrying option for residents'

(Atkinson and Flint, 2004: 334). Their conclusion, based on a study of four neighbourhoods, is 'that there is limited viability to a policy project' which seeks to 'empower residents' to fight crime and disorder. 'In affluent areas', they argue, 'taxpayers view these processes as something already paid for' whilst in deprived areas fear of reprisals prevents 'effective action' (Atkinson and Flint, 2004: 348).

However, other commentators take a different view. The former Home Secretary, David Blunkett, in a report published in 2009, argued that 'It would be a positive change for the public to have a greater say in crime prevention measures in their locality' (Blunkett, 2009: 19). The report also argues that local communities should be given the option to pay higher local taxes for greater service provision such as neighbourhood policing.

In an apparent attempt to boost civic engagement in respect of crime control, the Conservative/Liberal Democrat coalition government have set in place plans for directly elected local police and crime commissioners, to come into effect in 2011. The government argues that that the policy will make the police more accountable and will give local people more of a say in local policing matters. Theresa May, the Home Secretary, has argued that the proposals signal the most radical change to policing in the last fifty years 'by transferring power back to the people' (Home Office, 2010: 3). The government talks of how elected commissioners 'will empower the public' by giving them a voice and by strengthening accountability and trans-parency' (Home Office, 2010: 8).

The proposals have met with a mixed response. Critics, including the police, have expressed concern that policing could become too politicised. Rob Garnham, Chairman of the Association of Police Authorities and a Conservative councillor, argued that it was the wrong policy at the wrong time. For Garnham, there was no evidence that the public wanted more politicians or elections, or indeed that the proposed reforms would help reduce crime (BBC News online, 1 December 2010).

Other commentators have struck a more positive note. Louise Casey, Commissioner for Victims and Witnesses, has given the proposals a broad welcome, arguing that it would make local police forces more accountable and more responsive to local demands (BBC News online, 1 December 2010). Blair Gibbs, of the Policy Exchange think tank, has argued that the new model would 'make police chiefs truly accountable for the first time' (BBC News online, 1 December 2010).

Roth takes a more balanced view. He acknowledges that that police and crime commissioners 'should improve police visibility and give citizens a channel through which they can address their concerns' but cautions that 'electoral considerations could influence the actions and focus of police and crime commissioners, and that these will become too politicised' (Roth, 2010: 4).

Privatisation, marketisation and the choice agenda

The last thirty years have witnessed major change in both the delivery and nature of local public services with an increased market for private sector providers. There has also been an increasing emphasis on individual choice and personalisation in the delivery of local services. What has been the impact of these developments on local communities and civic engagement?

The personalisation of public services, whose stated aim is to give service users greater choice with services tailored to their particular needs and requirements, has been a key tenet in the local services' reform agenda over the last decade and a half. However, with the increasing emphasis on choice, decisions around local services are seen as less and less predicated on the impact on the collective experience of the local community, but instead are viewed as a matter for individual preference. Whilst there are obvious merits in policies that seek to tailor services to meet the needs of individual needs and preferences, there are also inherent dangers in such an approach.

Of course it goes without saying that local public services should be about quality education for young people, care for the elderly and the like but they also have another important dimension. They can act as a setting for civic engagement and community cohesion. This can include referenda on the level of local council tax, discussions at local community forums on recycling policy and community campaigns to oppose the closure of public libraries. Local services are part of the public realm. This links back to our discussion in Chapter 1 on public value. Proponents of the notion of public value argue that one of the key roles public services play is in strengthening civic engagement and building social capital. Marketisation and privatisation can undermine this.

The choice agenda presents other problems. I have already discussed the 'usual suspects' problem when policy makers draw up new strategies to boost civic engagement and community empowerment. A similar problem presents itself with the choice agenda. In this process some groups and individuals have an inbuilt advantage. The educated and the articulate, quick of mind and fleet of foot, can see their choices take preference over others.

The 'big society' and localism

Since it came to power in May 2010 the Conservative/Liberal Democrat coalition government has laid great stress on the twin policies of localism and creating the so-called 'big society' as the key to greater civic engagement in the shaping and delivery of local services. The Decentralisation and Localism Bill 2010, for example, gives local community groups the right to bid to deliver local services and to buy community assets. Such policy ideas are still in development but it is possible to make some initial assessment of the philosophy that underpins them and the potential impact on elected local government, local communities and civic engagement.

During the May 2010 General Election campaign David Cameron spoke on a number of occasions about his desire to create a 'big society' in Britain. What does this mean? Critics point to its vagueness and ill-defined nature. Even some Conservative supporters appear to have difficulty with the concept. In a speech to the Community Service Volunteers (CSV) in the House of Lords on 9 November 2010, Tim Loughton, the Children's Minister, said 'The trouble is that most people don't know what the big society really means, least of all the unfortunate ministers who have to articulate it' (*Guardian*, 10 November, 2010).

The candour of Loughton notwithstanding, the coalition government has sought to set out the philosophy underpinning notions of a 'big society' and what outcomes flow from it. David Cameron, for example, in a speech in Liverpool in July 2010, attempted to set out his vision of the 'big society'. 'You can call it liberalism. You can call it empowerment. You can call it freedom. You can call it responsibility', Cameron said, but 'I call it the Big Society' (*Guardian*, 19 July 2010).

Cameron argued that the 'big society' represented 'a huge culture change' which involved the 'most dramatic redistribution of power from elites in Whitehall to the man and woman on the street' (*Guardian*, 19 July 2010). The talk of a big society seems to tune with another idea expounded by the Conservative Party: the notion of the post-bureaucratic age (Conservative Party, 2009). This concept has been taken into government with the Decentralisation and Localism Bill. For Cameron, the purpose of the Bill was to 'reverse years of creeping state control and return power to people, communities and councils. We have an optimistic vision that supports people to work in the interests of their communities, rather than telling them what to do' (CLG Press Release, 28 May 2010).

Returning to this theme in his speech in Liverpool, Cameron argued the kind of 'top down, top heavy' government that we had witnessed in recent times 'had the effect of sapping responsibility, local innovation and civic action'. The solution for Cameron is to 'create communities with oomph – neighbourhoods who are in charge of their own destiny' and who 'can shape the world around them'. For Cameron, government has an important role to play as a facilitator in shaping and growing the 'big society'. It should 'foster and support a new culture of voluntarism, philanthropy and social action' (*Guardian*, 19 July 2010).

However, the idea of the 'big society' can be criticised on a number of levels. To illustrate this, let us take the example of a 'big society' project put forward by coalition government ministers, namely the Balsall Heath Neighbourhood Forum in Birmingham. On a visit in September 2010, the Decentralisation Minister, Greg Clark, praised the work of the forum and the community in tackling anti-social behaviour and restoring community pride. He said that he was 'delighted to meet the pioneering residents of Balsall Heath' and witness 'real proof of the value of community participation'. The thousand plus members of the Neighbourhood Forum were for

Clark 'the Big Society in action and other community groups can look to them as a perfect example of people power' (CLG Press Release, 21 September 2010).

Yet to link developments in Balsall Heath to the coalition government's idea of the big society and the notion of a cultural shift in the relation between civil society and government is disingenuous to say the least. The improvements in Balsall Heath, once a notorious red light area, are the product of work going back ten years or more. They are just one example of the myriad of volunteering and civic engagement that I examined in Chapter 2. The 'big society', if we are to use that phrase, has been in operation over a longer period than that of the coalition government.

So what lies behind the coalition government's 'big society' agenda? At best, it could be viewed as an act of political window dressing, a public relations branding exercise, giving the illusion of a big new policy idea when in reality it is nothing of the sort. At worst, it can be seen as part of a broader new right agenda to radically shrink both the central and local state. Cameron has argued that 'power' must be pushed away 'from central government to local government' (*Guardian*, 19 July 2010). However, the local authority expenditure cuts that resulted after October 2010 could have profound effects for elected local government and in a seeming paradox are a major threat to the volunteerism and civic engagement that lie at the heart of the so-called 'big society'.

In general terms, local authority budgets in England will be reduced in the region of 30 per cent in the period 2011–15. Evidence is emerging that seems to suggest that such cuts are having an impact on the voluntary and social enterprise sector. For example, the recently created Office for Civil Society (OCS), which replaced the Office of the Third Sector set up by the previous Labour government, cut its grant to organisations that encourage volunteering by £11 million. Sir Stuart Etherington, Chief Executive of the NCVO, warned in a speech to the annual NCVO conference in November 2010 that the 'big society' idea was being imperilled by the cuts in grants by local councils to the voluntary sector (*Guardian* online, 23 November 2010). Dame Elisabeth Hoodless, the former Executive Director of CSV, has warned that the budget cuts are 'destroying the volunteer army' and as a consequence are undermining the vision of the 'big society' (BBC News online, 7 February 2011).

Against a background of cuts to local services, the drive towards the 'big society' has been met with some scepticism amongst activists within the community development sector, a sector that would seem central to its viability. For example, Julian Dobson, Editorial Director of the sector's *New Start Magazine*, has said that 'there are areas around which conversations can happen, but at the moment we are seeing situations where people are feeling assaulted – not surprisingly, because many of them are going to lose their jobs and their livelihoods' (*Guardian*, 6 October 2010).

One organisation set up to push the agenda is the Big Society Network. It planned to hold a series of town hall style meetings. In August 2010 it sent a note to various voluntary sector leaders stating that it would be 'hosting a series of public meetings to engage with individuals, those active in civil society and social entrepreneurs on all aspects of the big society' (*Guardian*, 6 October 2010). By the end of 2010, only one such meeting had taken place. As reported by the *Guardian*, the meeting in Stockport 'ended up in acrimonious exchanges over spending cuts' (*Guardian*, 6 October 2010).

There are also question marks over the network's grass roots credibility. A Freedom of Information Act request by the *Guardian* found that five CLG staff had been seconded to the network since 2010 (*Guardian*, 6 October 2010). Yet the 'big society' still appears to be an important aspect of government thinking. Writing in February 2011, David Cameron rejected the criticism that the 'big society' idea was 'cover for cuts'. Instead it was an agenda that was about 'devolving power' and 'building a bigger, stronger, more active society' (*Observer*, 13 February 2011). This is a controversy that is set to run and run.

Innovation in local public services

Despite the limited policy and financial autonomy over the last thirty years, local councils have been able to act creatively and have responded in imaginative ways to shape local services and boost civic engagement. The 1980s and 1990s saw local authorities such Walsall, the London Borough of Tower Hamlets and the London Borough of Islington set in place decentralisation strategies that had a significant impact on how services were delivered.

More recently such innovative approaches have come to the fore. In the wake of the credit crunch local authorities will be increasingly faced with difficult decisions when it comes to service delivery. In this regard the LGiU launched an initiative with a number of other organisations, including the NALC, called 'Small is Beautiful' in 2009. Despite the downward pressure on local authority budgets, the LGiU is of the view that there is still a 'need to rebuild the sense of responsibility and connectedness that our communities feel they have lost' (LGiU, 2009a). To this end it is the small-budget services, most likely to be susceptible to cuts, which the LGiU argues have the 'greatest potential to build local pride, community relationships and sense of place' (LGiU, 2009a). Examples of such services include home library services, cultural services, volunteer development, heritage services and museums. Under the 'Small is Beautiful' initiative local authorities submit examples of how such apparently small-scale services can with 'ingenuity and innovation' help to 'turn a small service into a big community impact' (LGiU, 2009a).

Taking a similar approach, the Improvement and Development Agency (IDeA) argue that innovation is the key for local authorities if they wish successfully to engage with local communities and help strengthen their development (IDeA, 8 September 2009).

Responding to the innovation call, a number of local authorities have set out new approaches to local service delivery. Most prominent of these are the so-called 'John Lewis' model associated with the London Borough of Lambeth, the 'Easy Council' model that has been pioneered in the London Borough of Barnet and the 'Virtual Council' model associated with Suffolk County Council. These three models represent divergent and conflicting strategies as regards service delivery and community engagement.

The so-called 'John Lewis' model is principally associated with the Labour-controlled London Borough of Lambeth. It takes its name from the John Lewis department store group that operates as a mutual where the staff are partners in the organisation, having a say in company policy and taking a share of the profits. Its relevance to local public services comes out of a paper produced by the government's Innovation Unit (based in the Cabinet Office) in December 2009. It looked at the potential for what might be termed cooperative and mutual governance in local public services, whereby service producers and service users operate in partnership to affect both the delivery and nature of such services (Craig *et al.*, 2009).

Craig *et al.* start off with the general observation that public services have learned much from the workings of the private sector. They argue, for example, that the focus on citizens as consumers has led to some improvements in local public services. Yet such a view is contested. Craig *et al.* themselves concede that such 'approaches are subject to diminishing returns'. Indeed not everything in the private sector garden is rosy. As they note, 'the credit crunch and the subsequent economic down turn has freed our political imagination from the idea that this is the only game in town'. The key challenge ahead is that 'of engaging citizens and service users and harnessing their energy and creativity' (Craig *et al.*, 2009: 4). Craig *et al.* make a key point here and in doing so make an implicit criticism of the last Labour government's failure to deliver sufficiently on its empowerment and engagement agenda. They go on to argue that local public services need to draw on the approaches to mutual and cooperative forms of governance employed by the likes of John Lewis and other retailers like the Coop (Craig *et al.*, 2009:4). There needs to be reciprocity in local public services. 'Can we really expect citizens', they ask, 'to take on responsibility for their own health, learning and carbon footprint if public services do not give them greater rights to shape their work?' (Craig *et al.*, 2009: 5).

Such a mutualism agenda does appear attractive at first glance but there are obstacles and uncertainties. First, the interests of service providers and service users may not always complement each other and this may lead to conflict. Second, evidence suggests (see Chapter 3) that only a minority of service users are likely to become involved. This might not necessary be a problem if any benefits of mutualism are widely spread but there remains the danger of capture by 'a partial group of citizens' (Craig *et al.*, 2009: 5). Third, local government professionals, with their expertise and time in the job have an inbuilt advantage over many service uses. Thus professional capture remains an ever-present danger.

Such barriers notwithstanding, how can mutualism in local public services be operationalised on a practical level? In this regard let us focus on the London Borough of Lambeth. Faced with cuts in its budget in the order of £80 million in the period 2011–14, Lambeth has been looking at alternative ways to deliver local services. The approach adopted in Lambeth, according to Council Leader Steve Reed, is to involve users in providing local services 'at lower costs' (*Guardian*, 18 February 2010).

But what does Reed's vision mean in practice? In 2009, Lambeth Council appointed local resident Sue Sheehan to a position in the Council. Founder of a vegetable-growing cooperative in Balham, she was given the task of rolling out similar schemes across Lambeth. By the end of 2009, fifty had been established (*Guardian*, 18 February 2010). This is a relatively small-scale project but it does us some insight into how the John Lewis model might be developed. Indeed the council, in partnership with local community groups and other interested parties, has more ambitious plans which could bring cooperative and mutual governance to community centres and primary schools.

One ambitious plan has involved the abandoned former site of Lilian Baylis secondary school. The site sits in an area of high deprivation with very limited recreation facilities. Local community groups and local residents in partnership with North Southwark and North Lambeth Sport Action Zone (SAZ), the local MP and Lambeth Council put forward proposals to use the site and open up the building for community use. In 2006, SAZ were given access to the site. Since then, sporting and recreational developments on the site have 'opened up opportunities for participation that previously did not exist. Labelled as a community hub, a range of sports is on offer. There are also classes in art, education and music. The aim of the project is to create a place that is based in the community and, with council support, is led by the community'.

Building on such developments, the council set out its strategy in a document entitled *The Cooperative Council*, which was published in the autumn of 2010. In the foreword to the document, Council Leader Steve Reed speaks of the challenge of delivering 'services which meet local needs in a period of tighter funding' (Lambeth, 2010: 2). Forming a partnership with service users and service providers is the way that Lambeth seeks to meet this challenge. To this end, Lambeth Council has set up a Cooperative Council Commission made up of local citizens, community groups, interested partners and politicians to shape and set the agenda. The aim of this process says Reed is to 'make Lambeth the first co-operative council and ultimately the first co-operative borough' (Lambeth, 2010: 2).

In its strategy paper, the Council talks of the need to re-examine its principles, culture, governance, and 'crucially our relationship with citizens' (Lambeth, 2010: 4). It sets out a future vision (looking to 2014) for local services built on 'A new relationship between citizens, our communities and public services where power and responsibility is shared more equally' (Lambeth, 2010: 4). It is a policy very much in its infancy and any substantive analysis of its impact will have to wait until a future date. But it is a challenging agenda. Indeed Lambeth council asks itself the question, 'How can we provide opportunities for citizens to engage with public service provision ... in their everyday lives in ways that demonstrate choice, real influence and mutual understanding' (Lambeth, 2010: 46).

The ideas coming out of Lambeth chime to some extent with the idea of the 'big society'. For example, in opposition, the Conservative Leader David Cameron sought to position himself on traditional Labour terrain by talking of local authority workers forming cooperatives to deliver local services. He did this in a speech in Manchester on 8 November 2007 when he launched the Conservative Cooperative Movement (BBC News online, 8 November 2007). However, at the local level Conservative-controlled local councils have focused on what one might term a marketised cut back model.

One such model is the London Borough of Barnet's so-called 'Easy Council' model or, to give its official title, *The Future Shape of the Council*. The aims of this model were set out in a policy paper discussed at a meeting of the council's cabinet on 6 July 2009. The context here is the same as that for the London Borough of Lambeth, how to meet the challenge of delivering local services with a significantly reduced local budget. The paper talks of meeting this challenge by means of a 'relentless drive on efficiency' including further privatisation of local services (Barnet, 2009: 50). But it also talks of partnership working, of developing a new relationship with citizens and revitalising the way citizens interact with public services (Barnet, 2009: 50). The rhetoric here is in some ways similar to that employed in Lambeth. The prescriptions on offer are however radically different.

The Barnet model views community engagement and participation through the prism of choice and the market. Residents receive a set of basic services funded from the council tax and central government grant but if they want services beyond this basic level they have to make an additional financial contribution. This has drawn comparison with the business model of certain budget airlines such as Easy Jet, hence the 'Easy Council' label.

The approach adopted by Barnet has come in for much criticism and has encountered a number of difficulties. For example, proposals for a fast-track planning system (residents would pay more if they wanted their planning application to be dealt with more quickly) were put on hold after doubts were raised about the legality of such an approach. Furthermore, in December 2009, a High Court decision prevented Barnet from removing twenty-four-hour live-in wardens from sheltered housing. The High Court backed the view of elderly residents that such a move contravened the Disability Discrimination Act 2005 and also broke existing tenancy agreements. Commenting in the *Guardian* on 24 September 2010, the then Leader of the Labour group on Barnet Council, Alison Moore, argued that the 'Conservatives had persisted with Future Shape on a wish and a prayer without working out what the real purpose and value of it is' (*Guardian*, 24 September 2010). Such criticism from such a quarter might not be surprising but it is not confined to political opponents. In September 2010, an audit by Grant Thompson stated that the *Future Shape of the Council* project lacked an adequate analysis of the costs and benefits. The audit stated that 'Further work is required to develop the programme vision and the organisational blue print'. It also argued that the Council had failed so far to make a business case for its proposals (*Guardian*, 24 September 2010).

Another model of innovation to be considered is that of Conservative-controlled Suffolk County Council. Suffolk has been labelled the 'Virtual Authority' in some circles, based on its proposals to outsource many of its services to both social enterprises and private sector companies. The Council's plans are set out in a strategy paper entitled *The New Strategic Direction Explained* (Suffolk, 2010). In broad terms the aim is for Suffolk to become a radical enabling local authority, with limited responsibility for direct service delivery. It is the plan to phase in the outsourcing of the majority of Council services. By such means the Council hopes to reduce its £1 billion+ budget by some 30 per cent over four years, in line with the cuts to local authority budgets as set out in the October 2010 comprehensive spending review. A work force in the region of 27,000 could be reduced to just a few hundred (*Guardian*, 23 September 2010).

For Council Leader Jeremy Pembroke, without such radical reform, 'the cuts to local services would have been much deeper' (*Guardian*, 23 September 2010). In its strategy paper, the Council talks of changing its role 'from an organisation that that provides services to one which focuses on its role as a community leader and advocate' (Suffolk, 2010: 3). In practical terms this means divesting itself from some services it currently operates and outsourcing them to the private sector, social enterprises and community organisations. For example, local communities and staff might take direct responsibility for the running of local libraries, an idea that has some echoes in the Cooperative Council model in Lambeth. But there is a further strand to the reform process, with Pembroke arguing that 'by becoming an enabling authority, we will give local people the opportunity to decide what level of service they want' (*Guardian*, 23 September 2010). Such an approach has much in common with the Barnet model where individual choice and preferences in local services (a quasi-market) are seen as a key motor of civic engagement.

Local services and the private sector

It is not only services provided by statutory bodies that have the potential to build stronger communities and develop social capital. The private sector has a role to play here. Yet over recent years we have witnessed an emerging pattern of private sector retrenchment especially in certain rural areas and deprived inner-city communities. Post offices (which one might categorise as quasi-market organisations), local banks and building societies, and local community pubs provide us with three case studies.

Post offices

Local post offices provide an array of services including the payment of pensions, road tax renewals and banking services such as foreign currency. Indeed in a number of areas they fill the void created by the withdrawal of commercial banks. However, their functions go well beyond this. They can act as a community hub, a meeting place for local people helping to combat social isolation. They can provide a focus for community identity and community cohesion, a place to chat and interact. But there are specific groups of people such as the elderly for whom the local post office is a life-line. Indeed the coalition government acknowledges that 'the post office is more than a commercial entity and serves a distinct social purpose' (BIS, 2010: 3). The Business and Enterprise select committee of the House of Commons spoke of the community value of local post offices (House of Commons, 2009c: 3).

Yet in recent years the local post office network has come under strain and questions are being asked about its long-term survival. Some of the core services that it provides are under threat or have been withdrawn. For example, many people now have their pensions paid directly into their bank accounts. Road tax can be easily renewed online or by phone. Other services have been taken over by commercial competitors. For example, in 2006 the post office lost the contract for the renewal of television licenses to the private sector company Pay Point. In a further blow, it has been announced that, from 2012, the contract for processing benefit cheques will also be given to Pay Point. The five-year contract is worth £20 million (*Guardian*, 4 March 2011).

The threat to local post offices has also to be viewed in the context of plans by the Coalition government to privatise the parent company Royal Mail. Despite the announcement by the government that the Post Office will remain under public ownership, doubts have been raised about the future viability of the local post office network. The National Federation of Sub-Postmasters (NFSP), for example, has raised concerns about the future of the local post office network if it is separated from the Royal Mail and fails to hold on to contracts to process benefit payments and deliver other government services (*Guardian*, 8 November 2010). The number of post office branches has gone down over the last decade from over 18,000 in 2001 to currently in the region of 11,500. In the period 2003–9, 5,000 branches (28 per cent of the network) were shut under the then Labour government's closure programme (BIS, 2010: 8).

Such a policy was based on the view that 'falling customer numbers and revenues should be addressed by removing capacity from the post office network' (BIS, 2010: 8). Such a policy approach highlights a clear dilemma for local post offices. On the one hand they have to operate within commercial boundaries but at the same time, as I noted above, they have broader social obligations.

The closure programme attracted strong opposition in many quarters including user groups, local people and politicians. For example, a 4 million-strong petition, opposing the government's closure programme was handed into Downing Street on 18 October 2006 (*Guardian*, 19 October 2006). Such a large-scale closure programme does seem to suggest a lack of joined up thinking on the part of decision makers and does not take into account the externalities that may arise. If you close the post office, you lose an important community hub. This can lead to social exclusion with potential costs to other public agencies such as mental health and welfare services. Boarded-up post offices could lead to a downward spiral of dereliction and decay.

Various strategies have been put forward which attempt to put the future of the post office network on a secure footing. In the May 2010 General Election the Labour Party in its manifesto put forward the idea of a 'People's Bank' based on the local post office network. The Conservative Party and the Liberal Democrats in their coalition agreement (this formed the basis for their governing coalition) said that they would look at the case for developing new sources of revenue such as the creation of a Post Office Bank (H.M. Government, 2010a).

However, Ed Davey, the Postal Affairs Minister, subsequently announced on 9 November 2010 that it would not be going ahead with plans to set up such a bank (*Guardian*, 10 November 2010). This decision came in for strong criticism from the New Economics Foundation (NEF). Its Executive Director, Stewart Wallis, argued that it was a major setback for financial inclusion and local economic development. Such a bank, he argued, would have opened up 'Financial services to the millions of people across the UK who have no bank account and no means of getting one. It would have strengthened the social glue of local communities' (NEF, 11 November 2010).

A further government report raised the possibility that post offices might become a mutual organisation, with their operation carried out by staff and local communities (BIS, 2010: 3). This is a superficially attractive idea in terms of boosting civic engagement. The same report also talks of central government support for 'greater involvement of local authorities in planning and delivering local service provision' (BIS, 2010: 3). Indeed a number of local authorities has been involved in projects to secure the future of post offices, working in partnership with local actors. One such example is Sheffield City Council. Using powers enshrined in the Sustainable Communities Act 2007, the Council and Post Office Ltd set up a pilot project in 2010, working in partnership with the NFSP and local communities, including Sheffield's seven community assemblies. The aim of the pilot project is to secure a long-term sustainable future for the local post office network by 'making better use of post offices across the city and enabling local people and businesses to access a range of public services in their community' (BIS, 2010: 15). Under the plan local people will, for example, be able to pay their council tax and rent at any of the city's seventy-eight post offices rather than using a single cash office in the city centre, thereby putting more revenue and business into the local post office network (BIS, 2010: 15).

In 2008, Conservative-controlled Essex County Council entered into negotiations with the Post Office to buy fifteen of the thirty-one post offices due for closure in its area. Council Leader Lord Hanningfield argued that 'If the public want post offices then it is up to us. It is our job to provide them' (*Guardian*, 12 March 2008). To make the future of these post offices sustainable, Essex Council (in a move similar to that adopted in Sheffield) planned to combine postal services with council services. It spoke of bringing the post office branch network 'into the family of local government services' (Essex County Council, 2008: 5). However, local budget pressures have put these proposals in doubt.

Local banks, building societies and financial exclusion

The last fifteen years has seen a succession of bank and building society branch closure, many of them in poorer urban areas. This has had a major impact on financial inclusion and the health of local communities.

For example, a 2006 study by Professor Andrew Leyshon of Nottingham University found that between 1995 and 2003 4,041 bank and building society branches closed across the UK. Of these closures, the study found, upwards of 3,000 were located in poorer urban areas. Leyshon talked of a twin-track approach to such closures that threatened to widen the gap between poorer and more affluent areas. In areas where branches closed local people faced higher transport costs and a feeling of abandonment (BBC News online, 23 February 2006). Research by the Campaign for Community Banking shows that in the period from 1990 to 2010, a total of 7,388 bank branches closed, a reduction of 43 per cent in the network.

Such a large-scale closure programme has major implications for financial inclusion and the vitality of local communities. Currently, around 1–5 million people do not have access to a bank account, with just under 8 million people unable to access mainstream credit (*Inside Government*, 2 December 2010). It is argued that 'Access to banking is key to the survival of retail and other services in many medium sized rural communities and in less well-off suburbs, estates and inner cities' (Campaign for Community Banking, 2011). Financial exclusion has more of an impact on some groups than others. Especially affected are those living on low incomes, single parents and those who are unable to find work due to sickness or disability (European Commission, 2008; Finney and Kempson, 2009).

In an attempt to wrestle with these problems, the Labour government set up the Financial Inclusion Task Force in 2005. Its stated aim was that every household in Britain should have access to, and be able to benefit from, basic banking services (H.M. Treasury, December 2010: 2). In the opinion of the Taskforce 'access to basic banking facilities is just as important' as it was a decade or so ago (H.M. Treasury, December 2010: 1). Increasingly, access to consumer services requires the capability to make direct payments.

There have, however, been a number of initiatives. For example, in 2006 the government hosted an ATM summit with representatives of the banks and building society that looked at the issue of availability of no charge ATMs in deprived areas. As a result, a task force was set up and a deal was brokered in which banks and building societies agreed to provide 600 new free-to-use cash machines (*Guardian*, 12 June 2006). Banks such as Nat West operate a system of mobile banking in some areas that would otherwise be deprived of face-to-face commercial financial services. It has also been suggested that withdrawals and deposits could be done through retail networks such as Paypoint as many millions of customers already make payments this way (H.M. Treasury, 2010: 10).

The Financial Inclusion Task Force believes that, despite real difficulties, 'strong progress has been made ... to bring poorer households into retail banking' (H.M. Treasury, December 2010: 11). Others take a different view. The Campaign for Community Banking is highly critical of what it calls 'continued inaction on the part of the government' (Campaign for Community Banking, 2011). It argues that the impact of the credit crunch necessitates urgent action and requires new thinking about community banking if we are to ensure the sustainability of local communities (Campaign for Community Banking, 2011).

Local community pubs

The local pub, once a familiar feature in local communities up and down the country, is under threat. Pub closures are showing an increasing upward trend; in 2007 just over 1,400 pubs closed, compared to just over 200 in 2006. In the last three years this trend has continued. Data produced by the by the British Beer and Pub Association (BBPA) shows that in the region of 2,400 pubs closed in 2009. As Muir argues, 'Community pubs serving their local residential community have been hit the hardest' (Muir, 2009: 14). Cheap supermarket alcohol, the smoking ban, changing life styles and the credit crunch of 2008 have all played a key role in this decline.

But why should this be of concern? After all, there is a growing body of evidence that increased alcohol consumption over the last decade presents a serious public health danger. Therefore, fewer pubs means less alcohol consumed and more healthy people. However, such a view misses an important point. Local pubs play an important role providing opportunities for social interaction and warding off isolation and thus help shape and strengthen social capital. As one customer of a local pub in Tonbridge put it, 'I want to drink here because most of us know each other. Even if you come on your own, there's always someone to talk to' (*Guardian*, 21 October 2008). Research by Muir shows that community pubs provide a meeting place where 'social networks are strengthened and extended'. In a survey the pub ranked highest as the place where people 'get together with others in their neighbourhood' (Muir, 2009: 5).

A report by the All-Party Parliamentary Beer Group (APPBG) has highlighted the potential threat that local communities face with the increasing number of pub closures. It talks of the importance of community pubs as social hubs not only for social gatherings but as meeting places for local community groups. It argues that 'A pub's function room can be enormously important community facility' (APPBG, 2008: 12). It also talks of the role that community pubs play in supporting local charities, arguing that often the existence of the pub is the crucial catalyst as well as the focal point for the activity (APGGB, 2008: 11). There need to be changes to the regulatory regime and the duty on alcohol to help community pubs to operate on a sound footing (APPBG, 2008: 42). The report also called on DCMS to look at ways in which access to grants and other financial assistance to community pubs could be improved (APPBG, 2008: 45). The ideas and suggestions of the APPBG met with a generally positive response from DCMS, accepting or part accepting twenty-three of its thirty-one recommendations and supporting a number of measures designed to support community pubs (DCMS, 2009b). Indeed in March 2010, CLG announced a £3 million package of support as part of the Community Owned Pubs Support Programme to be led by the Plunkett Foundation. However, in August 2010, CLG announced that it was cutting the programme (*Social Enterprise*, 8 September 2010); eighty-two communities were affected.

In the context of demands on public expenditure and the impact of the credit crunch, the pressures on community pubs can only intensify. There are, however, other initiatives. The Plunkett Foundation, for example, has stated that it will continue its programme of work to try and keep community pubs open. Working in conjunction with organisations such as Cooperatives UK and Cooperative and Community Finance, it is developing plans to support local community pubs. Gerard Devlin of Cooperatives UK argues that 'the cooperative model offers a viable and exciting solution to the issues facing many pubs at present' (*Social Enterprise*, 8 September 2010).

Social enterprise, community initiatives and local services

There are a myriad of local services run and organised by social enterprise and community organisations operating in what has been described as the social economy. For Tallon, the social economy is neither part of the public (state) sector nor the private sector (Tallon, 2010: 150). Sometimes described as the third sector of the economy, it operates within a culture where personal profit is not the driving force. Instead as Tallon notes 'recent efforts have sought to build and promote the social economy as a way of tacking the problem of urban social disadvantage and exclusion' (Tallon, 2010:150). Activity within the social economy includes house building, exchanging skills and services, providing loans, providing transport and running community shops. For Tallon, the social economy has brought a number of benefits. These include the supply of goods and services to the local community and the creation of new jobs and pathways into employment. But he also argues that there are broader benefits in both community capacity building and the enhancement of local democracy (Tallon, 2010: 150). This section will focus on two areas of activity within the social economy. These are credit unions and community owned shops.

Credit unions

As the commercial high street banks continue to disengage from a number of our urban areas, other alternative forms of financial support have emerged which aim to fill some of the gap that the banks have left. One example is that of credit unions. Credit unions are financial cooperatives run and owned by their members. They provide a source of credit to those on low incomes, people who would be unlikely to obtain credit from the conventional high street banks and as a consequence often have to turn to so-called 'loan sharks', often paying punitive levels of interest.

Today there are in the region of 780 credit unions with over 814,000 members and assets of around £900 million. Such numbers seem relatively small when compared to the USA, for example, where a staggering 86 million people belong to credit unions, but they are nonetheless a growing and increasingly important part of the local financial landscape. Credit unions are a good example of the social capital I talked about in Chapter 1 where community interaction builds networks of trust and confidence and access to decision makers and sources of support.

The scope of credit unions increased significantly in 2007 when a number of them introduced current accounts for their members. In today's increasingly complex financial world it has become more and more difficult to operate as an individual without a current account. The vast majority of us have our wages and salaries paid into a current account. We pay our bills using our current accounts. For most of us the current account has become as much an inevitable part of life as death and taxes. And yet, as I noted above, for a significant minority of people on low incomes getting access to a current account is difficult. The result is financial exclusion.

This is where credit unions are potentially important. A total of eighteen credit unions now offer current accounts, with 15,000 credit union members having access to such a facility. This number is expected to grow (*Guardian*, 10 January 2009). Credit union current accounts come with a debit card for use in shops and for withdrawing money from cash machines. They can also be used to set up direct debits to pay for utility bills and the like. Given that utility companies charge less to customers who pay by direct debit, this helps tackle financial exclusion and reduces the financial burden on those who would not normally have access to such facilities.

For Tallon, there are four key advantages of credit unions. First, they encourage regular saving. Second, they give access to affordable loans. Third, they reduce the possibility of exploitation by loan sharks. Fourth, they help strengthen civil society (Tallon, 2010: 151). Credit unions do have their problems, however. For example, questions have also been raised about the capacity of some credit unions to function effectively. Goth *et al.* looked at the workings of fifteen credit unions. They noted the difficulty that credit unions had in attracting suitably qualified people on to their governing boards. (Goth *et al.*, 2006: 48). They highlighted a number of areas of failure including 'knowledge of risk management' and 'familiarity with asset liability management' (Goth *et al.*, 2006: 48). Goth *et al.* noted that 'many boards have a considerable number of directors with no ability to read and interpret financial statements' (Goth *et al.*, 2006: 48). On a more general level, the authors were critical of credit unions that focused 'exclusively on low income communities' which might create the impression that credit unions were 'the poor man's bank' (Goth *et al.*, 2006: 47). Rather 'the needs of the socially and financially excluded are best served' when the focus is on 'mobilising the monies of the rich as well as the poor' (Goth *et al.*, 2006: 47).

Despite such difficulties, Goth *et al.* acknowledge that there is a growing recognition that credit unions have an important role in the provision of affordable credit, and the UK government is supportive of plans to see the sector grow and develop (Goth *et al.*, 2006).

Community owned shops

The establishment of community owned village shops has been a growing trend over the last twenty years, as many local communities take the view that community ownership is the only viable way to keep basic retail services. According to data published by the Village Retail Services Association (VIRSA), average turnover for such shops is around £100,000 per year. The average shop employs just under one-and-a-half full-time equivalent staff backed up by a team of twenty-five volunteers. On average, each shop has in the region of 100 member shareholders from the local community. There are currently in the region of 250 community shops in the UK, the bulk of which have received start up support from the village core programme.

The village core programme supports the establishment of community owned shops in rural communities. This includes both the establishment of new community owned shops and the transfer of threatened commercial shops into community ownership. It is a partnership between VIRSA, the Esmée Fairbairn Foundation and Cooperative and Community Finance. It provides a start up grant of up to £20,000 per community owned rural shop, subject to matched funding from the local community.

A number of studies have analysed the impact that community owned village shops have had on their local communities. For example, research carried out by the Plunkett Foundation in 2004 pinpointed a number of benefits accruing from community shops. They have a real effect on the provision of essential retail services, especially for elderly and other vulnerable people without their own transport. They also have a significant impact on social cohesion and vibrancy within the community, a product of the dynamism and participative nature of such shops. They help shape and strengthen social capital. In addition they help to develop human capital by giving volunteers the opportunity to develop skills and work experience that subsequently can be of value in the world of paid work (Plunkett Foundation, 2004).

Survey evidence also suggests that community owned shops are 'reasonably robust enterprises', having been built on a tight web of community commitment' (Plunkett Foundation, 2005: 12). Though they are relatively small economic operations, they nonetheless 'have a disproportionate effect on community life', such as the services they offer and the number of members who have invested both time and money' (Plunkett Foundation, 2005: 12). Research also shows that although the vast majority of community owned shops received some initial financial support when they were being set up, only 43 per cent consider that they now require ongoing support. This may be taken as a positive indication of the sustainability of community owned shops (Plunkett Foundation, 2008). The government itself has described community owned shops as 'a success story' (Defra, 2005: 6). They make an important contribution to the vitality of local communities and the development of social capital.

Conclusion

The last two decades have witnessed important changes in the way public services are shaped and delivered. The traditional model of public service delivery, prevalent for much of the post-Second World War period, dominated by policy professionals and top-down in nature, has given way to a number of new approaches to public services. Whether it be in the context of local people as consumers of services expressing choices in a quasi-market or agendas which promote community empowerment and the 'big society', there has been an increasing emphasis on the participation of local people in how services are shaped and delivered.

No longer are decisions around public services the sole prerogative of state agencies. Increasingly, social enterprises and community organisations are making their presence felt as they take on responsibility for local services. However, such a trend is not just confined to the public sector. As private sector services contract and disappear in a number of our urban areas and inner cities, new forms of social enterprise have emerged such as community run shops, community run pubs and credit unions.

Such developments are not without controversy, as we have seen, but with the continuing pressures on public expenditure the emphasis of the current government on localism and the 'big society' they appear set to continue.

7

Regeneration and sustainability

Introduction

This chapter will be divided into three sections. First, there will be an analysis of the concept of sustainability, its application to local communities and what criteria have to be met if we are to achieve sustainable communities. Second, there will be a focus on key strategies at the both the national and local level to regenerate local areas and communities. The spotlight here will be on both physical and social regeneration and as such will be set within the context of our earlier discussion on the nature and meaning of sustainability. Third, there will be an analysis of various local initiatives to tackle climate change, a key element of the strategy to create sustainable local communities.

Sustainability and sustainable development

'Sustainability' and 'sustainable development' are relatively new concepts in public policy discourse. As a consequence, there is considerable debate both as to their meaning and their practical applicability. Some commentators ascribe different meanings to the two concepts (Jones and Evans, 2008: 85). It is a complex and ongoing debate, but for the purposes of this study I will be using sustainability and sustainable development interchangeably.

Since the Rio Summit of 1992, sustainability has become a key policy paradigm at global, national, regional and local level. At a UK level much of the policy agenda has been framed by the goals of sustainability; as Jones and Evans note, 'The mantra of sustainability lies at the core of the regeneration agenda' (Jones and Evans, 2008: 84). I shall return to this point presently.

For Jones and Evans the drive to sustainability 'is loaded with expectations of it being a magic bullet for delivering better cities' (Jones and Evans, 2008: 85). But sustainability is a much-contested concept in terms of both its meaning and its practical application. One widely accepted definition is that given by the 1987 UN Commission on Environment and Development, more commonly known as the Brundtland Commission. Brundtland defined sustainable development as 'Development that meets the needs of the present without compromising the ability of future generations to meet their own needs' (Brundtland Report, 1987). Yet even this definition is open to debate. For example, Jones and Evans note that Brundtland does not specify what constitutes a need nor does it spell out over 'what timescale the future should be considered' (Jones and Evans, 2008: 85). Notwithstanding such definitional difficulties, the drive towards sustainability represents an attempt to see beyond the economic and physical growth model that dominated public policy from the mid 1940s through to the 1980s. Instead it aims to look at policy proposals and policy solutions in a more integrated and holistic way. It encompasses, as Jones and Evans note, inclusiveness, social cohesion, the protection and enhancement of the natural environment and sustainable economic growth that involves the prudent use of economic resources.

Building on the work of Brundtland, the 1992 UN Conference on Environment and Development, more commonly known as the Rio Summit, set out three distinctive, but at the same time interrelated, components of sustainability. They were the environmental, the social (encompassing poverty reduction and social justice) and the economic. The challenge for sustainable development lies in attaining the appropriate balance between these three components. Of course different weightings have been given both at Rio and subsequently to each of these components, depending on the actors involved and the policy context. Sustainability is a highly politicised and values driven policy area. Indeed the complexity surrounding the concept of sustainability and its meaning has given rise to a literature in its own right.

One possible way to view sustainability is as a set of three circles; the point where these circles interlock is where sustainable development is taking place (see Figure 4). Yet such an explanatory framework fails to take sufficiently into account that we are governed by a set of real ecological limits. Perhaps a better way to view sustainability is as three concentric circles with economic growth and social development being carried on in the context of finite ecological resources (see Figure 5).

A number of key policy documents came out of the Rio Summit including Local Agenda 21. A key principle that emerged from these documents was 'subsidiarity, whereby international policy priorities are cascaded down through the national and regional tiers of government to the local level' (Jones and Evans, 2008: 85). The guiding principle was one of 'think global, act local'.

What makes the sustainable city?

In general terms, Bell and Lane have argued that 'The notion of human beings living in a community but not compromising social or environmental limitations is a key element to the notion of a sustainable city' (Bell and Lane, 2009: 648). It is about people, both individually and collectively,

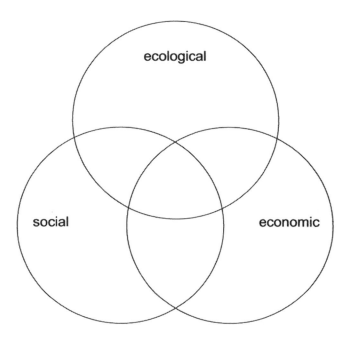

4 Sustainable development

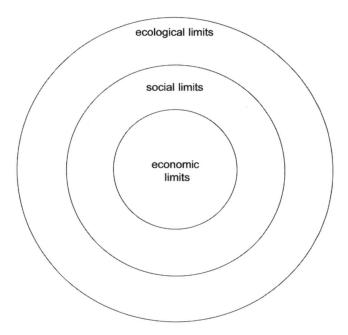

5 Sustainable development: the ecological limits

improving their quality of life based on a harmonious relationship with their physical and social environment.

Drilling down to the local level in Britain, what are the factors that need to be in place for cities and communities to be sustainable? In 2005 the 'Delivering Sustainable Communities' Summit was held in Manchester in an attempt to tease out some of the answers. The event was hosted by the then Deputy Prime Minister John Prescott and supported by a number of cabinet members. It brought together some 2,000 representatives from the public and private sectors, government, and the regeneration and building industries. The report-back from the summit provided a useful starting point as to what might constitute a sustainable community or city.

It argued that sustainable communities are places where people want to live and work. In addition, they should meet the diverse needs of both existing and future residents. They should also be sensitive to their environment and contribute to a high quality of life. Furthermore, they should be safe and inclusive, be well planned and run and offer equality of opportunity and good services for all. Finally, and crucially, the report acknowledged that there was no standard template that could be taken off the shelf. Policy responses had to be diverse reflecting the differing nature of local circumstances (Commission on Urban Life and Faith, 2006: 58).

However, the summit came in for some criticism. The Commission on Urban Life and Faith, for example, raised strong concerns about the overemphasis on 'material regeneration of urban communities' and power and profit' rather than looking at 'issues to do with how people lived and the quality of their living environment' (Commission on Urban Life and Faith, 2006: 58). The Commission argued that for cities to work and to be sustainable it is essential that the process begins 'with people, their well being, their happiness, and the understanding and use of their environment' (Commission on Urban Life and Faith, 2006: 59). Jones and Evans make a related point, noting how sustainability is based on a 'decentralised philosophy' which stresses that planning should be driven at the local level and that this process should involve local stakeholders' groups in decision making (Jones and Evans, 2008: 85). Bell and Lane develop this point, arguing that 'Unless sustainability is relevant to the individual and the community, at a very personal level, it will have little or no chance of engaging the community in dialogue' (Bell and Lane, 2009: 647). The government, too, has stressed the fact that 'It is for local people to decide what they think needs to be done to promote the sustainability of their area' (CLG, 2008d: 3).

As part of the work of the Commission on Urban Life and Faith, the Anglican Diocese of Newcastle held a series of 'Urban Hearings' in 2004 (Commission on Urban Life and Faith, 2006: 60). Based on the evidence it gleaned and responses received it found that a good (or sustainable) city:

- Values its inhabitants
- Is diverse and inclusive
- Is well led
- Attracts wealth creators but shares that wealth
- Has an active civil society
- Is dynamic
- Is a learning city
- Has opportunities for all
- Is a place in which people do not merely survive but live.

For the Commission 'However monumental its buildings, or successful its economy, people are always at the heart of a city' and as a consequence 'a sense of place needs to be understood as much in terms of its social and even spiritual value as its economic value' (Commission on Urban Life and Faith, 2006: 60). This vision of place ties into public policy strategies to promote local community cohesion. In the view of the government, a recognition of the value of diversity, equal opportunities, and a 'shared future vision and sense of belonging' lies at the heart of any definition of a sustainable community or city (CLG, 2009b: 12).

There have been a number of attempts to assess the efficacy of the sustainability agenda. The pressure group Forum for the Future has set up a sustainable cities index which tracks progress on sustainability in Britain's twenty largest cities, ranking them on issues with respect to environmental performance, quality of life and how they are addressing the challenges of climate change, recycling and biodiversity. In addition, the Sustainable Development Commission (since disbanded) developed plans for what it termed a 'local sustainable development lens', a voluntary basket of local indicators that could be used to guide and track progress towards sustainable development at the local level.

Regeneration

Jones and Evans argue that 'The goals of sustainable development', with its focus on alleviating social and environmental problems 'are ideally suited to regeneration' (Jones and Evans, 2008: 84). Urban regeneration was a key policy goal of the Labour government from 1997 to 2010 as it sought to bring life back to communities (in particular those in the industrialised north) still feeling the impact of the Thatcherite revolution of the 1980s, in terms of both job losses and social decay. Key to New Labour's regeneration strategy was the notion of partnership working, with central government working in tandem with other public bodies at both central and local level, the social enterprise sector, commercial companies and local communities. A key aspect of this partnership approach was the creation of LSPs. LSPs were set up as the main policy vehicle for delivering urban regeneration, and were charged with delivering strategic and joined up working at the local level.

As with other aspects of public policy the Labour government was not shy in coming in coming forward with ideas and proposals. These included the national strategy for neighbourhood renewal, the new deal for communities (NDC), the Sustainable Communities Plan (SCP) and the urban white paper *Towards an Urban Renaissance* (2000). The white paper owed much to the work of the Urban Task Force chaired by the architect Lord Rogers.

Yet as we have seen with other government initiatives over this period, quantity does not necessarily mean quality. With this in mind, this section will include a general analysis of some of the key elements of Labour's urban regeneration agenda together with a focus on some specific urban regeneration projects and their sustainability impact. It is important to note that regeneration is both a physical and a social process and in this context links directly to the discussion of sustainability in the first part of this chapter. Indeed, the Commission on Urban Life and Faith has argued that a 'person centred' and 'value driven' approach is the key to any successful urban regeneration scheme (Commission on Urban Life and Faith, 2006: 60).

Local and urban regeneration in the decade and a half of the last Labour government was a complex and crowded policy arena, with a welter of initiatives and policy pronouncements. This presents a challenge when seeking to assess the effectiveness of this particular policy agenda. It is, however, possible to draw out some broad themes. For Tallon, the Labour government broadly accepted the analysis of the previous Conservative government in respect of strategies to tackle the decay in inner cities 'which had largely been bypassed by national economic success, suggesting that the causes of urban decline lay in the areas themselves rather than in the wider social context' (Tallon, 2010: 79). Running alongside such continuity, however, there appeared differences both in tone and policy substance. For, as Tallon himself argues, a 'hallmark' of New Labour's agenda was the 'recognition of the interrelationship between the economic and social dimensions' in regeneration set within the context of what was termed the 'urban renaissance' (Tallon, 2010: 78).

Imrie highlights the view held by various commentators that the period of Conservative government from 1979 to 1990 was characterised as one of 'property led' regeneration, with limited emphasis on the economic and social needs of local people (Imrie 2009: 97). Concerning the Social Exclusion Unit, a policy initiative of the Labour government when it came into office in 1997, 'there was too much emphasis on physical renewal instead of better opportunities for local people' (Imrie, 2009: 97). Turning the city glitzy with an emphasis on prestigious office blocks and high-end apartments seemed to be the order of the day.

The 1990s witnessed apparent changes in regeneration policy. The talk now was of making the built environment sustainable and engaging local communities in the regeneration and development process. As Imrie notes, government programmes such as City Challenge and the Single Regeneration Budget (SRB) 'encouraged community involvement in regeneration' (Imrie, 2010: 97). It was a narrative that was to strengthen with the election of a Labour government in 1997. The 2000 urban white paper argued that regeneration should be inclusive and communities 'must be fully engaged in the process from the start and ... everyone must be included' (DETR, 2000).

I noted in Chapter 3 the difficulties that can arise when governments seek to boost participation and civic engagement in local communities. Tallon highlights a number of challenges in this regard:

- It requires time and appropriate resources if the process is not just to involve the usual suspects. Appropriate capacity building is required.
- Expectations about the extent of local community engagement need to be realistic.
- Communities are diverse entities: mediating the different interests that arise from this is a challenge.
- The competitive nature of much regeneration funding can 'drive wedges between communities' thus undermining collaboration and community cohesion (Tallon, 2010: 149).

Research by Taylor into community participation found significant levels of mistrust towards government in local communities with concerns about being co-opted in to government agendas (Taylor, 2007). To this one can add the danger of raised expectations amongst local communities as to what participation can achieve. And linked to this is the issue of consultation fatigue. But there are also two broader constraints. First, in its period in office New Labour put a strong emphasis on evidence-based policy. But, as Tallon argues, it is 'difficult to provide evidence that community involvement does make a difference' (Tallon. 2010: 150). Second, the target led and performance indicator culture of New Labour, wrapped up in a managerialist and centralist mentality, militated against involvement by local communities in making substantive decisions about how their area should be developed.

Government-commissioned research points to qualified success in respect of the NDC programme. On the positive side, there were signs of positive change in relation to place. This included a more positive attitude by local people to their local community and environment. There was a reduced fear of crime and increased confidence in the capacity of local agencies to combat it. On the other hand, progress on so-called 'people based outcomes', such as worklessness, health and education was slower (CLG, 2010b: 38–40). However, Tallon argues that there is evidence that NDCs saw improvements in local community involvement in regeneration initiatives (Tallon, 2010: 150).

Central to much of New Labour's policy agenda was an approach which sought to bring together the state and the market in what has been described as a 'Third Way' in respect of politics and policy making (Giddens, 1998). For some commentators such an agenda was problematic to say the least. Johnstone and Whitehead, for example, argue that the 'Third Way' can be best characterised as 'an uneasy and problematic marriage of the large scale anti-poverty programmes of the post war social democratic state, with the economic imperatives of Thatcherite neo-liberal urban policy (Johnstone and Whitehead, 2004: 9). New Labour did target significant regeneration resources on some of the most deprived urban areas of Britain and 'did address some of the inherent weaknesses of policies in the recent past, particularly reflected in the move away from property and economic dominated approaches' (Tallon, 2010: 104). Yet, as Tallon notes, 'It did not embrace the 'Keynesian redistributive economic policies characteristic of Labour administrations of the 1960s and 1970s, thus representing continuity with the approaches adopted by previous Conservative administrations' (Tallon, 2010: 82). Other commentators make the point more forcefully. Evans *et al.*, for example, argue that in fact 'speculator-led regeneration' has remained the dominant model since 1997 (Evans *et al.*, 2009: 683).

The debate continues about government's general ability to deliver long-term regeneration. Leunig *et al.*, looking through a neo-liberal lens, go so far as to argue that 'attempts to regenerate British cities over the past ten twenty or even fifty years have failed' (Leunig *et al.*, 2007: 5). Challenging the whole ethos of the regeneration agenda, they call instead for policies to actively encourage people from deprived urban areas in the north of England, for example, to relocate to London and the South East, arguing in effect that some areas are beyond regeneration (Leunig *et al.*, 2007: 5). Regeneration is a complex policy landscape.

Case studies in regeneration

In 2003 the then Labour government set out its proposals for sustainable communities (the SCP). It spoke of sustainable communities as 'places where people live and work now and in the future' (ODPM, 2003: 56). The plan set out some of the key principles that it considered underpinned sustainable communities. These included:

- A successful local economy to produce jobs
- Substantive engagement by local people in the planning and long term future of their community
- Good-quality local public services
- Effective local public transport infrastructure
- An appropriate mix of housing types to meets the needs of the local community
- A sense of place.

The purpose of the SCP was to give substance to the government's sustainability agenda with projects in specific areas. A key element of the Plan was the need to improve both housing quality and supply but also important was the objective 'to improve the quality of the public realm' (Jones and Evans, 2008: 90). Attention was to be given to the broader social and physical environment by improving public spaces, improving community facilities, and providing good-quality local public services. The creation of such a sense of place was an element in the Labour government's sustainability agenda. I will now seek to analyse how this mapped out in practice by focusing on two case studies of regeneration.

Case study 1: Salford Quays, Manchester

Salford is located to the west of the city of Manchester. Salford's docks, built in 1894, served the Manchester Ship Canal. At its height the docks employed up to 3,000 people. The docks went into gradual decline in the period from the Second World War until their eventual closure in 1982. The area encompassing the docks covered some 150 acres of land and 75 hectares of water. The closure of the docks and the job losses that went with it brought significant social problems to an area already suffering from high levels of unemployment. Salford City Council bought the land in 1983 and put forward a plan to develop the area that was branded as 'Salford Quays'. Over two decades later, as Jones and Evans note, 'Salford Quays is widely regarded as a model of successful regeneration, turning a large derelict area into a thriving mixed-use development' (Jones and Evans, 2008: 92). But does this optimistic analysis reflect the reality on the ground, and to what extent did the development plan for Salford Quays help to create a sustainable community?

Jones and Evans highlight a number of problems in this regard. First, little attention was paid to the wider needs of residents in Salford Quays. Priority was given to commercial and residential development 'at the expense of developing community services and spaces' (Jones and Evans, 2008: 93). Such a neglect of the public realm critically undermines attempts to build a local sustainable community. Second, Jones and Evans point out the isolated nature of the Salford Quays community. For them, it represented 'an island of owner occupied housing within a predominantly publicly owned housing area of Salford'. This was compounded by the fact that the new residents of Salford Quays tended to be wealthier than existing residents in the surrounding areas. The two communities existed largely in isolation from each other (Jones and Evans, 2008: 93). The potential such a situation creates for tension, resentment and social conflict cuts right across any notion of a sustainable and cohesive community.

Finally, Jones and Evans argue that the problems and issues identified in Salford Quays raise broader questions about 'the ability of regeneration projects to deliver sustainable communities'. Regeneration projects such as

Salford Quays tend to result in gentrification as 'more affluent people move into an area that has already been upgraded for them' (Jones and Evans, 2008: 93). The local property market may well be revitalised but existing local residents are excluded as house prices rise beyond their means. This is in direct conflict with objective set out in the SCP to provide an appropriate mix of housing types to meet the needs of the existing residents and so help support sustainable communities.

Case study 2: the redevelopment of King's Cross, London

The area in question compromised a 67-acre brown field site to the north of London Kings Cross and Saint Pancras train stations. It incorporated two local authorities: the London Boroughs of Camden and Islington. Planning permission to develop the site was granted in 2006. The site included a mixture of derelict and semi-derelict infrastructure with railway sidings, loading depots and warehouses. The site also contained a number of important listed buildings including the Granary and the Stanley Buildings. The development potential of the area came to prominence in 1987 when it was earmarked as the terminus for the high-speed rail link to Europe.

The redevelopment was heralded as a flagship of urban regeneration, in which the views of the local community would play a key role in determining policy priorities (Imrie, 2009: 93). Such community involvement is, as I discussed earlier, a central element of sustainable development. For the Commission for Architecture and the Built Environment (CABE), when promoting regeneration projects, it was 'crucial to understand the local geography of the community, the social and economic fabric of the neighbourhoods' (CABE, 2003: 97). Arup, the principal private contractor, talked of delivering 'benefits to local communities' (Arup, 2001: 10). To this end, the Kings Cross Development Forum was set up in 2002. It was a broad-based umbrella organisation representing a variety of local groups.

For Imrie, however, evidence showed that community engagement was both 'partial and piecemeal' (Imrie, 2009: 95). For the developer Argent there were real 'tensions and difficulties' in defining the nature of the community that should be involved (Imrie, 2009: 102). The field of community groups was a crowded one. Some were long established but many were of recent origin coalescing around regeneration initiatives. As Imrie notes, there were hundreds of organisations that potentially fitted 'into the government's understanding of who ought to be engaged' (Imrie, 2009: 105). This raises a number of questions. 'What sort of groups were to be involved? What was the best way to engage and inform them? How could such plural publics be managed? Such a situation makes the idea of community participation difficult in practice'. Imrie noted the frustration felt by some local community representatives having spent hours in meetings that seemed 'to lead to no change' (Imrie, 2010: 109).

In conclusion, Imrie asks the question whether King's Cross did herald a new wave of property development, bringing in its wake a 'new politics of consultative and participative processes' (Imrie, 2009: 108). For Imrie, there is little evidence in this regard. Rather, he argues that Argent's approach to engagement simply did not allow any substantive input into the planning and development process. Indeed, the initial proposal for a mixed-use development incorporating commercial, office, retail and residential spaces remained largely in place (Imrie, 2009: 108).

Regeneration and sustainability: some concluding remarks

Since these case studies on regeneration were undertaken events have moved on as Britain has felt the full force of the global credit crunch of 2008 and 2009. The subsequent economic downturn saw unemployment increase and many building projects put on hold. The economic climate is uncertain. The large-scale public expenditure cuts (announced by the coalition government in the 2010 Comprehensive Spending Review, CSR) have only added to this uncertainty. This presents a major challenge to the sustainability agenda.

Commentators such as Evans *et al.* strike a more optimistic tone, arguing that 'The credit crunch suddenly makes it possible to challenge dominant political narratives of market led regeneration, which have privileged the generation of wealth for developers and investors' (Evans *et al.*, 2009: 683). They do not deny that the state and large private developers can deliver sustainable development but 'rather that they need to be simultaneously more creative and more patient in order to deliver something more sustainable in the widest sense of a development that is diverse, socially inclusive, environmentally friendly and economically durable' (Evans *et al.*, 2009: 694). But this would require a major cultural change. Evans *et al.* voice their support for what they call 'organic regeneration', where ideas for regenerating communities come from local people themselves. In this regard they point to the Transition Town movement that adopts an 'avowedly small-scale and grass roots' approach, challenging the view that sustainable development 'demands a large scale, rapid intervention' (Evans *et al.*, 2009: 693). I shall return to the subject of Transition Towns shortly.

Tackling climate change at the local level

The issue of climate change is one that has global, national and local ramifications and encapsulates well the idea of the global to the local. In other words, the issue of climate change has global and local causes and necessitates both global and local solutions.

There is now overwhelming consensus amongst scientists and the international community that the climate change that the world is experiencing is the result of human action, specifically the increased emissions of carbon dioxide into the earth's atmosphere by the burning of fossils fuels, what have become commonly know as 'greenhouse gases' (Giddens, 2009; Lynas, 2007; Stern, 2006).

In 1992, the Rio Summit set out the global challenges of sustainable development. One of the policy documents that came out of Rio was the Climate Change Protocol. This Protocol took on greater policy substance in 1997 when the majority of developed nations (the USA was a notable exception) signed up to an agreement in Kyoto, Japan, which set targets on the reduction of greenhouse gases. The targets set committed the signatories to a reduction in greenhouse gases of 5 per cent by 2012, using 1990 as the base line. There has been limited progress at recent global summits in Copenhagen, Denmark and Cancún, Mexico, to agree a new set of targets beyond 2010 (the so-called 'Kyoto 2'). However, the UK Parliament passed the Climate Change Act 2008, which commits the UK government to reduce greenhouse gases by 80 per cent by 2050. Vigorous debates continue about how achievable this target is. This section looks at a number of policy proposals and initiatives that aim to reduce greenhouse gases and tackle climate change.

Eco-towns

In December 2007 the Eco-towns initiative was launched. They were to be new towns that, in the words of the government, would be 'exemplar green developments of a minimum of five thousand homes'. They would be designed to meet the highest standards of sustainability, including low- and zero-carbon technologies and good public transport. An initial shortlist of fifteen locations in England as potential Eco-towns was announced in April 2008. In July 2009, the then Housing Minister, John Healey, announced plans for four such Eco-towns. In December of the same year, the Minister announced proposals for a second wave of Eco-towns with nine local authorities setting out outline plans. Ahead of the climate change talks in Copenhagen in late December 2009, John Healey stated that the proposals signalled a 'real and radical momentum to change and to re think how we design our towns and homes for the future' (CLG Press Release, 1 December 2009).

The proposals met with a mixed response. The Campaign to Protect Rural England (CPRE) wanted the plans scaled back and instead called for a major focus on the redevelopment of brown field sites (*Guardian*, 17 July 2009). The architect, Richard Rogers, who had chaired the Urban Task Force, was highly critical, stating that 'eco-towns are one of the biggest mistakes the government can make'. For him they were 'in no way environmentally sustainable' (PropertyWeek.com, 22 May 2008). The LGA took a more balanced view. Whilst not opposed in principle to the eco-towns, it expressed concern about the top-down nature of the proposal. For the LGA, 'eco-towns can only be sustainable over the long term with the buy in, support and commitment of local councils and communities from the outset' (LGA, 2008b: 3). John Alker, of the UK Green Building Council, made a similar point, arguing that if such plans 'are linked to existing communities, have local support and are built to the very highest environmental standards, it can only be a good thing' (*Guardian*, 17 July 2009).

However, recent developments have put the whole eco-towns project in some doubt. In July 2010, Grant Shapps, the Housing Minister in the Conservative/Liberal Democrat coalition government, wrote to all local authorities promoting eco-towns informing them that the 2010/11 grants for the projects would be halved. In addition, any such project would have to meet a set of government criteria that would include a value for money and sustainability audit (House of Commons Library, 2010). With continuing downward pressure on public expenditure, the future for eco-towns as originally conceived remains uncertain.

Tackling climate change locally

At the local level, there have been a number of local initiatives, many of them emanating from Local Agenda 21 of the Rio Summit, designed to tackle climate change and to meet the UK's commitments on the reduction of green house gas emissions.

Transition Initiatives (formerly called Transition Towns), for example, are a good example of bottom-up community-led action on climate change. In the words of the Transition Network, 'A Transition Initiative is a community led response to the pressures of climate change' and 'fossil fuel depletion' (Transition Network.org, 2011). For Chatterton and Cutler, 'A Transition Initiative is a community that is unleashing its own latent collective genius to look Peak Oil and Climate Change squarely in the eye' (Chatterton and Cutler, 2007: 2). It is an agenda that stresses the dangers of an economic system that is so heavily dependent on fossil fuels and calls for urgent action to move towards a more low-carbon economy. Without doubt this is a major policy challenge. But Transition Initiatives is backed up by a growing national network of villages, towns and cities around Britain. There are in excess of fifty such Initiatives nationally, Totnes (in Devon) being the first. But there is also a global network with over sixty such initiatives in countries such as the USA, Australia and New Zealand.

Elected local government has also been involved in a number of initiatives to tackle climate change. For, as Buckingham and Theobold argue, local authorities 'have the capacity to facilitate and support local community actions and initiatives for environmental sustainability' and also play an important role in putting forward 'new ideas and approaches' (Buckingham and Theobold, 2003: 3).

For example, to date 216 local councils have signed up to the so-called '10/10' campaign. By signing up, organisations and individuals commit themselves to reducing their green house gas emissions by 10 per cent each year. Another key initiative is the Nottingham Declaration on Climate

Change. Launched in 2000, the Declaration has now been signed by more than 300 English local authorities. Scottish and Welsh local authorities have signed their own versions. The Declaration 'acknowledges the increasing impact that climate will change will have on local communities' and commits the signatories 'to tackling the causes and effects of a changing climate' (Energy Savings Trust, 2011).

The LGA, the representative body for local councils, argues that 'Tackling climate change must be at the centre of local government's vision for their communities' (LGA, 2007b: 8). It is not one competing priority amongst others but 'it is the single priority which overrides all others' (LGA, 2007b: 8). Indeed, as the LGiU notes, 'Many local authorities are already taking the lead with plans to reduce their own and the wider community's emissions'. 'But a step change will be needed', the LGiU argues, 'to meet the challenging targets of reducing carbon emissions' (LGiU, 2009b: 4).

Indeed the LGA has spoken of the public policy challenges of achieving greater energy efficiency and thus reducing green house gas emissions. It calculates, for example, that some 10 million homes still require basic insulation. To tackle the issue of domestic energy efficiency, it calls for a more integrated policy approach designed to bring together the plethora of government funding streams to support 'systematic area based programmes to cut household fuel bills' by £300 each year, so reducing the carbon footprint by 20 per cent (LGA, 2009a: 4). For the LGA, local councils with their democratic mandate have a key role to play as a voice for local residents (LGA, 2009a: 5). For the LGiU, local councillors are crucial here. In their role as 'community leaders [they] are very tuned in to their local communities and they are best placed to communicate the issues to their constituents' (LGiU, 2010: 5). But for local strategies to be effective, argues the LGA, there needs to be active community engagement in both the design and implementation of such strategies (LGA, 2009b: 4). Working in partnership with other local councils and private companies is also vital (LGA, 2009b: 14). Central government also has laid great emphasis on the importance of partnership working in tackling climate change, highlighting the important contribution that third sector organisations such as environmental groups, faith groups, youth organisations and trade unions can make (H.M. Government, 2010c: 10). 'The third sector shapes the future by mobilising and inspiring others to tackle climate change and maximising the social, economic and environmental opportunities of action' (H.M. Government, 2010c: 8).

The LGA has argued that 'Developing a sustainable low carbon economy should be an integral consideration in every decision a council takes' (LGA, 2009a: 5). This is a challenging policy objective. Yet there are examples on the ground of policy innovation by local councils (see LGA, 2009b). Reading Borough Council, for example, set up its Heatseekers scheme to identify those homes in the area without insulation. All private homes are being photographed using thermal imaging to show where insulation is needed and a comprehensive review of the council's housing stock is being carried out. Devon County Council, in partnership with a number of local actors, has been promoting renewable energy in an attempt to boost the local economy. This has led to over 100 installations in small and medium-sized firms. The council has given out grants and provided advice and information on other funding streams. In 2005, Harrogate Borough Council introduced a trial programme introducing ground source heat pumps (an efficient energy source) into a number of social housing units. The trial proved a success and the technology has now been rolled out across other social housing units (LGA, 2009b: 11).

Cambridge City Council has been involved in several initiatives. Since 1996, the energy efficiency of housing in the city has improved by 40 per cent. The Council uses lower-emission fuels in its vehicles and requires renewable energy generation in new developments. In October 2007, it launched a Climate Change Charter. This is a means by which local organisations can pledge their commitment to tackling climate change through their procedures and activities (Cambridge City Council, 2008). In July 2009, the Mayor of London published his 'environment programme for the capital'. It talks of reshaping London as a low-carbon economy and putting in place large-scale programmes that can deliver significant green house gas reductions. For example, it talks of rolling out a retrofit programme of homes in the capital that could reduce emissions of green house gases by 2 million tonnes per year. Reference is also made to support for more sustainable energy sources (GLA, 2009).

Darlington Borough Council (in the north east of England) has been involved in a five-year project to reduce local traffic levels (see Friends of the Earth, 2009). Darlington was selected as one of three sustainable travel demonstration towns (the others were Peterborough and Worcester), with grant funding for schemes to reduce traffic levels. These have included free bicycle training in local schools, the introduction of travel plans by local businesses and other local organisations (designed to encourage, for example, the use of public transport and car sharing schemes) and free travel advice for all residents in Darlington. There have been some tangible outcomes from the project. By 2008, there had been a 9 per cent reduction in car journeys as people switched to public transport. Indeed, use of public transport went up by 18 per cent. In the same year significant increases were recorded for journeys by foot and bicycle (Friends of the Earth, 2009: 34).

Local councils have also been working with the Carbon Trust to develop the Local Authority Carbon Management Programme. Set up in 2001, the Carbon Trust is an independent UK-wide company funded by the climate change levy and government. One of its key roles is to support the development of UK-based low-carbon technologies. Over 140 local authorities have received technical and management support in an effort to reduce green house gas emissions. There have been a number of policy responses to this.

Torbay Council (in Devon), for example, has committed itself to a significant reduction in green house gases from its own operations with a particular emphasis on energy usage, travel and transport and procurement policy. It is also its stated aim to actively encourage all sectors in the community 'to take the opportunity to reduce their own greenhouse gas emissions and to make public their commitment to action' (Torbay, 2008). The council has adopted a strategic plan to reduce the annual carbon emissions created by its own operations by 20 per cent by the year 2012. Colchester Borough Council seeks to reduce green house gas emissions from its buildings by 25 per cent by 2012. The Council argues that 'By reducing our own emissions we can provide an example to others, enabling us to act as leaders in the wider community' (Colchester Borough Council, 2008: 7). Cambridge City Council has committed itself to a 20 per cent cut in greenhouse gases by 2020 and a reduction of 89 per cent by 2050 (Cambridge City Council, 2008). In London, the Mayor has made commitments of a 60 per cent reduction in green house gases by 2025 (GLA, 2009: 12).

There are clearly a variety of initiatives at the local level that seek to tackle climate change and promote a more sustainable way of living. Many local councils have made specific commitments to reduced their green house gas emissions. But questions remain as to the substantive impact of such policies. The LGA, whilst recognising that there are some 'outstanding examples of local council leadership' in tackling climate change, has called for a 'more urgent and consistent authority wide approach ... by each and every local authority' (LGA, 2007b: 9). The environmental lobby group, Friends of the Earth, has called for 'a step change in local action by local councils'. It has argued that much greater ambition is 'needed in local emissions cuts if councils are to play their part in meeting the national targets set out in the Climate Change Act' (Friends of the Earth, 2009: 4). Friends of the Earth readily accepts that 'local government is in a strong position to lead and co-ordinate' action against climate change and that 'many councils are taking climate change very seriously', but argues that 'most councils are being left behind' (Friends of the Earth, 2010: 1). What is required is 'A nationwide system' that will support 'councils and ensure emissions come down in every local authority' (Friends of the Earth, 2010: 1). Accordingly, Friends of the Earth has called for all local councils to have a local carbon budget and to set out a firm commitment (with a detailed action plan) to cut emissions in their area by 40 per cent by 2020. But they also argue that support from central government is vital in the form of more resources to develop green technologies (Friends of the Earth, 2011). The prospects for such central government support in the current climate of large-scale cuts in public expenditure are uncertain to say the least.

Conclusion

This chapter has looked at three interrelated areas: the meaning of the concept of sustainability and its practical application for local communities, the extent to which regeneration can contribute to sustainable communities, and lastly attempts at the local level to tackle climate change and promote environmental sustainability.

Policies with regard to sustainability have often been based on high hopes and the best of intentions. They stem from a clear and legitimate recognition that the old ways of working are no longer an option. A new paradigm has emerged that recognises the fragility of both our physical environment and our social fabric. There is a growing acceptance that environmental, social and economic sustainability are key to creating a dynamic local polity, together with vibrant and engaged local communities. But setting in place policies to deal with this reality presents major challenges.

Perhaps when all is said and done the most appropriate way forward is to *satisfice*. Instead of trying to set out to achieve the goal of sustainable communities and cities, what we should be perhaps doing in the short to medium term is working for a city or community much less unsustainable than we have now. By such an approach, and with the benefits of lessons learned and the strengthening of local social capital, the types of local communities and social networks might develop which could put us on the road to a long-term sustainable future.

Conclusion

The arrival of Margaret Thatcher's Conservative government in 1979 marked a period of deep uncertainty and turbulence in the world of local government. A centralising agenda of financial restrictions, policy directives and privatisation served to undermine the rationale of local democracy itself. Indeed, writing in 1982, Alexander argued that 'unless conscious efforts are made to revive it, the end of local government may be in sight' (Alexander, 1982: 2). It has been argued elsewhere that despite the 'mighty onslaught from the centre' local government 'stoutly defended its position' and managed to carve out a creative autonomy in a number of policy areas (Atkinson and Wilks-Heeg, 2000: 270). In other words, though showing some signs of wear and tear local government and local democracy remained healthy and strong.

But what is the diagnosis in 2011? New Labour was elected in 1997 on a wave of optimism in many circles. Nowhere was this optimism more pronounced than in the world of local government. After eighteen years of successive Conservative administrations deeply hostile to large sections of local government, here at last was a government that appeared once again to value it. Certainly the mood music improved as the government talked of reinvigorating local government and local democracy. There was a constant flow of policy briefings, green papers and Acts of Parliament.

And yet New Labour's agenda was often contradictory as an ever-increasing number of centrally driven targets cut through the notion of local autonomy. Little was conceded by way of more policy and fiscal autonomy for local government. It is true that there was great emphasis on attempts to boost local civic engagement and political participation. This was to be welcomed. And yet the suspicion remained that this was part of an agenda to 'hollow out' the role of local government in favour of a rather disparate notion of community empowerment.

This is not to deny the crucial importance of community activity. Indeed, I have noted in this book countless examples of community organisations, social enterprises and individuals making a real difference to the shaping of local services and a major contribution to local democracy. Such activity is essential to the health of the local body politic. But just as elected local government needs empowered communities to be effective, so too do local communities need empowered local government.

The New Labour agenda for local government and local democracy was full of ideas but it was often piecemeal and fragmented, driven more by technocratic solutions than broader values. In essence, what was missing was a broader vision of the role of elected local government and local democracy in the twenty-first century. This was its fundamental weakness.

The current Conservative/Liberal Democrat coalition government does claim to have a vision in the twin concepts of the 'big society' and localism. Yet, as I have noted earlier, these are vague and contested concepts. In its coalition agreement, the government talks of its 'determination to oversee a radical redistribution of power away from Westminster and Whitehall to councils, communities and homes across the nation' (H.M. Government, 2010a: 7). The self-styled localist agenda is linked to the 'big society'. The big society', argues the government, 'is what happens when people work together for the common good'. In this way we achieve 'our collective goals in ways that are more diverse, more local and more personal' (H.M. Government, 2010b: 2). In its own words the government is 'committed to decentralisation which is the biggest thing government can do to build the big society' (CLG, 2010d: 2).

At first glance this seems like music to the ears of those who believe that a vibrant local democracy, encouraging a creative local government and active local communities, is an essential ingredient of the national body politic. Yet, as Sir Michael Lyons has cogently argued, 'The proof of the localist pudding will be in the central ingredients' (*Local Government Chronicle*, 6 January 2011). Indeed the government itself concedes that 'Decentralisation is easy to pay lip service to' (H.M. Government 2010b: 2).

Looking through the policy details there does appear to be evidence that the government means what it says about decentralisation and localism. There is a commitment to lift the burden of red tape on local councils, and there is to be less ring fencing of the central government grant, allowing local councils to make spending decisions based on local priorities. There is to be a general power of competence for local government (H.M. Government, 2010b). On a broader level, there is talk of empowering 'communities to do things their way' (H.M. Government, 2010b). This includes the right to bid to run local services and to bid to buy community assets. Grounds for optimism one might think.

On the surface, such policy measures suggest considerable room for manoeuvre and for creative responses for both local government and local communities. But is all as it seems? The introduction of a power of general competence for local government, replacing the long-standing constitutional doctrine of *ultra vires*, does seem to indicate greater policy freedom for local government. Yet as Andy Sawford, the Chief Executive of LGiU, has noted, there are many limitations and qualifications on how local councils may use the power (*Guardian* online, 22 December 2010). In addition, to take full advantage of this power of general competence local authorities need adequate resources. Yet as we noted earlier in this book local authorities face budget cuts of some 30 per cent in the period 2010–11 as a result of the government's 2010 CSR.

Proposals to allow local community groups to bid to run local services also appear attractive on the surface. But they are part of a broader agenda to transform the way local services are shaped and delivered. As David Cameron says, 'We will create a new presumption that public services should be open to a range of providers' (*Guardian*, 21 February 2011). This includes not just community groups and the social enterprise sector but large-scale private operators. This whole policy agenda marks a qualitative change in the way local services are delivered, the consequences of which could be significant for local government.

This stratagem on public services feeds into a broader discourse about the role of the state. Some commentators, and I include myself here, argue that the sub-text to the 'big society' and localism agenda, together with policies to cut the budget deficit, is an ideological strategy designed to reconfigure and shrink significantly the role of the state at both national and local level. This does not bode well for local government. One might even term it a local ConDemocracy!

However, there is an alternative scenario. The coalition government itself states 'that the days of big government are over' and goes on to argue 'that the time has come to disperse power more widely in Britain' (H.M. Government, 2010b: 4). If we take this statement at face value, government policies, instead of being viewed as a threat, might well provide an opportunity for local government. Local government has in the past demonstrated its ability to meet difficult challenges and reinvent and sustain itself. I noted in Chapter 6 recent examples of local councils developing new ways of working in the difficult current climate. How local government fares in the longer term only time will tell.

Perhaps we should return to the words of Robert Putnam. In the Introduction to this book I spoke of his view that the local space has a potential and a vibrancy thanks to its cultivation by 'assiduous civic gardeners' (Putnam, 2000: 16). We can view local government itself as a garden. Like all gardens, it has its fair share of weeds, pests and other problems. Each year the coming seasons present both opportunities and challenges with the winter political frosts a threat to its plants, flowers and roots. But then comes the fresh optimism of spring and the summer sun that brings rejuvenation and new life. Just as the physical garden ebbs and flows, waxes and wanes with the seasons, so does the garden of local democracy with the oncoming of each political season.

Bibliography

Books and journals

Adonis, A. and S. Twigg, 1997. *The Cross We Bear: Electoral Reform for Local Government*, London, Fabian Society.

Alexander, A., 1982. *The Politics of Local Government in the United Kingdom*, London, Fabian Society.

All-Party Parliamentary Beer Group, 2008. *Community Pub Inquiry*, London, House of Commons.

Arup, 2001. *Our Principles for a Human City*, London, Arup.

Atkinson, D., 1994. *The Common Sense of Community*, London, Demos.

Atkinson, H., 2008. 'Democracy and Empowerment in London's Neighbourhoods', *Local Economy*, Vol. 23, No. 4, pp. 325–331.

Atkinson, H. and S. Wilks-Heeg, 2000. *Local Government from Thatcher to Blair: The Politics of Creative Autonomy*, Cambridge, Polity Press.

Atkinson, R. and J. Flint, 2004. 'Order Born of Chaos? The Capacity for Informal Social Control in Disempowered and Disorganised Neighbourhoods', *Policy and Politics*, Vol. 32, No. 3, pp. 333–350.

Bacon, N., S. James and V. Savage, 2007. *Transforming Neighbourhoods*, London, Young Foundation.

Barber, B., 1998. *A Place for US*, New York, Hill & Wang.

Barker, E., 1962. *The Politics of Aristotle*, New York, Oxford University Press.

Barnardo's, 2005. *Give us a Chance*, London, Barnado's.

Barnet, London Borough of, 2009. *The Future Shape of the Council*, London, Barnet.

Baston, I., 2007. *Local Authority Elections in Scotland*, London, Electoral Reform Society.

Beetham, D., 1996. 'Theorising Democracy and Local Government', in D. King and G. Stoker (eds), *Rethinking Local Democracy*, London, Macmillan, pp. 28–49.

Beetham, D., A. Blick, H. Margetts and S. Weir, 2008. *Power and Participation in Modern Britain*, London, Democratic Audit.

Bell, S. and A. Lane, 2009. 'Creating Sustainable Communities', *Local*

Economy, Vol. 24, No. 6, pp. 646–657.

BIS (Department for Business, Innovation and Skills), 2010. *Securing the Post Office Network in the Digital Age*, London, HMSO.

Blair, T., 1998. *A New Vision for Local Government*, London, IPPR.

Blunkett, D., 2009. *A People's Police: Police Accountability in the Modern Era*, London. Home Office.

Bochel, H. and C. Bochel, 2010. 'Local Political Leadership and the Modernisation of Local Government', Vol. 36, No. 6, pp. 723–727.

Bogdanor, V., 2006. *The Rise and Fall of the Political Party*, in *The Political Party RIP?*, New Statesman, Political Studies Guide, 23 October, pp. 4–6.

Bottery, M., 2000. *Education, Policy and Ethics*, London, Continuum.

Bruntland Report, 1987. *World Commission on Environment and Development*, New York, United Nations.

Buckingham, S. and K. Theobold, 2003. *Local Environmental Sustainability*, Abington, Cambridge, Woodhead Publishers.

Butler, D., A. Adonis and T. Travers, 1994. *Failure in British Government: The Politics of the Poll Tax*, Oxford, Oxford University Press.

Cambridge City Council, 2008. *Cambridge Climate Change – Strategy and Action Plan, 2008-2011*.

Chandler, J.A., 1996. *Local Government Today*, Manchester, Manchester University Press.

Chandler, J.A., 2009. *Local Government Today*, Manchester, Manchester University Press.

Chandler, J.A., 2010. 'A Rationale for Local Government', *Local Government Studies*, Vol. 36, No. 1, pp. 5–20.

Chatterton, P. and A. Cutler, 2007. *The Rocky Road to the Transition Town Movement and What it Means for Social Justice*, Leeds, Trapese.

Chisholm, M. and S. Leach, 2008. *Botched Business: The Damaging Process of Reorganising Local Government 2006–2008*, Coleford, Gloucestershire, Douglas McLean Publishing.

Chisholm, M., and S. Leach, 2011. 'Dishonest Government – Local Government Reorganisation: England, 2000–2010', *Local Government Studies*, Vol. 37, No. 1, pp. 19–41.

Clarke, H., D. Sanders, M. Stewart and P. Whiteley, 2004. *Political Choice in Britain*, Oxford, Oxford University Press.

CLG (Department of Communities and Local Government), 2006a. *2005 Citizen Survey: Active Communities Topic Report*, London, CLG.

CLG, 2006b. *Strong and Prosperous Communities*, London CLG.

CLG, 2007a. *Community Empowerment Action Plan*, London, CLG.

CLG, 2007b. *Representing the Future: The Report of the Councillors' Commission*, London, CLG.

CLG, 2008a. *Communities in Control: Real People, Real Power*, London, CLG.

CLG, 2008b. *Communities in Control: Real People, Real Power – Summary*, London, CLG.

CLG, 2008c. *Practical Use of the Well Being Power*, London, CLG.

CLG, 2008d. *A Step by Step Guide to the Sustainable Communities Act*, London, CLG. CLG,

CLG, 2008e. *Citizenship Survey, April–September 2007*, Statistical Release 2, London, CLG.

CLG, 2009a. *Strengthening Local Democracy*, London, CLG.

CLG, 2009b. *Guidance on Building a Sense of Belonging*, London, CLG.

CLG, 2010a. *Citizenship Survey, 2000–10*, London, CLG.

CLG, 2010b, *The New Deal for Communities: A Final Assessment*, London, CLG.

CLG, 2010c. *National Evaluation of Participatory Budgeting in England*, London, CLG.

CLG, 2010d. *Draft Structural Plan*, London, CLG.

Cochrane, A., 2010. 'Exploring the Regional Politics of "Sustainability": Making Up Sustainable Communities in the South-East of England', *Environmental Policy and Governance*, Vol. 20, No. 6, pp. 370–381.

Colchester Borough Council, 2008. *Local Authority Carbon Management Programme.*

Commission for Architecture and the Built Environment (CABE), 2003. *Building Sustainable Communities*, London, CABE.

Commission for Local Democracy (CLD), 1995. *Taking Charge: The Rebirth of Local Democracy*, London, Municipal Journal Books.

Commission on Urban Life and Faith, 2006. *Faithful Cities: A Call for Celebration, Vision and Justice*, London, Church House Publishing.

Conservative Party, 2009. *Control Shift: Returning Power to Local Communities*, London, Conservative Party.

Copus, C., 2004. *Party Politics and Local Government*, Manchester, Manchester University Press.

Copus, C., 2006. *Leading the Localities: Executive Mayors in English Local Governance*, Manchester, Manchester University Press.

Copus, C., 2009. *English Elected Mayors: Developing a New Form of Political Leadership in England, or Moving on in the Same Old Style?*, Political Studies Association Annual Conference, 7–9 April, University of Manchester.

Copus, C. and H. van der Kolk, 2007. *Comparative Perspectives on Local Party Politics*, European Consortium on Political Research, 7–12 May, Helsinki.

Cornwall, A., 2008. *Democratising Engagement: What the UK Can Learn from International Experience*, London, Demos.

Council of Europe, 2007. *Local Authority Competences in Europe*, Strasbourg, Council of Europe.

Councillors' Commission, 2007. *Representing the Future*, London, CLG.

Craig, J., M. Horne and D. Morgan, 2009. *The Engagement Ethic: The Potential of Cooperative and Mutual Governance for Public Services*, London, Cabinet Office.

Curtice, J., B. Seyd and K. Thomson, 2008. 'Do Mayoral Elections Work? Evidence from London', *Political Studies*, Vol. 56, No. 3, pp. 653–678.

DCMS (Department for Culture, Media and Sport), 2009a. *Digital Britain, Final Report*, London, DCMS.

DCMS, 2009b. *Government Response to the All-Party Parliamentary Beer Group Community Pub Inquiry*, London, DCMS.

DCSF (Department for Children, Schools and Families), 2010. *The 21st Century: Implications for Governing Bodies*, London, HMSO.

Dearlove, J., 1979. *The Reorganisation of Local Government: Old Orthodoxies and a Political Perspective*, Cambridge, Cambridge University Press.

Defra (Department of the Environment, Food and Rural Affairs), 2005. *Sustainable Models of Community Retailing*, London, Defra.

Department of Health, 2010. *Equity and Excellence: Liberating the NHS*, London, HMSO.

DETR (Department of the Environment, Transport and the Regions), 2000. *Our Towns and Cities: The Future. Delivering An Urban Renaissance*, London, HMSO.

De Tocqueville, A., 1945. *Democracy in America*, 2 vols., New York: Knopf.

DLTR (Department of Local Government, Transport and the Regions), 2001. *Strong Local Leadership, Quality Public Services*, London HMSO.

Dorling, D., D. Vickers, B.Thomas, J. Pritchard and D. Ballas, 2008. *Changing UK: The Way We Live Now*, Sheffield, University of Sheffield.

Dungey, J., 2007. *Democracy Day*, London, Local Government Information Unit.

Dunleavy, P. and H. Margetts, 2010. 'The Second Wave of Digital Governance', paper presented to the American Political Science Association, 4 September.

Dunrose, C. and V. Lowndes, 2010. 'Neighbourhood Governance: Contested Rationales within a Multi Level System', *Local Government Studies*, Vol. 36, No. 3, pp. 341–359.

Edwards, M., 2004. *Civil Society*, Cambridge, Polity.

Edwards, M. 2008. *Civil Society*, Cambridge, Polity Press.

Electoral Commission, 2003. *The Shape of Things to Come*, London, Electoral Commission.

Electoral Commission, 2005. *Securing the Vote: Report and Recommendations*, London, Electoral Commission.

Electoral Commission, 2007a. *Local Elections: Pilot Schemes 2007*, London, Electoral Commission.

Electoral Commission, 2007b. *Electoral Pilot Scheme Evaluation: Swindon Borough Council*, London, Electoral Commission.

Electoral Commission, 2007c. *Electoral Pilot Scheme Evaluation: Shrewsbury and Atcham Borough Council*, London, Electoral Commission.

Electoral Commission, 2007d. *Electoral Pilot Scheme Evaluation: Sheffield City Council*, London, Electoral Commission.

Electoral Commission, 2007e. *Electoral Pilot Scheme Evaluation: Bedford Borough Council*, London Electoral Commission.

Electoral Commission, 2009. *Allegations of Electoral Malpractice at the May 2008 Elections in England and Wales*, London, Electoral Commission.

Electoral Reform Society, 2006. *The Great Local Vote Swindle*, London, Electoral Reform Society.

Essex County Council, 2008. *Counter Measures: A New Vision for Local Postal Services.*

Etzioni, A., 1993. *The Spirit of Community*, London, Fontana.

European Commission, 2008. *Financial Services Provision and Prevention of Financial Exclusion*, Brussels.

Evans, J., P. Jones and R. Krueger, 2009, 'Organic Regeneration and Sustainability or Can the Credit Crunch Save Our Cities?', *Local Environment*, Vol. 14, No. 7, pp. 683–698.

Farrelly, M., 2009. 'Citizen Participation and Neighbourhood Governance: Analysing Democratic Practice', *Local Government Studies*, Vol. 35, No. 4, pp. 387–400.

Farrelly, M. and H. Sullivan, 2010, 'Discourses of Democracy in Neighbourhood Governance', *Critical Policy Studies*, Vol. 4, No. 3, pp. 234–249.

Finney, A. and E. Kempson, 2009. *Regression Analysis of the Unbanked – Using the 2006–07 Family Resources Survey*, University of Bristol.

Friends of the Earth, 2009. *Cutting Carbon Locally – And How to Pay For It*, London, Friends of the Earth.

Friends of the Earth, 2010. *Briefing: Local Carbon Budgets*, London, Friends of the Earth, December.

Game, C., 2009. *Place-Shaping's Difficult if You Don't Have a Place: The Toponymy of English Shire Government*, Political Studies Association Annual Conference, 7-9 April, University of Manchester.

Giddens, A., 1998. *The Third Way: The Renewal of Social Democracy*, Cambridge, Polity.

Giddens, A., 2009. *The Politics of Climate Change*, Cambridge, Polity.

Gillett, S.E., W.H. Lehr and C. Osorio, 2003. *Local Government Broadband Initiatives*, Massachusetts Institute of Technology – Program on Internet and Telecoms Convergence, 18 September.

GLA (Greater London Authority), 2009. *Leading to a Greener London: An Environment Programme for the Capital*, London, GLA.

GLA, 2010. *Focus on London, 2010 – Population and Immigration*, London, GLA.

Goldsmith, M., 1986. *Essays on the Future of Local Government*, Wakefield, West Yorkshire Metropolitan County Council.

Goth, P., D. McKillop and C. Ferguson, 2006, *Building Better Credit Unions*, York, Joseph Rowntree Foundation.

Hague, R. and M. Harrop, 1987. *Comparative Politics and Government*, Basingstoke, Macmillan.

Hague, R. and M. Harrop., 2004. *Comparative Government and Politics*, Basingstoke, Palgrave Macmillan.

Hague, R. and M. Harrop, 2010. *Comparative Politics and Government*, Basingstoke, Palgrave Macmillan.

Hansard Society, 2006. *Audit of Political Engagement 3*, London, Hansard Society.

Hansard Society, 2009. *Audit of Political Engagement 6*, London, Hansard Society.

Hansard Society, 2010. *Audit of Political Engagement 7*, London, Hansard Society.

Hansard Society, 2011. *Audit of Political Engagement 8*, London, Hansard Society.

Healey, J., M. Gill and D. McHugh, 2005. *MPs and Politics in Our Time*, London, Dods Parliamentary Communications.

Heclo, H., 1969. 'The Councillor's Job', *Public Administration*, Vol. 47, No. 2, pp. 185–202.

Hill, D.M., 1974. *Democratic Theory and Local Government*, London, George Allen & Unwin.

H.M. Government, 2006. *Improving Community Involvement in Community Safety*, London, HMSO.

H.M. Government, 2007. *Creating Strong, Safe and Prosperous Communities – Statutory Guidance – Draft For Consultation*, London, HMSO.

H.M. Government, 2009. *Building Britain's Future*, London, HMSO.

H.M. Government, 2010a. *The Coalition: Our Programme for Government*, London, HMSO.

H.M. Government, 2010b. *Decentralisation and the Localism Bill: An Essential Guide*, London, HMSO.

H.M. Government, 2010c. *Shaping Our Future – The Joint Ministerial and Third Sector Task Force on Climate Change, the Environment and Sustainable Development*, London, HMSO.

H.M. Treasury, 2010. *Banking Services and Poorer Households*, London, HMSO, December.

Home Office, 2010. *Policing in the 21st Century: Reconnecting Police and the People*, London, HMSO.

Horner, L, R. Lekhi and R. Blaug, 2006. *Deliberative Democracy and the Role of Public Managers*, London, Work Foundation.

House of Commons, 1998. 'Cabinets, Committees and Elected Mayors', Research Paper 93/98, London, House of Commons Library.

House of Commons, 2003. Public Administration Select Committee, *On Target? Government by Measurement*, London, HMSO.

House of Commons, 2008. Public Administration Committee, *From Citizen's Charter to Public Service Guarantees: Entitlements to Public Services*, London, HMSO.

House of Commons, 2009a. Communities and Local Government Select

Committee, *The Balance of Power: Central and Local Government*, London, HMSO.

House of Commons, 2009b. Public Administration Committee, *Good Government*, London, HMSO.

House of Commons, 2009c. Business and Enterprise Select Committee, *Post Offices – Securing the Future*, London, HMSO.

House of Commons Library, 1998. *Cabinets, Committees and Elected Mayors: Models of Decision Making and the Welsh Assembly*, March.

House of Commons Library, 2009. *Membership of UK Political Parties*, 17 August.

House of Commons Library, 2010. *Eco-Towns*, 5 November.

Imrie, R., 2009. 'An Exemplar for a Sustainable World City: Progressive Urban Change and the Redevelopment of King's Cross', in R. Imrie, L. Lees and M. Raco (eds), *Regenerating London*, London, Routledge.

Independent Commission on Alternative Voting Methods, 2002. *Elections in the 21st Century: From Paper Balloting to E-Voting*, London, Independent Commission on Alternative Voting Methods.

Ipsos MORI, 2008. *Charity Commission Study into Public Trust and Confidence in Charities*, London, Demos.

Johnstone, C. and M. Whitehead, 2004. 'Horizons and Barriers in British Urban Policy', in C. Johnstone and M. Whitehead (eds), *New Horizons in British Urban Policy: Perspectives on New Labour's Urban Renaissance*, Aldershot, Ashgate.

Jones, A., 2007. 'New Wine in Old Bottles? England's Parish and Town Councils and New Labour's Neighbourhood Experiment', *Local Economy*, Vol. 22, No. 3, pp. 227–242.

Jones, G.W., 1973. 'The Functions and Organisations of Councillors', *Public Administration*, Vol. 51, No. 2, pp. 135–146.

Jones, G.W. and J. Stewart, 1985. *The Case for Local Government*, London, George Allen & Unwin.

Jones, P. and J. Evans, 2008. *Urban Regeneration in the UK*, London, Sage.

Kitchin, H., S. Griggs, S. Rogers, C. Crawford, N. Mathur and L.Wilson, *Formative Evaluation of the Take Up and Implementation of the Well Being Power*, Birmingham, INLOGOV, University of Birmingham.

Lambeth, London Borough of, 2010. *The Cooperative Council – A New Settlement Between Citizens and Public Services. A New Approach to Public Service Delivery*, London, Lambeth.

Layfield Committee, 1976. *Report of the Committee of Enquiry into Local Government Finance*, Cmnd 653, London, HMSO.

Leach, S. and L. Pratchett, 2005. 'Local Government: A New Vision, Rhetoric or Reality?', *Parliamentary Affairs*, Vol. 58, No. 2, pp. 318–334.

Lepine, E., 2009. *Scrutiny, Public Participation and Democracy – Making the Connections*, Political Studies Association Annual Conference, 7–9 April, University of Manchester.

Leunig, T., J. Swaffield and O. Hartwich, 2007. *Cities Unlimited: Making Urban Regeneration Work*, London, Policy Exchange.

LGA (Local Government Association), 2007a. *Lifting the Burdens Taskforce*. London, LGA.

LGA, 2007b. *A Climate of Change – Final Report of the LGA Climate Change Commission*, London, LGA.

LGA, 2008a. *Local Elections 1 May 2008, Stand Up and Be Counted*, London, LGA.

LGA, 2008b. *Eco Towns: Back to the Future*, London, LGA.

LGA, 2009a. *The Economy or the Environment, Do I Need to Choose?*, London LGA.

LGA, 2009b, *From Kyoto to Kettering, Copenhagen to Croydon – Local Government's Manifesto for Building Low Carbon Communities*, London, LGA.

LGA, 2010. *A Tale of Twelve Cities: What will the Government's Localism Bill Really Mean?*, London, LGA, 25 November.

LGA, 2011. *LGA Responses to the Localism Bill*, Press Release, 18 January.

LGiU (Local Government Information Unit), 2009a. *Small is Beautiful – Mission: To Find Local Initiatives with Big Potential*, London, LGiU.

LGiU, 2009b. *Carbon Trading Councils*, London, LGiU.

LGiU, 2010. *Getting Ready for a Changing Climate*, London, LGiU.

London Civic Forum, 2011. *Parish Councils – Could they Work in London?*, Event Report, 9 February.

Lynas, M., 2007. *Six Degrees: Our Future on a Hotter Plant*, London, Fourth Estate.

Lyons, M., 2007. *Lyons Inquiry into Local Government, Place Shaping; A Shared Ambition for the Future of Local Government*, Executive Summary, London, HMSO.

McLellan, D., 1980a. *The Thought of Karl Marx*, London, Macmillan.

McLellan, D., 1980b. *Marxism After Marx*, London, Macmillan.

Marquetti, A., 2004. 'Building a New Form of Local State: Participatory Budgeting in Porto Alegre, Brazil', in E.K. Hassen, A. Marquetti, A. Mathew and P. Harrid, *Contesting Public Services*, Johannesburg, Naledi.

Mason, W. and J. McMahon, 2008. *Freedom for Public Services*, London, Centre for Policy Studies.

Mill, J.S., 1975. *Three Essays on Liberty, Representative Government and The Subjection of Women*. London, Oxford University Press.

Ministry of Justice, 2009. Letter from Ministry of Justice, 20 August.

Mulgan, G. and F. Bury, 2006. 'Local Government and the Case for Double Devolution', in G. Mulgan and F. Bury (eds), *Double Devolution: The Renewal of Local Government*, London, The Young Foundation.

Muir, R., 2009. *Pubs and Places: The Social Value of Community Pubs*, London, IPPR.

ODPM (Office of the Deputy Prime Minister), 2003. *Sustainable*

Communities: Building for The Future, London, HMSO.

ODPM, 2004. *The Future of Local Government: Developing a 10 Year Vision Plan*, London, ODPM.

ODPM, 2005. *Citizen Engagement and Public Services: Why Neighbourhoods Matter*, London, ODPM.

O'Reilly, D. and M. Reed, 2010. 'Leaderism: An Evolution of Managerialism in UK Public Sector Reform', *Public Administration*, Vol. 88, No. 4, pp. 960–978.

Orr, K. and R. Vance, 2009. 'Traditions of Local Government', *Public Administration*, Vol. 187. No. 3, pp. 655–677.

Pattie, C., P. Seyd. and P. Whiteley, 2003. 'Citizenship and Civic Engagement: Attitudes and Behaviour in Britain', *Political Studies*, Vol. 51, No. 3, pp. 443–468.

Phillips, H., 2007. *Strengthening Democracy: Fair and Sustainable Funding of Political Parties*, London, HMSO.

Plunkett Foundation, 2004. *Assessing the Impact of Social Enterprise in Rural England*, Woodstock, Oxford.

Plunkett Foundation, 2005. *Community Owned Village Shops in England*, Woodstock, Oxford.

Plunkett Foundation, 2008. *Community Owned Rural Shops*, Woodstock, Oxford.

Power Inquiry, 2006. *The Report of Power: An Independent Inquiry into Britain's Democracy*, London, Power Commission.

Pratchett, L., 1999. 'New Fashions in Public Participation: Towards Greater Democracy?', *Parliamentary Affairs*, Vol. 52, No. 4, pp. 621–622.

Pratchett, L., 2004. 'Local Autonomy, Local Democracy and the New Localism', *Political Studies*, Vol. 5, No. 2, pp. 358–375.

Prince's Trust, 2008. *The Truth About Youth*, Press Release, London, Prince's Trust, 2 November.

Putnam, R., 2000. *Bowling Alone*, New York, Simon & Schuster.

Pycroft, C., 1995. 'Restructuring Local Government', *Public Policy and Administration*, Vol. 10, No. 1, pp. 49–62.

Renwick, A., 2010. *The Politics of Electoral Reform: Changing the Rules of Democracy*. Cambridge, Cambridge University Press.

Renwick, A., 2011. *A Citizens Guide to Electoral Reform*, London, Biteback Publishers.

Rhodes, R.A.W., 1981. *Control and Power in Central/Local Relations*, Farnborough, Gower.

Roth, O., 2010. *A Fair Cop? Elected Police Commissioners, Democracy and Local Accountability*, London, New Local Government Network.

Rowson, J., S. Broome and A. Jones, 2010. *Connected Communities: How Social Networks Power and Sustain the Big Society*, London, RSA.

Runswick, A., 2004. *Life Support for Local Parties: An Analysis of the Decline of Local Political Parties and the Case for State Support for Local Activism*,

London, New Politics Network.

Scottish Parliament, 2002. *Local Government in Scotland Bill – A Power of Well Being*, Edinburgh, Scottish Parliament.

Sharpe, E., 1970. 'Theories and Values of Local Government', *Political Studies*, Vol. 18, No. 2, pp. 153–174.

Skidmore, P., K. Bound and H. Lownsbrough, 2006. *Community Participation: Who Benefits?*, York, Joseph Rowntree Foundation.

Smith, G., 2005. *Beyond the Ballot*, London, Power Inquiry.

Smith, M.J., 2010. 'From Big Society to Big Government: Changing the State/Society Balance', *Parliamentary Affairs*, Vol. 63, No. 4, pp. 818–833.

Stern, N., 2006. *Stern Review on Economics of Climate Change*, London, HMSO.

Stevens, A., 2008. 'An Introduction to Parish Councils', in *Micro-Democracy: Parish Power in London?*, London, LondonSays.org.

Stewart, J., 2003. *Modernising British Local Government: An Assessment of Labour's Reform Programme*, Basingstoke, Palgrave Macmillan.

Stewart, J., E. Kendall and A. Coote, 1994. *Citizens' Juries*, London IPPR.

Stoker, G., 2003. *Transforming Local Governance*, Basingstoke, Palgrave Macmillan.

Suffolk County Council, 2010. *The New Strategic Direction Explained – Council Services to be Delivered Differently in the Future.*

Sullivan, H., M. Smith, A. Root and D. Moran, 2001. *Area Committees and Neighbourhood Management*, York, Joseph Rowntree Foundation.

Sullivan, W.M., 1986. *Reconstructing Public Philosophy*, Los Angeles, University of California Press.

Sutherland Commission, 2002. *Improving Local Democracy in Wales: Report of the Commission on Local Government Electoral Arrangements in Wales*, Cardiff, Welsh Assembly Government.

Tallon, A., 2010, *Urban Regeneration in the UK*, London, Routledge.

Taylor, M., 2007. ''Community Participation in the Real World: Opportunities and Pitfalls in New Governance Spaces'. *Urban Studies*, Vol. 44, No. 2, pp. 291–317.

Torbay Council, 2008. *Carbon Management Plan: Working Together to Reduce our Carbon Emissions.*

Vella, A. and M. Morad, 2011. 'Taming the Metropolis; Revisiting the Prospect of Achieving Sustainable Communities', *Local Economy*, Vol. 26, No. 1, pp. 52–59.

Verheul, W.J. and L. Schaap, 2010. 'Strong Leaders? The Challenges and Pitfalls in Mayoral Leadership', *Public Administration*, Vol. 88, No. 2, pp. 439–454.

Whiteley, P., 2003. 'The State of Participation in Britain', *Parliamentary Affairs*, Vol. 56, No. 4, pp. 610–615.

Widdicombe, D., 1986. *The Conduct of Local Authority Business: Committee of Inquiry into the Conduct of Local Authority Business*, Cmnd 9797–9801, London, HMSO.

Wilks-Heeg, S., 2010a. 'A Slow and Painful Death? Political Parties and Local Democracy in Two Northern Towns', *Local Government Studies*, Vol. 36, No, 3, pp. 381–399.

Wilks-Heeg, S., 2010b. *Constitution Committee Inquiry into 'Referendums in the UK's Constitutional Experience' – Written Submission by Democratic Audit*, 3 January.

Wilks-Heeg, S. and S. Clayton, 2006. *Whose Town is it Anyway?: The State of Democracy in Two Northern Towns*, York, Joseph Rowntree Foundation.

Wilson, D., 1999. 'Exploring the Limits of Public Participation in Local Government', *Parliamentary Affairs*, Vol. 52, No. 2, pp. 246–259.

Wilson, D. and C. Game, 1998. *Local Government in the United Kingdom*, Basingstoke, Macmillan

Women in Journalism, 2009. *Teenage Boys and the Media*, London, Women in Journalism.

Internet sources

BBC News Online, 7 May 2002. *Postal Voting Boosts Turnout*, http://news.bbc.co.uk/1/hi/uk_politics, accessed 22 October 2008.

BBC News Online, 23 February 2006. *Bank Closures to Hit Poor Hardest*, http://news.bbc.co.uk/I/hi/business/4740712.stm, accessed 23 February 2006.

BBC News Online, 5 July 2007. *E-Voters Not Boosting Turnout*, http://news.bbc. co.uk/1/hi/uk_politics, accessed 1 July 2008.

Brighton and Hove City Council, 2009. *Brighton and Hove's Citizens' Panels*, www.brighton-hove.gov.uk/index.cfm?request=c1139444, accessed 28 October 2009.

Bristol City Council, 2009. www.bristol.gov.uk/page/citizen-panel, accessed 21 July 2009.

British Beer and Pub Association, 2010, www.beerandpub.com.news, accessed 7 December 2010.

Campaign for Community Banking, 2011, www.communitybanking .org.uk/report, accessed 1 March 2011.

Cheshire East Council, 2011. *Local Strategic Partnership*, www.cheshireeast .gov.uk/community_and_living/local_strategic_partnerships.as..., accessed 6 May 2011.

Community Broadband Network (CBN), 2010. *The Future of Broadband is Community*, http://www.broadband-uk.coop/, accessed 7 September 2010.

Corby Borough Council, 2009. *Citizen Panels*, www.corby.gov.uk /COUNCILANDDEMOCRACY/COUNCILLORSDEMOC, accessed 22 April 2009.

Croydon, London Borough of, 2009. *Neighbourhood Partnerships*, www.croydononline.org/neighbourhood_partnerships, accessed 3 March 2009.

Energy Savings Trust, 2011. *Nottingham Declaration on Climate Change*, www.energysavings   trust.org.uk/nottingham/Nottingham-Declaration /The Declar... , accessed 8 January 2011.

ERS (Electoral Reform Society), 2009a. *Alternative Voting Methods*, www.electoral-reform.org.UK/article.php?id=4, accessed 29 July 2009.

ERS, 2009b. *Voting Systems*, www.electoral-reform.org.UK/article .php?id=48, accessed 29 July 2009.

Friends of the Earth, 2011. *Get Serious About C02*, www.foe.co .uk/campaigns/climate/get_serious/info.html, accessed 8 March 2011.

Hampton, K., 2001. *Broadband Neighbourhoods – Connected Communities*, http://portal.acm.org.cfm?id=634245, accessed 7 September 2010.

IDeA (Improvement and Development Agency), 2008a. *Coalition Government Plans – Implications for Local Partnerships Working*, www.idea.gov.uk/idk/core/page.do?pageId=20784973, accessed 6 May 2011.

IDeA, 2008b. *Lessons from the Pilot Studies*, www.idea.gov.uk/idk/core /page.do?pageId=7377264, accessed 1 May 2008.

IDeA, 2009. *Innovation in Local Public Services*, http://www. improvementnetwork.gov.uk/imp?core/page.do?pageID=1068545, accessed 8 September 2009.

Inside Government, 2012. *Working in Partnership to Tackle Financial Exclusion and Improve Financial Capability*, www.insidegovernment .co.uk/economic_dev/financial-exclusion/, accessed 8 December 2010.

Kirklees Council, 2009. *Area Committees – Your Area Your Voice*, www.kirklees.gov.uk/you-kmc-howcouncilworks/area-committee /AreaCo, accessed 22 April 2009.

Lambeth, London Borough of, 2010. *Future Kennington – Old Lillian Baylis School*, www.lambeth.gov.uk/Services/Environment/Regeneration /FutureLambeth/Futu, accessed 26 February 2010.

Leeds City Council, 2009. *Bramley and Stanningley Community Forum*, http://democracy.leeds.gov.uk.uk/ieListDocuments.aspx?CId=3615&Ver =4&, accessed 8 November 2009.

Leicestershire County Council, 2009. *Community Forums*, www.leicestershireforums.org/, accessed 22 April 2009.

Lewisham, London Borough of, 2009. *Local Assemblies*, http://www .lewisham.gov.uk/?CouncilAndDemocracy/ElectedRepresentatives /Council, accessed 22 April 2009.

Lewisham, London Borough of, 2011. *Lewisham Strategic Partnership*, www.lewishamstrategicpartnership.org.uk/, accessed 6 May 2011.

Maire, S., 2008. *Good Parliament, Bad Governance*, www.unlockedemocracy .org.uk/?p=1023, accessed 8 May 2008.

Moore. M. 2007. *Making Sense of Public Value*, www.nationalschool.gov.uk, accessed 17 May 2007.

NEF (New Economics Foundation), 2010. *Government's Rejection of Post*

Office Plans is Short Sighted, www.neweconomics.org/press-releases /government%E2%80%99s-rejection-of..., accessed 7 December 2010.

Norris, P., 2004. *Voter Turnout in Western Europe*, www.idea.int/publications /voterturnout-weurope/Full Report.pdf, accessed 2 March 2011.

North East Lincolnshire Council, 2011, *Local Strategic Partnership (LSP)*, www.nelincs.gov.uk/community-people-and-living/local-strategic-partnership/, accessed 6 May 2011.

O'Brien, R., 1999. *Philosophical History of the Idea of Civil Society*, www.web.net/-robrien/papers/civhist, accessed 25 October 2008.

Oxford City Council, 2009. *Welcome to Oxford CSW Area Committee*, www.oxford.gov.uk/council/central-south-and-wst.cfm, accessed 22 April 2009.

PropertWeek.com, 22 May 2008. *Rogers Attacks Eco-Towns as Big Mistake*, www.propertweek.com/news/rogers-attacks-eco-towns-as-a -big-mistake /3114, accessed 19 January 2011.

Ritchie, K., 2008. *Electoral Reform Society: Putting People in Control*, http://www.politics.co.uk/opinion-formers/electoral-reform -society/article/electoral-reform-society-putting-thepeople-in-control, accessed 14 June 2011.

Sawford, A., 2010. *The Localism Bill: The Key Points for Local Government*, www.guardian.co.uk/local-government-network/2010/dec/22/localism-bill-councils-key-points, accessed 3 February 2011.

Social Enterprise, 2010. *Coops to Step in to Support Community Pubs*, www.socialenterpriselive.com/section/news/community/20100909/co -ops-step-, accessed 7 December 2010.

Thurrock Council, 2009. *Thurrock Community Forums*, www. thurrockcommunityforums.org.uk/Contents/Text/Index.asp?Siteld =777&, accessed 22 April 2009.

Transition Network.org, 2011. *What is Transition Initiative?*, http://www. transitionnetwork.org.org/support/what-transition-initiative, accessed 8 March 2011.

Walzer, M., 2007. *Canadian Liberal Renewal Commission, Task Force on Engagement*, www.the planningdesk.com/renewal-pdf, accessed 2 April 2011.

Watford Borough Council, 2009. *Citizen Panels*, http://www.watford .gov.uk/ccm/council-and-democracy/consultations/citi, accessed 22 April 2009.

Woods, M., B. Edwards, J. Anderson and G.. Gardner, 2011. *Participation, Power and Rural Community Governance in England and Wales*, www.aber.ac.uk, New Political Geographies, accessed 22 February 2011.

Index

Numbers in *italics* refer to figures